TAIJI

The Story Of The Japan Dolphins

'Be charitable to all beings, for Love is the representative of God'
–Ko-ji-ki, Hachiman Kasuga of the Shinto tradition

TAIJI

THE STORY OF THE JAPAN DOLPHINS

☙✿☙

Len Varley

Copyright © 2023 Len Varley

All rights reserved.

No part of this publication may be reproduced,
distributed, or transmitted in any form or by any means,
including photocopying, recording, or other electronic or mechanical methods,
without the prior written permission of the publisher,
except in the case of brief quotations embodied in critical reviews
and certain other noncommercial uses permitted by copyright law.

For permission requests contact the publisher at the address below.

ISBN: 978-1-7384582-0-2 (Paperback)
ISBN: 978-1-7384582-1-9 (Hardcover)
ISBN: 978-1-7384582-2-6 (eBook)

Cover design by Diana Buidoso – Design Crowd

Len Varley Publishing
PO Box 331E
East Devonport TAS 7310
Australia

CHAPTERS

FOREWORD by Leah Lemieux

INTRODUCTION

PART I – THE COVE

1 – THE BLACK STREAM.....2

2 – TAIJI....35

3 – DRIVE HUNT....50

4 – A FALL FROM GRACE....60

5 – A MEMORIAL FOR THE WHALES....74

6 – NAMI....82

7 – WHALE MUSEUM....88

PART II – DEEPER WATER

8 – KUMANO....100

9 – THE SQUID....111

10 – COLORS....114

11 – FAITH & HOPE....122

12 – THE FOUR....133

13 – BLUE DAY....149

14 – BREATHE....154

CHAPTERS

PART III – THE NAIL
15 – DIVINE WIND....160
16 – THE NAIL WHICH STICKS UP....166
17 – PEST CONTROL....177
18 – ROCK PAPER SCISSORS....188

PART IV – SPIRIT
19 – SPIRIT....198
20 – BIG IN JAPAN....215
21 – HINDSIGHT IS 2020....229

ABOUT THE AUTHOR....234

Foreword

By Leah Lemieux

There is a wave.

A wave, composed and driven by connected and passionate individuals around the earth who have recognized that our destructive human tendencies have put us in an untenable global situation and that we are in dire need of positive changes. This wave swept me up into the complex world of dolphin conservation over twenty years ago and I've been riding it ever since.

I first met Len in Taiji in early 2011. It was a chaotic time; the town was flooded with activists from at least 12 different countries and we were amid a terrible killing streak, with dozens of beautiful striped dolphins being slaughtered day after day. It was hard to hope–that the situation could ever get better, could ever change. Only a year later, I was back in Taiji and so was Len and though the dolphin slaughter had not stopped, the numbers being killed had dropped markedly. The presence of individuals in Taiji to investigate and document the dolphins' demise was important, not only to keep track of the numbers being butchered for poisoned meat but also the numbers being shipped to captive marine attractions around the world. But bearing witness wasn't enough. We were working toward positive change.

The situation in Taiji is a complex one and highly charged for a number of reasons. In Japan issues about whaling are purposely twisted in the media and almost always discussed in terms of aggressive foreigners assaulting Japan's hallowed traditional ways of hunting dolphins and whales. The fact that mechanization and greed have left very few if any traditional aspects of the hunt intact is assiduously ignored. Further, issues about the lucrative international trade in live dolphins and the toxicity of dolphin meat are purposefully avoided and quickly side-tracked amid incendiary claims of racism, and cultural imperialism. Time and time again, this switches attention away from the fact that traditional whaling has long been taken over by modernized fishing methods and that it's actually the money from selling dolphins into captivity that makes the whole enterprise in Taiji worth the hunters' time and effort.

Making conscious daily efforts to remain courteous, to learn about local customs and language is truly an essential part of helping the Japanese overcome the media-spun distrust that's been sown, regarding foreigners who support the cessation of cetacean slaughter. Only when both sides come to see each other as human beings, rather than monsters, can bridges towards a brighter future begin to be built.

I found Len to be a consummate diplomatic presence, with a keen and winning mixture of strength, seriousness, humor, understanding and a quick and open mind infused with heart and soul. It's truly been a pleasure working with him through circumstances, which are to say the least, often trying. From time to time, curious pro-whalers have asked me why I do this work. I explain to them that dolphins saved my life, while I was swimming off the coast of Hawaii years ago–and I am trying to repay the favor.

This kind of story gives people pause, as the argument is typically made that there is nothing special about these creatures. Yet seeing first-hand the passion on all sides of the dolphin slaughter issue, the incredible international efforts pouring forth to help save them, it's clear that even if we cannot explain *why*, there truly IS something remarkable about cetaceans and the effect they have upon us. And there's more. Leading edge science is now telling us that dolphins and whales appear to meet the criteria of non-human *Persons*. This is not to be confused with the biological term *Homo sapiens*, which applies only to our species. Rather, this is a philosophical distinction that in today's world, morally qualifies Persons to basic rights, like freedom from slavery and the right to life. Following this line of reasoning, it becomes more important than ever to raise awareness about the plight of whales and dolphins and their marine environment. Working at the charged border between life and death in Taiji, one sees how the battles playing out there–the struggle to replace ignorance with understanding, to arbitrate peace with would-be adversaries, to protect Nature's fragile beauty, to temper the traditions of the past with a path toward a brighter future–mirror a struggle we see taking place in many quarters all around the world.

Thus, have the dolphins of Japan become a beacon species, representing this battle for the flourishing of Life over greed and commerce; freedom over tyranny and injustice and compassion over conflict. We are the cause of the harm and we carry also the cure within us, if we can reconnect, envision, mobilize and transform the people and situations around us. Death wakes us up to the preciousness of Life. We realize the stakes are high and the price of indifference is ruin. The universal fascination and love of dolphins and whales presents humanity with a serious challenge, asking each of us–what have we got to give towards creating positive change in this world? Its starts by getting connected, educated, empowered and involved to stand up, speak out and reach out. Social media networks and video sharing makes it easier than ever to connect, find out what is happening, join movements, inject support where it is most needed and educate others.

Which brings us back to that wave sweeping the world. In opening the pages of this book, we invite you to enter the dolphins' story, to join us; to ride the wave and dare the deeper water....

Leah Lemieux
Author - 'Rekindling the Waters'

Introduction

> "Long have you timidly waded, holding a plank by the shore.
> Now I will you to be a bold swimmer,
> To jump off in the midst of the sea, and rise again
> and nod to me and shout, and laughingly dash with your hair"
> —WALT WHITMAN - 'Leaves of Grass'

I realize that for many readers, picking up this book for the first time is a daunting proposition. I've been told by several people that before they began reading, they felt somewhat challenged by the subject matter, and wary of hearing the plight of Taiji's dolphins.

I must begin by saying I recognize and respect these sentiments, and for this reason I thank you for your motivation and your bravery in reading my words. That having been said, I think it is perhaps warranted that I assure you that there is a greater depth to this story than the simple recounting of a slaughter. One of the things that draws me to dolphins is their spirit; their practical demonstration that life cannot be all work and no play. Goodness, they are the only species outside of human beings who enjoy recreational sex! They demonstrate perfect qualities of altruism–there are many recorded instances of dolphins deliberately saving the lives of humans. For this reason, they were admired and protected by ancient civilizations. They possess the highest commitment to family and social bonding–orcas, for example, will spend their entire life with their family group (I was ready to leave home at nineteen!) It is recognized that they have a complex language, and at least one species of dolphin actually gives themselves individual names which they recognize each other by. Bottlenose dolphins have even been recorded talking about other dolphins–using the signature names of others in their pod!

With that in mind, any book which I write about them could not justifiably dwell solely on tales of death or imprisonment. As much as there is darkness here, there is also light. There is frustration, but there is also hope and positivity. And all through it, the dolphins show us the way to a deeper connection, and a deeper understanding of our place in All That Is. This, I believe is their gift to us, and so please do read this book with that concept in mind. My own interaction with the dolphins led me to a wider world, and I hope that you will similarly experience this as you read my words.

Most people who pick up this book will likely do so with a preconceived notion about Japan and its relationship with whales and dolphins. Most will know that Japan maintains a regimen of whaling in the Southern Oceans, carried out loosely under the guise of 'scientific research'. And some readers will very likely have heard of the Cove and Taiji–the Japanese coastal village which harbors the small industry which slaughters up to two thousand dolphins annually, and is responsible for the capture and supply of live specimens to the world's marine amusement parks.

My motivation for writing this book was twofold–firstly to give you, the reader, an accurate rendering of the dynamic on the ground in Taiji. And secondly; to present you with the wider story which confronted me there. In so doing I would also like to dispel the element of racism that has developed as people become understandably angry and frustrated with the dolphin hunters. I seek to address the angry claims that we are dealing with an entirely monstrous race of beings. Don't get me wrong; I believe to this day that the slaughter and capture of a self-aware marine mammal is an antiquated notion which has no place in present day. It is a cruel and unnecessary practice perpetuated and supported by a minority, and in that respect the Japanese are no better or worse than many other nations and cultures.

When challenged to defend this claim, I simply refer people to the fact that each year some three thousand dolphins meet their deaths needlessly as by-catch in American fisheries. Canadian sealers still bludgeon young seals to death for their pelts. And on the west coast of Australia, fishermen have routinely baited their pots with live kittens to attract more lobsters.

So, who are the monsters? *We* are the monsters–the human race. And so, when we challenge others to change their ways, we must remain conscious of that fact. We must *inspire* change, rather than aggressively *demand* it.

In truth I think it would be fair to say that at first, I went to Taiji angry and openly prepared to demand change. I tried to understand how and why a group of people would carry out the cruel acts that they do. Three trips to Taiji and some years later, my desire to advocate for change has not diminished; to the contrary it has only become stronger. I was drawn to Taiji, just like many others, to play a part in bringing about change. I hope that in some small way I have contributed to that process. And you can too, simply by *being* the change that you wish to see in the world, to quote the famous words of the Mahatma.

There is something to be said for inspiring change. My partner Jackie refers to it as 'sowing seeds' and in that respect her reckoning is perfect. If you slash a field of weeds, they will simply grow back. But if you plant a stand of trees, they will choke the weeds out as they grow.

So once again, thank you for your courage in reading this.
I now speak on behalf of the Taiji dolphins....

PART I

THE COVE

Kumano's salt tears
Water on ancient rock weeps
Blue water turned red

CHAPTER ONE

The Black Stream

TAIJI JOURNAL – February 2012

5am. Through the fog of my half sleep a muffled incessant chirp emanates from my equipment bag somewhere at the foot of the bed. The unfamiliar room is pitch dark and I fumble to find the source of the offending sound–my mobile phone set with a five o'clock wake-up alarm. In the measured silence of my still unfamiliar quarters, it sounds harshly foreign and abrasive. Like a drunken somnambulist I rummage blindly through binoculars, video equipment and computer accessories, cursing soundly and emphatically under my breath. The annoying audio cricket remains tantalizingly out of reach.

There appears to be a little-known law of physics which states that the item of technology that you require at any given moment is always located at the greatest possible distance from your grasp. I swear that mobile phone was right at the top of the bag when I packed it.

Ahhh, that's it! I packed the bag in the southern hemisphere and now I'm opening it in the northern hemisphere. I vaguely recall a thing called *Coriolis Effect* from my aviation days. That's the phenomenon that causes water to swirl in a clockwise direction as it drains out of your sink in the southern hemisphere and anti-clockwise in the northern hemisphere. Maybe it also applies to the contents of hand luggage as well as water flow. What was on top is now at the

The Black Stream

bottom! I marvel at how my mind works at totally ridiculous hours of the morning, and I thank the gods that nobody is listening.

I am in Katsuura, Japan. A pretty little resort village built around a bustling harbor which is home to a fleet of tuna fishing trawlers. Overlooking the harbor, my small single hotel room is silent except for the asthmatic wheeze of the air-conditioner set in the wall, keeping the room in a close artificial warmth. Sliding the window open in the pre-dawn silence, the vacuum of my little sleeping cell is broken and the shock breath of cold clear air invades the dark room with an audible sigh. Down in the narrow street below, the harbor is starting to wake in anticipation of the return of the tuna boats, heavy with the night's harvest. Muffled noise is already starting to rise from the wharf below.

In a few short hours the concrete under-croft across the docks will be filled with row upon row of plump blue steel bullets–highly prized Bluefin tuna that populate the rich Kuroshio Current which flows down along Japan's Pacific south-east coast. Originating from the Philippines before travelling hundreds of miles north to Japan, this fast-flowing nutrient rich warm ocean current supports a teeming multitude of marine species in a breathtakingly massive ecosystem. It also goes by the name of the 'Black Stream' in deference to the characteristic dark aquamarine coloration of its water.

I am laboring the point in describing this offshore current for a particular reason. It plays a very large and pivotal role in the battle which I am about to describe to you. Any changes in the architecture of this current, together with small water temperature fluctuations within its aqueous limits, will change the face of the battlefield off the beautifully picturesque stretch of Japanese coastline. Drawn to the rich feeding grounds of this deep blue flow are roving pods of whales and dolphins. Many of the species navigating these wild offshore waters I have never seen before in my homeland on Australia's west coast. Though my time in Japan was relatively short, I very quickly came to know and love these unfamiliar species who, prior to my first journey here last year, had only been images in a textbook. I very quickly discovered that each species is distinctly different in their characteristics and behavior.

For example; there are the small and nimble deep-sea dwellers, the striped dolphins. They typically travel in large pods numbering in the hundreds. Because of their smaller size, they breach regularly for air, and they actually conserve energy by leaping routinely on long voyages. Breaching frenetically and leaping skywards they churn a vast swath of ocean in a blaze of froth with silvery flashes and powerful tail flicks.

Then there are the mighty Risso's. Blocky and snub-nosed, their jet grey flanks distinctively etched with a crisscross graffiti of long pale-white scar markings. The Risso's dolphins are slow, graceful and deliberate by comparison. Definite, focused and reliable; making slow and calculated breaches in order to draw breath. I feel the peace and the grace of the ocean when I am in their presence. Like their smaller cousins the striped dolphins, the Risso's dolphins generally inhabit deep water and it is only by virtue of the fact that they are chased into shallow water by the hunters that we even get to see them here in Japan.

The bottlenoses, on the other hand are regular inhabitants of the shallows, and I already know them intimately from my home town in Australia. Gentle and playful, often with a cheeky glint in their eyes; I have often shared the river with them back at home on my kayak. Suddenly ignoring me to chase silvery fish into the shallows, the river dolphins have no problem with spraying an onlooker with brackish river water as they dive off opportunistically in pursuit of dinner. Massive, grey and slab-sided, they leave me awestruck with their subtle yet commanding presence and their obvious intellect.

Standing at the open Katsuura hotel window watching the first watery yellow tendrils of dawn sunlight silhouetting the jagged coastline, an ominous shiver runs through me. It is not so much the cold still air which causes it. Rather it is the recollection of the struggle which will be fought almost daily in the beautiful deep blue waters not so far from where I now stand. Here the dynamic between man and dolphin is vastly different to my hometown experiences. For several months it will be struggle for life and for freedom. Until recent times, precious few have stood in defense of the dolphins. It is the reason that I have returned to this place. And I am not the only one.

The geography books will tell you that the Kuroshio Current cuts a swath of dark water approximately one kilometer deep and one hundred kilometers wide along its journey of some three thousand miles; drawing in vast legions of diverse marine life along its path. It carries an imposing fifty million tonnes of sea water past Japan's southeast coast each second.

As awe inspiring as these statistics are, there is another element to the 'Black Stream.' In a deeper sense, the true reach of the Kuroshio seems to be something far greater than mere physical size. In 2012 there is an additional intangible dimension which could not have been factored into the textbooks. You see, it is this same dark rich current that is indirectly responsible for drawing terrestrial life forms from all across the globe here to Japan in the defense of the whales and dolphins that navigate its flow.

It has drawn me north from the sunburnt continent of Australia as surely as it has drawn many others from across the globe–from Canada, from the United Kingdom, New Zealand, South Africa, the United States and from points across Europe.

The rasping buzz of a fisherman's small white van rises from the street below and draws my attention back to the world outside. Katsuura harbor is waking in the chill stillness underneath a cloudless sky, pinpricked by the subtle yellow glow of the harbor lights. The air is calm and it causes a sudden catch of breath in my chest. Ordinarily I would stand captivated by the natural serenity and beauty of such a predawn scene. Ordinarily I would savor the warmth and the sharp pungent aroma of a morning coffee. Lost in the peaceful reverie of my own quiet thoughts as the world wakes up around me; lit by the eastern glow of sunrise. But not here. Not today. The perfect weather conditions can mean only one thing–it is a perfect day for the hunters.

Very quickly I fall back into the familiarity of the morning ritual I learnt just a year ago in this very place. This is now my second trip to Japan, and the old routine quickly returns. By the diffuse glow of my laptop perched on the tiny cluttered desk, I eat a quick breakfast of porridge and fruit whilst laying out the equipment I will need for the day ahead. My earlier fumbling search for my phone has hastened proceedings somewhat, and most of my gear now lies in a semi-neat array on my bed. Just after six o'clock a soft knocking on my hotel room door announces that Kerry, New Zealand activist and marine mammal rescue expert, is packed and ready to roll. An Aussie and a Kiwi in the land of the rising Sun. The irony of our pre-dawn assault is not lost on me–the Anzacs are ready to head for the Cove.

Out through the main doors of the hotel, Katsuura harbor is dark, and the string of long-line tuna vessels is still out. Our car, wedged into a cramped spot alongside the side wall of the hotel side is freezing to the touch. The road out of Katsuura wends its way through timeless hills painted in a verdant green of cedar trees and lush vegetation; meandering around the coast and into Taiji village, just a few kilometers away. At this time of the morning however the undulating terrain simply appears as towering charcoal shapes in the darkness, the alien sodium yellow of streetlights on the narrow road bleeding through the mantle of pre-dawn black. Threading its way through long stone tunnels the road meets up again with the wild blue of the Pacific and meanders toward our destination.

Although we are living in rented accommodation in the tuna fishing town, the object of our attention is the neighboring coastal village just a short drive away. Taiji. It is ancient, picturesque. And they hunt dolphins there.

As we get closer the good-natured banter slowly recedes. A cold dread has been gradually insinuating itself on the short drive from our home base of Katsuura and I now feel numb despite the all-pervading warmth of the car's heater. It is always an unknown as to how we will be greeted, and the recent aggression resulting in the imprisonment of an activist has added to that concern. Few words are now spoken between us as we drive on in silence along the now familiar route, each of us lost in our personal memories of the past, and the chilling prospect of what the immediate future might hold.

Despite the pre-dawn dark I have the odd sensation that we are alone, yet starkly naked and exposed; the small car and its two occupants nothing more than a micro-organism laid bare on a microscope specimen slide. Perhaps it is just my own paranoia, I think to myself. It seems to me as though our slow winding transit through this dark foreign world is being scrutinized by an unseen presence. As if lending further weight to this unsettling sensation, our movement past the notorious Cove is noted by several sets of eyes.

Dislodging itself from the darkness, the black and white shape of a police patrol car heaves into view and takes up station in an apparent escort position in front of us. The local police vehicles always appear slightly anachronistic to me; heavy squarish and boxy, they are reminiscent of old 1950's Russian KGB vehicles. The parallel only serves to make its presence even more ominous and foreboding. The knot in my stomach pulls a little tighter as its red roof lights flash and intermittently bathe the cliffs around the cove in an ominous crimson glow. I shiver and wonder if this is a portent of things to come. Kerry and I curse roundly in unison; our selection of expletives is almost comically identical.

Any hope of anonymity as we pass the Fishermen's Co-operative building and the imposing lines of drive boats berthed around Taiji harbor is now lost as we beetle crawl our way through Taiji township behind our garishly lit escort. Even in the washed greys of early dawn, we stick out like proverbial dogs' balls. This is not the big cosmopolitan city of Osaka or Tokyo, where tourists and Westerners are commonplace. This is more like the Wild West; little rural villages where people who speak English are the exception rather than the rule. The only Westerners around these parts are activists and protestors. The tourists who make the pilgrimage to trek the holy sites in the nearby mountains rarely come down here.

Instinctively I pull my navy-blue woolen beanie further down over my eyes as we pass the slab concrete sides of the fishermen's outpost. Through the concrete pillars I can plainly see the hunched forms huddled close around the cozy fire lit in a forty-four gallon drum alongside the harbor bulwarks. The dolphin hunters. In the orange glow of flying embers, I recognize the familiar overalls and white Wellington boots. Navigation lights are already glowing red and green on a few of the banger boats, confirming our gnawing fear.

Today they will be hunting for dolphins.

Taiji – Wakayama prefecture. The birthplace of Japanese whaling. Population 3,225.
Within the hour a dozen pristine white fishing boats will depart Taiji harbor, the steep mountain walls reflecting the throaty roar of their diesel engines. Once clear of the rocky sea wall that marks the harbor entrance, they will fan out and head for the open coastal waters of the Pacific. Their destination is an area a few nautical miles offshore which they refer to as *shiome*; a zone of disturbed water where the passing Kuroshio Current mixes and eddies with the local coastal current. Here they will sit in wait for their prey–passing pods of dolphins or small whales, drawn here by the rich abundance of fish and squid.

Out here beyond the harbor on the long finger of rocky land forming the lookout point, we watch the white tail position lights of the banger boat fleet flitting their way towards the horizon like errant fireflies. The dolphin hunters' boats are referred to as 'bangers' by the activists; so named because of the banging noise they employ to drive or herd the dolphins towards land. The banging is courtesy of a long metal pole they dip into the water from each boat. Hammering on the pole creates a loud 'banging' sound underwater which scares the dolphins and forces them to flee. It is primitive but effective.

In the pre-dawn stillness the seas are still calm and smooth, the offshore winds no more than a fleeting zephyr, and this is no good at all for the dolphins. Rough choppy seas and cloudy skies make it harder for the hunters to spot the surfacing dolphins–grey against the camouflaging grey water. The weather today favors the hunters.

Away in the mid-distance, small fishing boats with their distinctive black triangular staysails idly ply the becalmed waters. Like burly players in a rugby scrum, the banger boats navigate their way purposefully through the clutch of smaller fishing boats, slowly disappearing to become little more than small white smudges on the horizon. Small evil white smudges. I know that on the aft decks and the fly-bridges the crews will be scanning the seas for the tell-tale breach of dorsal fins. For us there is now nothing to do but watch and wait. Distant but familiar memories of this place have been flooding back since we left the hotel. The recollection is bittersweet.

The lookout is beautifully picturesque and the steely greys start to give way to color with the approach of the rising sun. Lush greenery surrounds our vantage point, and a grove of ancient gnarly tree trunks and pretty forested areas with breathtaking splashes of colorful flowers mark the long stretch of path back up to the car park at the foot of the peninsula. As I cast a glance back along the moss-covered stone pathway, three uniforms appear from underneath the umbrella of green foliage. Blue jacketed, gold braided; these are the three Special Task Force police who we now recognize as being our earlier escort through the deserted streets of Taiji township.

Despite the rising knot in my gut, I decide to stay on the front foot and I stride to meet them openly as they approach. Tensions have been running high prior to our arrival here with the recent arrest, and the subsequent seizure and search of other activists' laptops and camera equipment. The exact charges and the circumstances surrounding the incident still remain unclear to us at this point. What we do know is that one activist is currently incarcerated in the local Shingu prison, and other members of his group were subject to a police raid at their Katsuura hotel base just a few days prior to our arrival in-country.

Unsure of just what kind of reception to expect, we bow polite but cautious greetings to the police officials. I am more than a little surprised when the lead officer greets us by name in a polite and articulate English speaking voice. Leah Lemieux, the leading Save Japan Dolphins group representative currently here on the ground in Taiji, has already supplied our names to the police in advance, smoothing the way for our arrival. Although still cautious of us and not completely sure of our agenda here in the small fishing village, the three police are nonetheless polite and open with us. Their body language, demeanor and genuinely kind words find me warming to them immediately. With the necessary check of passports and personal details completed, the uniformed trio excuse themselves with polite bows and leave us to continue our surveillance of the drive boat fleet.

The morning steadily wears on, turning into a typical winter day in the pretty little coastal village. Thin watery sunlight infuses a cloudless sky of ice blue. The wild blue of the Pacific stretches out in front of me to become a graceful curve at the horizon. Scanning the watery arc through binoculars is a painfully tedious process and we take turns, alternately sweeping the blur of horizon.

The boats which left harbor in the predawn dark now enjoy anonymity in the distance. Blowing sea spray and the presence of other fishing boats and passing ships all but hide their location from our sight. Despite the sun the cold is bracing, and I alternately glance at close in objects with my naked eye to readjust my focus and counter the rising eyestrain. As the hours pass, so too do the number of times I have to break my concentration from the arduous task of scanning the distant waters. It is nearing mid-morning when an ominous sign appears in the far distance. A growing formation of white shapes has started to develop. Emerging from the distant haze several shapes resolve themselves slowly into the fleet of banger boats now slowly converging into a classic drive formation. This deliberate maneuver is always the first sign to confirm our worst fear–it means that the hunters have located a pod.

Life underwater carries a different set of sensory priorities compared to land dwellers. For us as human beings, sight is the primary sense. We use it for spatial awareness, for balance and for recognizing others. Cetaceans exist in a highly sonic environment, simply because sound is capable of travelling far greater distances than light underwater. So, for marine mammals, it is all about sound and hearing. Sounds projected by marine mammals can travel for many miles. Light by comparison will only travel a few hundred meters before it is scattered and absorbed. Water is thus a far more effective transport medium than air for carrying sound, and cetaceans have evolved sensory apparatus to best capitalize on this. In fact, the natural equipment a dolphin carries is nothing short of amazing. Toothed whales and dolphins possess highly sophisticated echolocation sonar (short for 'Sound Navigation and Ranging') which they use for hunting, foraging and navigation. Beaming a controlled stream of sonic clicks and buzzes, they listen for a reflected return echo in the same way that man-made radar systems listen for reflected radio waves in the atmosphere. It is believed that a dolphin's inbuilt sonar can actually help it to form a three-dimensional image of the surrounding environment. It is in fact so perfect that a dolphin can distinguish between two different types of metal buried in sand. For all our technological ability, humans to this day still cannot build sonar equipment with this level of discrimination.

In Taiji this highly sensitive hearing ability sadly becomes the dolphins' undoing. Despite the amazing sophistication of the dolphin's echolocation system, a primitively simple method is used by the hunters to counteract and confuse it. What's the worst thing you could do to somebody with hyper-sensitive hearing? Make a lot of noise, of course.

Each of the twelve drive hunting boats is equipped with a long metal pole which flares at one end into a bell shape; like the mouth of a trumpet. Placed into the water and hammered on the other end with a mallet, the resultant soundwaves fan readily through the salt water, overwhelming and confusing the dolphins' hypersensitive hearing mechanism. They simply turn and flee from the source of the sound. With the fleet of banger boats drawing up around and behind a fleeing pod, the dolphins can thus be shepherded like a flock of sheep and corralled towards the coast. And into the killing cove.

It is late morning when it happens. A line of distant white hulled boats looms larger, heading steadily toward us. Then, in the mid-distance, within the zone occupied by the ragged clutch of tiny sailboats, a distinct line of breakers appears, only to disappear almost as suddenly as it formed. These however are not natural ocean waves or white-caps, and we scan the area closely through binoculars. Tightly bunched and positioned to landward of the looming fleet of banger boats, the sudden concentrated points of rough white water mark the presence of a dolphin pod, breaching suddenly to draw air before diving swiftly down into deep water.

Several sets of eyes now confirm the sighting; it is definitely a pod of dolphins. However, at this long range the quick breaches aren't quite enough to permit us to determine the species as yet. There are however characteristic trademarks which give a good idea as to the identity of the beautiful creatures now being menacingly stalked just offshore from our lookout. A large number of dolphins means they may be striped dolphins or Risso's, which tend to travel in big numbers. Fast, repetitive breaching may indicate one of the smaller species of dolphins like the striped or the Pacific white-sided dolphins. The bigger dolphin species like pilot whales, Risso's and bottlenoses can stay submerged for longer periods and won't break the surface quite as often.

With conditions of near perfect visibility and calm seas, the distant pod has the odds currently stacked against them. Long minutes pass and I methodically sweep my binoculars across the horizon around the last point of the pod sighting using a technique learnt from my flying days to visually spot oncoming traffic. Suddenly in my field of view, the blue-grey ocean surface yields to the flash of dark triangular dorsals. This time however, they are seawards of the pursuing boats. I smile grimly, knowing that the pod has evaded the boats by staying down deep, doubling back and heading back out to sea. I have seen the big Risso's dolphins do this before; staying low in the water and passing quietly underneath the hulls of the pursuing boats. Will they be able to keep it up long enough to escape the hunters?

I suddenly become aware of just how tightly I am clutching one of the smooth grey stones I picked up hours earlier. Each one of us here on the lookout is mentally willing the dolphins to head to open sea. And for a while the pod does just that. A strange thing happens at this point in proceedings. Time and again, usually just around the point a pod was sighted and being driven, I would notice a sudden drop in temperature. I discovered it wasn't just me. Often the others would also remark about the sudden cold; sometimes it would simply be evidenced by an increase in the stomping of feet, shivering, hands clasped to bodies for warmth. I think I've worked out what is happening. Long hours of waiting have passed by. The sudden shock of the impending capture pumps adrenaline into the body. The 'fight or flight' mechanism causes blood to divert from organs to muscles and the anxiety response causes the body's core temperature to drop. Watching the pods feverish attempts at evasion out in the waters directly in front of me, I realize that we are also vicariously experiencing the emotions of the pod. The difference is that at the end of the day we are able to return home. It is now obvious to the pod that they are deliberately being targeted and pursued. No matter which way they turn the boats intercept and move in relentlessly. These dolphins do not naturally inhabit the shallows and the closer they are driven toward land, so their sense of panic begins to increase.

This time though the pod behaves quite uncharacteristically. Long minutes pass and the dolphins do not breach again. They are taking the tactic of staying low to the extreme and delaying the breaking of the calm water's surface. Knowing that the dolphins must eventually surface to breathe, the hunters slow their boats to a crawl and take to scanning the water's surface, looking for the tell-tale flash of dorsal fins. The fact that the pod is underwater for long periods confirms that this is one of the bigger dolphin species; maybe the blunt nosed Risso's, or perhaps even a small herd of pilot whales. A closer glimpse of the dorsal fin profile or body coloration will narrow this down. Yet still the pod remains non-compliant and out of sight. Long minutes pass. I would be more than happy not to make their acquaintance today, and simply seeing that line of beautifully sleek dorsal fins disappearing into open ocean would be the perfect conclusion to the day.

Over the course of a two-hour period the tussle continues at sea. Several more times the deep diving pod eludes the fleet of drive boats, leaving them wheeling in circles in a desperate attempt to relocate the fleeing herd. Several times they go deep and stay down, only to resurface at a distance, well clear of the bangers. Several times they swim under the hulls of the circling boats. And still they have not remained topside long enough for positive identification. By late morning however, events take a sudden turn for the worse when the pod appears to mistakenly turn in towards land. In a moment the balance has swung.

Seizing on this miscalculation the gleaming white boats accelerate, each blowing angry dark puffs of oily smoke from their funnels as they pull in close behind their prey. Painfully slowly the pod is maneuvered closer toward our position until finally they pass along the long rocky finger of land where we are standing. Behind us is Taiji harbor. As they pass below us heading toward the harbor, they still barely breach the water's surface as they rise to take air. We can now hear the breathy blows of the pod as they pass by; they are so painfully close to us. And then a flash of the tall curving falcate dorsal fins (think of the shape of a fin on a surfboard) and blunt snouts reveal them to be a small pod of Risso's dolphins. We can easily make out the distinct shape and scribbly white patterns across their flanks. Blazing past us, a solitary drive boat makes brisk headway back into the harbor. He is tasked with the job of returning to dock ahead of the others in order to prepare the small boats (called skiffs) bearing the nets which will rope the catch securely into the dark waters of the killing Cove. And it is then that all too familiar sound begins, like the hammering of so many coffin nails. The dull metallic thuds ring out and reverberate through the chill winter air. The rocks of the surrounding cliffs quickly take up the grim chorus and echo back the staccato beats.

Running alongside the rocky finger of land, back towards Taiji harbor and the outlying Cove, is a long stretch of water which we often refer to as 'the Funnel'. A passage of naturally deep water leading towards the harbor mouth, it forms a natural transit route along which the hapless pod is shepherded by their unwanted escort of surrounding banger boats. From ten gleaming white banger boats the metal poles are hammered in unison to further drive the pod in the desired direction. It is very likely a one-way trip from this point.

'We're going to have to move, and really soon people' says Leah commandingly.

Her lilting Canadian accent is terse and crisp, emotions held tightly in check. I grunt an incoherent reply, hearing my voice pitch slightly higher than usual in the grim tension of the moment. Again, the memories flood back as we gather up equipment and back-packs before making a hasty dash back along the picturesque little peninsula to the car. To our right, down through the tangle of trees and undergrowth they parallel us, heading in the same direction. Like the dolphins, my world has become suddenly sonic; the fevered crunching of stones underfoot as we run, the baritone thrum of diesels rising through the undergrowth, the occasional breathy blows of the pod, the whole stern symphony punctuated by the incessant metallic chorus of the banger poles echoing on the slab sides of the rocky outcrop, like some erratic heartbeat. It makes the hairs on my neck stand on end. I stub my toe on the rough pathway and swear roundly and fervently under my breath, self-consciously recognizing my broad Aussie twang sounding in sharp contrast to the Canadian's drawl and the distant American accents of the other activists. Taiji is rapidly becoming an international melting pot, in the defense of the dolphins.

Fumbling awkwardly on the run, I pull the car keys from my hip pocket. I feel far from home. Toughen up...*focus*. Backpacks are thrown into the backseats and video equipment stowed. A chorus of car doors slam. Retracing our path from earlier this morning back down the hill and around the long harbor, we relocate to Takababe Hill; thick with a lush forest it forms a natural wall to one side of the killing cove. A grassy swath of open parkland on the top of it permits a view straight down into the cove below.

Now, having navigated our way back along the narrow meandering roads of the ancient village to the small car park overlooking the bay, we hastily tote the equipment bags; scurrying under their weight towards the base of the towering hill. The few words that pass between us are curt and breathlessly businesslike. No words are really needed to explain exactly where our hearts and our minds are at this moment. We each know only too well what this point of the journey represents. If the pod is unable to make an eleventh-hour escape at this point, their final resting place lies in the still waters on the other side of this hill.

On my first visit here last year, one of the first things that I did was to stand quietly and feel the energy of this place. Moving air and flowing water will always endow a place with a clear energy and freshness that we resonate in harmony with. Here in the hills which line the coast, one can almost sense that this clear energy is tainted; there is an undertone of brooding tension underscoring it. A great many fearful deaths have occurred here whilst life has continued on around it, almost perfectly unaware of the travesty that has taken place. It is that duality and the sense of fractured energy that starts to insinuate itself on me, but today there is precious little time for navel gazing and quiet contemplation as we rush to the staircase. Breathlessly, we make the hasty climb up the hundreds of rough-hewn stone steps that cut their way through the dense canopy of foliage that cloaks Takababe Hill.

The blood is pounding in my temples and my leg muscles are taut with the effort as I pause briefly to catch my breath, turning at the midway point to glance back down the ancient stone walkway. After our breathy passing, the scene has already returned to a contented sun-dappled solitude. That strange duality. The air is crisp and thin; offering no heat to warm my protesting quads. A sudden sharp cry issues from a circling raptor. I can just make him out through the thick canopy overhead. Eyeing the graceful brown hawk wheeling slowly in the gathering thermals above the hill, I am again left in sober wonderment at the glaring disconnect between worlds; the gaping schism between the timeless beauty and serenity of this perfect natural world; so removed and oblivious to the churning chaos and panic in the world of water down at the base of the hill. Punctuating its sudden maneuver with a single shrill call, the hawk banks to seawards, the five long flight feathers on its wingtips held rigid like a ballerina's gracefully outstretched fingers. Our brief rest over, I run up the remaining flight of steps to the hill summit, anticipating the arrival of the banger boats carefully shepherding their catch through the shallows.

Breaking through the filtered half-light of the rainforest canopy, the neatly manicured grass area on the hilltop park stands in a bright sharp focus, bathed in a blaze of late morning sun. Below our lofty vantage point, standing out in a stark relief against the blue-grey of coastal waters are the gleaming white hulls of the drive boats, idling at low speed around the rocky tracing of coastline. By comparison with the earlier frantic maneuvering in the offshore waters, the movements of the banger boats are now steady and measured; almost leisurely. The reason for this quantum change becomes immediately obvious; the waters ahead of the lead boat break and churn with the slow breaching of a small scattering of tall falcate dorsal fins. The pod is clearly exhausted from the long pursuit. The dolphins knew that their best chance of evasion lay in staying as low and as deep as possible, and they had almost managed it today. But the Risso's are not as nimble as their smaller cousins. Slower moving and relatively leisurely, their foraging for food takes place far offshore. They are what is known as a *pelagic*, or deep-water species. Born a dark grey color, their bodies lighten with advancing age due to the myriad crisscrossing of white marks lining their flanks. It is said that these markings are caused by large squid, which is one of their preferred foods of choice. Being ocean dwellers, they are not used to being in the shallows so close to land. The hunters take care not to panic them unduly; not so much for the dolphins' wellbeing, but to ensure they don't scatter feverishly and escape. Out beyond the rocky coastline I attempt to count the grey-white bodies as they surface and circle warily.

Two small skiffs motor around on either side of the small group, a fisherman occasionally throwing a large heavy weight attached to a rope into the water in order to muster the big mammals. The group numbers just over half a dozen individuals. Even with a small 'sub-pod' of this size it is difficult to obtain an accurate head count as the group circles and weaves erratically.

Their body language shows them to be confused and bone tired from the deadly game of hide and seek they have been forced to play with the hunters for the past two hours.

Pulling back from the view through my binoculars I become aware of the throng of people suddenly milling around me; the blue uniforms of the Special Police Task Force. The blue capped provincial Wakayama police representatives, typically more aloof and disdainful by comparison. Three members of the Task Force bow in polite recognition. There is the undertone of shared understanding in their body language. Taiji town officials, dressed casually and standing sullen and aloof, refuse to make eye contact with me. Clearly, they would much rather I wasn't there. The Western activists; a knot of black and white skull and cross bones marking the darker presence of Sea Shepherd; by comparison, the colorful clothing of the wonderful ladies who make up our little group–Kerry and Masako, Tia and Leah from Save Japan Dolphins; looking for all the world like some gathering of guardian angels. I am thankful they are all here for the dolphins. Ric O'Barry, who stood watch with us through the long cold hours of the morning at the Lookout now keeps a vigil at the Cove beach down below us. Although surrounded as I am by the human element, I still feel somehow solitary and alone; lost in my own private thoughts.

The muted backdrop of accompanying sound seems somehow surreal and remote after our frenzied rush; the distant throb of diesels, the off-hand small talk of the activists in low undertones, occasional metallic clicks of cameras and the lonely call of hawks wheeling overhead. Ahead of the slow procession rounding the rocky head land, a skiff carrying two dolphin trainers has already navigated its way into the cove. Since the Risso's is a species with captivity potential; the two trainers, presumably from nearby Dolphin Base, will assess the pod at close quarters in order to select the best specimens.

It is really the live captures that drive this little industry. This diminutive little village hosts the world's principal exporter of dolphins to the world's marine parks and aquariums, this is where the big money is made. And wherever there is money there is invariably greed and exploitation. That is the naked truth of present-day Taiji. Not proud tradition or culture. No matter what people may say, this is all about money. The bitter reality is that it is the youngest dolphins that will likely become the prize for the watching trainers, who have now disembarked the skiff to stand on the nearby rocks awaiting the hunters. Juvenile dolphins can be broken and trained, ready for a life given to providing entertainment for the crowds of paying customers at scores of marine amusement parks and oceanariums. They are also the most likely candidates for the in-house breeding programs of marine parks. Their family and pod elders will be slaughtered first, before they are transported away in canvas slings. The dolphin trainers will always profess their love for these creatures, yet whenever there is a live capture selection to be done, they will routinely watch the accompanying slaughter without comment or protest.

The stillness is broken harshly by the jarring buzz-saw rasp of outboard motors from below us in the cove. With the holding nets deployed around the mouth of the bay, the skiffs cleave the still waters and deftly circle the small pod while the two trainers look on. It soon becomes apparent just what they are doing; the small boats are keeping the dolphins confined to a small area of the cove so that the trainers can carefully assess them and select the best specimens for captivity. Today their selection is a relatively easy one. The count is quickly confirmed at seven Risso's dolphins; five adults and two juveniles.

Several times the two members of the Taiji town council discreetly attempt to gain a tactical advantage by positioning themselves at the best viewing points, thereby blocking our view. Their plan doesn't work, and they find themselves very quickly part of a thick knot of activists who politely bow and excuse themselves before wedging themselves in discreetly around the two slightly built locals. It presents an almost comical picture; tousled blonde Cove angels in bright colored scarves, yours truly looking to all and sundry like a nightclub bouncer in a dark woolen beanie, sunglasses and hoodie, and two somewhat scrawny town officials doing their level best to appear like relaxed casual sightseers, whilst studiously avoiding any eye contact with any of us. But far from being relaxed and no doubt feeling themselves the odd ones out in the world's strangest rugby scrum, the pair eventually disengage somewhat reluctantly and re-group at a safe distance in an activist free zone of the park. From the corner of my eye I weigh up their body language. We are like that annoying guest who overstays his welcome at a party. Gone are the days when the local hunters could carry on their business quietly and in relative secrecy.

The ancient spirits of Kumano seem almost possessed of a wry sense of humor. These days whenever *iruka* (dolphins) are hunted it seems the gods are wont to open large cans of activists and sprinkle the contents liberally over the emerald green top of Takababe Hill. These cloying Westerners with their zoom lenses and their video cameras; the *gaijin* (foreigners) who mourn the death of a 'fish'. In a quiet moment's reflection, I wonder how the hunters will look back on these days in the years to come. And how will their hearts speak to them as they cast their minds back across the years?

The whole business reminded me of a very similar whaling town much closer to home.

☙❦❧

For as long as I can remember I have loved the ocean. I competed in school swim teams throughout my primary and high school years, and while away the timeless days of summer break in the surf at the sun-drenched beaches of Scarborough and Cottesloe. As a young boy growing up in the early seventies, my summer holidays were spent in south-western Australia, swimming and surfing on beautiful unspoiled beaches in little country towns with names like Busselton and Margaret River. I fondly remember the long beaches of golden white sand, baking under a blazing summer sun and a sky painted like a glossy postcard in the most perfect blue. It is almost unspoiled wilderness country, wild rocky coastlines and big surf. Inland lies the vast expanse of dense forest and bushland.

Kangaroos are plentiful here and quite happily share the camping areas with humans; bounding out suddenly from the darkening fringes of the surrounding bushland as dusk falls. It truly is the lucky country. As awe inspiring as this unspoiled natural beauty was, I also remember the stark contrast of a darker element overshadowing the wilderness of the south-west. From my teen years I can still clearly recall the Dantesque scene of a whale being hauled onto the flensing deck of the whaling station in the peaceful little holiday township of Albany. It was only a few miles from the beach where I spent the long lazy summer days in the beating surf. I can still see that curiously squalid and surreal picture in my mind's eye.

In those days the local radio station would broadcast the impending arrival of a harpoon ship with a whale in tow. Having heard that a whaler was returning, Dad had woken my brother and me in the small hours of the morning, before bundling us half-asleep into the family station wagon to make the short, bumpy drive along the wild southern coastline to witness the scene. In those days there was no such thing as occupational health and safety considerations–we simply walked into the whaling station, nodded a casual greeting to the workers and literally stood right on the corner of the flensing deck amidst the noise and the chaos. Directly in front of us were the massive iron holes, set like so many vast and gaping black eyes sunk into the concrete ramp; dropping down into the giant burner pots below where the oil was decanted from the blubber. I recall the scene as being strangely surreal–an ethereal vision of Hades under an industrial blaze of yellow sodium lights. The massive grey bulk of the whale was being swiftly dissected by a team of sweating, disheveled men with huge flensing knives, lit from the pits below by the eerie orange glow from the flensing pots. Despite the apparent chaos there was a workmanlike precision about it all.

To this day many people are unaware that, right up until 1978, Australia was a whaling nation. In the south-west of the state of Western Australia lies the coastal whaling town of Albany. It has a strikingly similar heritage to the little Japanese village of Taiji. Looking out onto the wild restless blue of the Southern Ocean, Albany is endowed with a large natural harbor and a proximity to the bounty of the great southern sea. Capitalizing on the passing trade of French and American whaling vessels, the early settlers established small bay whaling stations to support the transient industry. The foreign seafaring traffic that had originally prompted the colonizing of Albany became a lucrative source of potential income for the fledgling township. Originally settled in the manner of so many Australian towns as a convict settlement, the destiny of Albany was immediately being shaped by the influence of the foreign whalers.

By the mid-1800's whaling had reached a peak with as many as three hundred whaling ships from the American Yankee whaling fleet plying the waters off the southern coastline of Australia. This time period was also to become a turning point for many of the Western whaling nations; with the discovery of petroleum oil, the demand for whale oil went heavily into decline, and with it went the great whaling fleets.

Albany, however, now had an established link with the sea and the taste of whaling. In the early 1900's a Norwegian company negotiated the rights to establish a permanent whaling operation in the little coastal town, with a fleet of modern steam driven harpoon vessels. The Cheynes Beach Whaling Company was born. Over the ensuing years, the fledgling company grew and established itself firmly as one of the economic mainstays of the little coastal town. Despite disruption by two world wars in the early decades of the 20th century, the whalers continued their trade; further decimating the migrating pods of southern right whales and humpbacks.

Public sentiment towards whaling slowly changed over time, and my relationship with Albany was formed in those years of change and growing environmental awareness. As a young boy I have fond memories of the 1970's as a decade of fashion faux-pas; platform shoes, bell-bottom flares and androgynous shoulder length hair. And I'm almost embarrassed to confess, I possessed all three! To coin a modern term, it was a decade of epic fashion fail. But it was also a decade of trying things on to see what fit–we seemed like a generation in search of ourselves. Born out of the hippie movement of the sixties, the seventies saw a pubescent growth-spurt in environmental consciousness. With the Apollo moon landings of the late 1960's, mankind was beginning to see itself from a sobering new perspective– as a solitary ark in space. The first color photographs of the Earth viewed from space began to sink into mass consciousness. There we were, hung suspended in all our glory–vulnerable and fragile. So now we began to perceive our home planet from an entirely new perspective; as a sparkling yet delicate gem, lonely against the vast backdrop of deep space. We began to grasp the beauty and the fragility of life on planet Earth.

Subsequently, the 1970's saw the rumblings of a fundamental mind shift with regards to the protection and conservation of whales. In 1972 the United States passed the Marine Mammal Protection Act, prohibiting the hunting and killing of cetaceans domestically. Popular culture was beginning to embrace whales and dolphins as intelligent and engaging creatures. With shows like 'Flipper', television and film were paving the way with depictions of dolphins as playful and charismatic mammals of the deep, possessed of distinctly individual personalities.

It was an era that marked the beginning of the Western world's love affair with whales and dolphins. When Roger Payne, a biologist and environmentalist, revealed recordings of humpback whale song, the public were introduced to a hitherto unknown depth of sentiment and intelligence that these mighty marine mammals possessed. *They could sing!* Enchanting and wistful, we learnt that their complex melodies were being sung across hundreds of miles of open ocean, seeking out their distant kin. Whale song became the latest craze wherever New Age records and cassette tapes were sold. Whale song meditation tapes. Whale song set against string symphonies. The whales were being given a voice and more people were starting to take up their call.

'Save the Whale' protests were taking to the streets of London en-masse, marching to the amplified backdrop of a hauntingly beautiful soundtrack—the song of the humpback whales. The 'Save the Whales' catch-cry was becoming deeply ingrained in pop culture, appearing on posters, bumper stickers and T-shirts. In the great southern land of Australia, the seeds of a fledgling anti-whaling movement were also tentatively starting to make their presence felt. With the support of activists from the recently born Canadian Greenpeace organization, a small group of protesters began putting pressure on the Cheynes Beach whalers to cease their whaling activities. Poorly equipped and ill-experienced in boat craft, the activists put to sea in small zodiacs, much to the surprise and annoyance of the experienced seafarers aboard the four harpoon ships.

The captains and crews aboard the whalers found their presence frustrating and their poor attempts at seamanship foolhardy and reckless on the unforgiving swells of the Southern Ocean. Many was the time that a harpoon would be fired dangerously low over the heads of the shaggy zodiac occupants who had deliberately placed themselves between the harpoon ships and the fleeing whales. Foolhardy they may well have been, but the actions of Greenpeace in the coastal waters off Australia's rugged south-west tip were coming to the attention of the Australian population, who by and large did not share the small town's whaling sentiments. The actions of one young Australian girl touched the nation, when the daughter of the then Prime Minister of Australia, Malcolm Fraser submitted an anti-whaling plea in a school project. It seemed to echo the sentiments of greater Australia, and the anti-whaling cause began to gather greater momentum. The days of whaling in Australia were numbered. But before the flensing decks lay abandoned and bleached by sun, the town of Albany refused to give in without a fight. Ugly scenes developed as whalers and activists clashed. Violence threatened when the whalers called on the services of local outlaw bikie gang 'God's Garbage' during a protest at the gates of the whaling station. The townsfolk of Albany held grave concerns for their economic future. Theirs was a whaling town, and for the whalers themselves it was the only life that they knew. They were not going to surrender to the growing weight of public opposition without a fight. The writing however was on the wall. Under the weight of public pressure, the Cheynes Beach Whaling Station finally collapsed and closed its doors forever. The last whale was taken at Albany, Western Australia on 20th November 1978.

ൟ❈ൠ

High up over Takababe Hill, the ever-present brown hawks wheel endlessly and sound their plaintive cries. Down in the Cove below, one skiff is routinely circling and mustering the small group, its outboard noise continuous and grating, rather like an annoying lawn mower on a peaceful Sunday morning.

For almost half an hour the incessant maneuvers continue in the waters of Hatajiri Bay, directly below our vantage point. The exhaust smoke from the small boat's motor clouds the air above the water, and its nasal drone grates on my nerves. If it has this effect on me standing high above, I can only begin to imagine the effect on the hypersensitive hearing of the seven dolphins circling tired and confused in the waters below. My own personal discomfort pales in comparison to what they are presently going through. After almost thirty minutes of slow constant circling, the skiffs begin to change pattern and maneuver in towards the pod. They are preparing for the slaughter. My stomach knots as I watch the occupants of the skiff begin to shepherd the blocky grey Risso's under the makeshift marquee of blue tarpaulins directly below us. This is the killing area; tarped off to prevent us from documenting the final proceedings.

This marks the end for these gentle dolphins, now discreetly hidden from our cameras and prying eyes. Those sorts of photographs make for bad press. Blocked from our view with the open skiffs drawn in around the open end of the marquee, there is now nothing for us to do but wait. The killing process is mercifully fast today; the dull heavy thud of bodies against the floorboards of skiffs marks the passage of these majestic ocean dwellers. My heart aches in my chest. The open boat, now loaded to the gunwales and riding low in the water, slowly navigates its way out of the killing Cove. Its precious cargo is hidden from view under heavy blue-green tarpaulins.

There is a momentary pause and confusion. The second skiff draws out from the covering marquee of stretched blue tarpaulins with what appears to be a sling strapped along one side. With binoculars trained we catch glimpses of the departing boat from our vantage point up above. There appears to be a young dolphin alive and held snugly in the cradle, lashed against one side of the motorboat. Such are the lengths that the dolphin hunters go to in order to hide the grim work from watching eyes that it is not until later when we carefully review the video footage of the second skiff's departure for Taiji harbor that something else becomes evident. The dark outlines of not one but *two* small dorsals show against the shadowed sides of the white hull. There are two juvenile dolphins slung low to the waterline against the flank of the open boat. The pair of youngsters will be transferred to a series of floating pens in the mouth of the harbor. Here they will undergo basic training by local trainers before being sold to a marine amusement park.

Whilst it is not my intent in this work to dwell on the cruel mechanics of dolphin slaughter, I do need to point something important out to you. Hidden from our gaze under the marquee in the shallows of the Cove, the two youngsters were held in those final minutes whilst their mothers and the remainder of their group were cruelly slaughtered.

More damningly, there are another two sentient, self-aware beings also standing by and bearing witness. The two dolphin trainers who have watched the carnage belong to a group which universally lays claim to a devotion and a love for dolphins. It leads me to wonder just how they rationalize the brutal events of the day against their self-professed love for their charges. I have learned over years of experience that the industry is wrought with many hypocrisies and incongruities. The International Marine Animal Trainers Association (IMATA) recently ran its annual conference. The major sponsor for the event was the Dutch company which operated a fleet of fishing 'super trawlers' which have been banned from some nation's waters due to the damaging nature of its operation. The by-catch from these trawlers includes dolphins and other marine mammals and remains controversial to this day.

After today's drive hunt and the subsequent slaughter in the killing Cove, two youngsters are all that remain; now swimming in the confines of small sea pens in Taiji harbor. Their destiny is to be broken in and trained by the local dolphin trainers. Their immediate survival will depend on how quickly they can transition and adjust to a shock change in diet, environment and social conditions. Theirs is an uncertain future. A deep-water dolphin that rarely comes into contact with land; this has likely been the young dolphins' first encounter with land dwellers. This has been their introduction to the human race.

Perhaps you may be wondering what became of the little coastal whaling town of Albany, Western Australia? Australia by world standards is a relatively new nation. Its history is one of convict settlement dating back a mere two centuries to the time that Europeans settled in the colony now called Sydney on the eastern Pacific coast. Although it cannot boast an ancient heritage, the small coastal town of Albany is fairly similar to Taiji in certain respects. From the early days of its founding, Albany was heavily influenced by the transient whalers that regularly navigated its waters. The town grew to maturity in the shadow of a coastal whaling station. When activists and public pressure threatened the closure of Cheynes Beach whaling station in the latter part of the 1970's, the town was in an uproar of concern regarding their economic future and the well-being of the townspeople.

A couple of years before I first went to Japan, I celebrated my birthday in Albany. I visited the derelict whaling station, now preserved for all to see as a natural history museum. Shivering, in part from the bone-numbing chill rolling in from the Southern Ocean, and the tremor which comes from the outpouring of memory, I stood on the windswept deck of the old harpoon ship which now lies silent in dry-dock as a static display; a mute testament to a violent past. I was the only person on the ship that day, and the whaling station was all but deserted, being a weekday. It was eerie. Actually, wandering in and out of the cramped rooms in the belly of that old whaling ship, it felt for all the world as though I was some forlorn soul condemned to roam the seas like Davey Jones. Gazing out from the harpoon ship's high deck onto the grey unforgiving waters of King George Sound, I wondered what it must have been like to have lived all those years ago in a culture of whales and whaling.

The main reason I made the five-hour drive to Albany to celebrate my birthday was to go whale watching. The high point was my trip out into the waters of King George Sound aboard a whale watching catamaran under full sail and to watch several massive black Southern right whales, churning their way south with their young in tow, nestled alongside for protection. One even followed us back into the harbor; surfacing curiously alongside our hull!

At that time of the year, they were making the long and arduous journey to the bottom of the world; drawn inexorably southwards toward the great ice continent of Antarctica and its rich feeding grounds.

You see, today Albany is a whale *watching* town.
Those who speak out in defense of the dolphin slaughter industry in Taiji claim that financial hardship will beset the town should the industry be closed. And yet the little town of Albany didn't die the day they stopped whaling in 1978. Quite to the contrary, the coastal settlement went from strength to strength over the ensuing years. Today tourism has taken the place of whaling. Today there are still spotters manning the high ground looking out onto the wild Southern Ocean. They are still looking for whales just like times gone by; however, it is a vast industry of whale watching that has taken the place of whale slaughter. It is quite telling that some of the captains who once manned the steam driven harpoon ships in the halcyon days of Aussie whaling have come out on record, stating publicly that the killing of whales was wrong. But it was their livelihood and their means of income.

In more recent times many of those former captains have again crossed paths with the Greenpeace activists who were the thorns in their side all those years ago. Only now they meet in friendship and not with raised voices of anger and frustration like times past. The men who once hunted and killed these mighty creatures have since stood up at rallies and spoken out in their defense. Sadly, a lot of damage was done to the population numbers of the great southern right whales, and the species is only just beginning to recover from it, decades later. Whales, unlike fish do not give birth in large numbers, and like other mammals their young take years to reach breeding age themselves.

The forced closure of their industry ultimately forced the whalers to seek out other means of employment; many took to the sea as fishermen whilst others left to work the nearby coal mines. But survive they did, as did the town of Albany, which has grown to be a thriving city in modern day. How then, will the dolphin hunters of Taiji look back on their past in the years to come?

ଓ୫❀ଌଠ

Five kilometers to the north of Taiji lies the resort town of Katsuura. Originally developed as a pilgrim's waypoint town for travelers visiting the nearby Shinto shrine high in the mountains, today the Katsuura fishing port also reaps the rewards of the rich coastal environment. It is the base for one of Japan's largest tuna fishing industries. Just like Taiji, Katsuura lies in the formidable embrace of the steep mountains of the Kii peninsula, clinging to the hilly coastline with its harbor area nestled into the secluded safe haven of Katsuura bay. Looking out across the lively harbor area with its rows of white hulled fishing vessels, a large multi-story complex sits squat and businesslike on the far dock. Its high walls are festooned with huge colorful murals the size of billboards; a lobster and a giant school of Bluefin tuna stare out dramatically across the busy harbor waters. This sprawling warehouse complex which occupies the length of the far harbor docks is the local fisheries processing building and fish market. The sheer size and imposing dimensions of the graphic displays high on its walls is in itself testament to the relative importance of this industry to the Japanese locals. When you consider it against the relative dimension of its surroundings–small streets overlooked by equally small houses, and everywhere the small cars which typify Japan, you realize that anything which is presented with such Godzilla-like enormity must be something that psychologically holds a great weight of importance for the Japanese. Just like Taiji, evidence of Katsuura's relationship with the sea is to be found on every street and every corner.

There is a major difference between the neighboring towns that is interesting to note. Katsuura's murals and effigies all relate to fish–and in particular to tuna–and the whales and dolphins whose images adorn the Taiji streets not five kilometers away are conspicuous by their absence. The village streets adjoining the harbor area are not unlike a Japanese version of Chinatown–the narrow cluttered streetscapes festooned with hanging sprays of pale pink and white flowers. Rising above them each lamp post carries a hanging mural of a leaping Bluefin tuna; the pendulous white balls of streetlights all hanging enclosed in wire 'lobster pot' cages. Beautiful old glass fishing floats decorate a small stone bridge near the harbor, and everywhere there are dazzling splashes of bright color that assault the senses.

So, it intrigues me that in a town just five kilometers from the whaling village of Taiji–the birthplace of Japanese whaling–there is scant recognition of whales or dolphins here.

Katsuura is a fishing town and more specifically it is a key player in the vast and lucrative Bluefin tuna long-line industry. Fishing using this method involves miles of line laid out with multiple hooks and indiscriminately catches large amounts of marine life; amongst the by-catch a large number of sharks are also caught as a result. The Fisheries Agency of Japan instructs the tuna long-line fishermen to bring back both fins and carcass together when they land shark fins so that the by-catch can be recorded. A number of major pelagic shark species are caught by the tuna long-line fishery including blue shark, big eye thresher shark, oceanic white tip shark, silky and Mako shark. Katsuura is also home to one of the three largest morning fish markets in Japan, the scale of which is both stunning and sobering to view.

Putting a further perspective on this, the Katsuura market is tiny and relatively sedate when compared to Japan's massive main fish market located in Tokyo. The Tsukiji fish market covers an area equivalent to forty-size football fields and it is said to be the largest fish market in the world. Approximately 42,000 people will pass through the market every day in 4,500 vehicles. 20,000 fish retailers and 7,500 wholesalers trade almost five hundred different varieties of marine products at the market daily.

In 2010, a Bluefin tuna weighing 232 kilograms sold for ¥16.28 million yen. That's one big fish. Big dollars too. One hundred and seventy-five thousand US dollars, to be precise.

Just like other regions of the world, Bluefin tuna stocks in Japan are now severely depleted by over-fishing–the species is on the verge of collapse and is listed as critically endangered in the eastern Atlantic Ocean and the Mediterranean Sea. The Japanese nation alone consumes three quarters of *all* the Bluefin tuna caught in the world's oceans.

In March 2010 a proposal to totally ban the trade in the critically endangered Atlantic Bluefin tuna failed at the Convention on International Trade in Endangered Species (CITES). Sixty-eight member nations including Japan voted against the proposal. To add insult to injury, the highlight of the menu that night was.... Bluefin tuna sushi. What hope do we have? It is interesting to note that just a couple of years later, I presented CITES–an international organization which supposedly protects endangered species–with a scientific report showing that the depletion of local populations of up to seven different dolphin species in Japanese coastal waters was beyond their ability to reproduce and replenish their population numbers. In other words, local Japanese dolphin populations would go into serious decline if their slaughter and capture continued at present levels. The report was completely ignored by CITES, who refused to even acknowledge it.

And so, what does the future hold for Japan's whales and dolphins? Well, despite their heavy reliance on seafood, it is of interest to note that in a survey conducted in 2008 by the Nippon

Research Centre, 95% of Japanese respondents indicated they either consume whale meat rarely or never at all. Sadly, there is another cultural mindset that works against the welfare of whales and dolphins here in Japan. With the steadily reducing fish stocks, there is a perception that whales and dolphins are simply pests. They are eating all of the fish! Recent history shows that the concept of 'pest control' has become a recurrent theme in Japan's view of the treatment of whales and dolphins.

The International Whaling Commission (IWC) makes the following statement in their publication 'Whales and Whaling':

'The Japanese research programs have revealed that whales compete with fisheries in the waters around Japan as they feed on sardine, Pacific saury, pollock, salmon, squid and other species that humans utilize as fishery resources. Many whale species are known to have increased at a rate of 4% since the moratorium was placed on commercial whaling.

This means that their populations have doubled in the seas around Japan since then. During this time, the catch of Japanese fisheries has gone down from twelve million tons in the 1980s to less than six million tons today. Competition between whales and fisheries is an issue that cannot be overlooked from the perspective of fisheries resource management.'

Simply put, the Japanese mindset is: *Those pesky whales and dolphins are eating all of our fish!*

CHAPTER TWO

Taiji

S. Hamanaka, Taiji Town Mayor on behalf of the People of Taiji, Japan. Address to the International Whaling Commission (IWC) meeting–1994.

A Message from the People of Taiji, Japan:

"The village of Taiji, where we live is located on the southern part of the Japanese archipelago at the tip of the peninsula which extends into the Pacific Ocean. Steep mountains which are covered with dense forests come to the shoreline and fall sharply into the ocean. With flat land suitable for farming being so limited, the people of Taiji must depend on the resources available from the sea. As far back as our knowledge of history can tell, the people of Taiji have been catching a variety of whales.

For people without farming, whales have been an important source of food as well as commodity for exchange to obtain rice and vegetables from the farmers. Particularly, since the 17th century when Yorimoto Wada and Yoriharu Wada, the well-respected founding fathers of Taiji Kujiri Gumi (Taiji Whaling Group), invented net whaling, whaling has become the most important subsistence activity and industry for villagers. This has continued into the modern period after Japan opened its doors to the west. Whaling is the very activity we have learned from our ancestors and lived by for many generations.

Because of those historical reasons, we consider ourselves to be 'a whaling people.' We are proud of our own heritage and want to hand it down to the next generations. Thus, it was a traumatic experience that our values were attacked fiercely by western environmentalists and animal right activists, and the International Whaling Commission (IWC) mercilessly forced us to stop whaling. The impact of the whaling ban has been tremendous. Many villagers lost their proud occupations and important means of livelihood, and wounds and scars were made in the heart of many men and women.

No matter how viciously the environmentalists and animal right activists condemn us, we will not give up whaling. We simply cannot do that, because it would mean to us not only a significant economic loss but also a loss of our pride and the unique culture of our own. A small village like Taiji would be wiped out completely by the massive forces of industrialization and commercialization without a pride for its own heritage and a strong sense of community identity.

Although Japan is one of the world's most advanced industrialized nations, there are a number of small communities which are still dependent on traditional subsistence activities based on natural resources and maintain traditional values which contrast sharply with the increasing influence of urban and western values. Taiji is one such community, and we want it to remain that way and we are trying so hard for that.

We believe our views on nature and its utilization, which have been accumulated and nurtured by generations of experience right here in Taiji, are not only valuable for ourselves but potentially for many other coastal peoples who suffer from environmental deterioration caused by mishandling of the nature. Humans, the greatest predator on earth, need wisdom and technology tested by generations of experience in order to live in harmony with the nature. The nature is so diversified that our approaches to the nature need to be diversified. We should try to understand and respect unique adaptive values of the individual cultures in their own environment, and try to utilize and protect the nature rationally by making full use of those diversified cultures. Cultural imperialism which some western environmentalists are promoting, either knowingly or unknowingly, is harmful to both people and nature.

We believe we know more about our own sea in Taiji than anyone who lives hundreds or thousands of miles away from us. We also believe we are more concerned with its protection and assume more responsibilities than anybody else in the world. We are sure that the same view is shared by Alaskan Eskimos, Faroese, Greenlanders, Icelanders, Norwegians, and Russians in Chukotka as well. We hope many environmentally concerned people in the industrialized nations will understand our views and trust us as rational and humane people, and stop making whaling a 'scape goat' of the environmental crusade and making inhumane attacks on whaling people. Cultural diversity is just as important as biological diversity in order to protect the earth's environment. After all, it is only a diversified people who can really take tender care of a diversified nature and make truly rational and orderly use of it.

We people of Taiji need whaling and we have a right and a good reason to continue whaling. We hope our position is well understood by all the participants of the IWC meeting, and rational actions will be taken by the Commission. We urge the Commissioners to sincerely respond to our humble request of interim allocation of 50 Minke whales to alleviate our distress caused by the unreasonable and unjustified moratorium since 1988 for four small coastal whaling communities including Taiji."

TAIJI

☙❀❧

Situated on the southern-most point of Japan's main island of Honshu, Taiji is a pretty little coastal village facing onto the wild blue of the Pacific Ocean. Ringed by lush heavily forested mountains she is today an enigma–a contradiction. For an outsider who is not privy to what goes on here, it would be very easy to fall in love with this place. As indeed I did when I first journeyed there in the winter of January 2011. The winding roads snake through stone tunnels carved into the heart of rolling hills, growing thick with ancient cedar trees and verdant green growth. The air is fresh and pungent with the heady fragrance of wood. The surrounding Wakayama prefecture is called 'Country of tree (*ki-no-kuni*) blessed with forest'. Around the village of Taiji, this imposing high ground succumbs to the wild vigor of whitecaps perched atop aquamarine blue; the beaches dashed and dotted with pebbles and rocks of greys and browns, worn smooth by the restless Pacific tides. The deep blue sings of an ancient history laced with danger, echoed by the steep surrounding rock walls. In an almost zen-like study, a slab-sided rock mound erupts from the sea near the harbor mouth reflecting the pale sunlight in muted hues of tans and pale browns. It is surmounted by a solitary gnarled tree in bonsai form, its calloused trunk bent seawards as though pointing the way to the Pacific for the benefit of the tiny boats departing the harbor.

It is my personal belief that the physical world in which we exist imprints across the world of spirit. There are doorways which exist between the two where the line blurs and the subtle influence of spirit can occasionally insinuate itself into our world of form and vibrational solidity. And if that is true then my first impressions of Taiji tell me that there is a deeper mystery here to be unlocked. There is an ancient power moving behind the veil here as if awaiting some sort of communion and reconnection. Those readers who have an

Taiji

affinity with the Star Wars epic will understand this observation–there are places here which are strong with the dark side of the Force. The more I have learnt about the history of this place and the region which surrounds it, the more I have come to believe in the validity of those first impressions.

In 2009 a movie called 'The Cove' brought the spotlight of world attention to this erstwhile timeless fishing village, labelling it 'the small town with a big secret'. But to begin to understand the Taiji of present day we must firstly look back on its past.

Taiji's heritage is its connection with '*hogei*', a term meaning whaling, which includes dolphins and small cetaceans. Historical records show that this connection with whaling dates back several centuries, with official sources citing 1606 as the year of the formal establishment of '*Kujira-gumi*', a large-scale organized whaling company. Diminutive though it may seem, this tiny coastal village is recognized as the birthplace of Japanese whaling. In those formative years, this took the form of coastal subsistence whaling. Venturing offshore in brightly painted open rowboats, teams of fishermen hunted the mighty whales that swam along the migratory routes close to shore.

In the years that followed, a fisherman named Taiji Kakuemon was credited with devising a net method of trapping passing whales known as '*amitori-ho*'. By casting heavy rope nets into the path of their prey, the great whales were worn down and slowed enough for the men in the fastest boats, shaped for speed and painted in sleek black lacquer, to cast their handheld harpoons and deal the death blow. This was well before the days of mass whaling characterized by the harpoon cannon, fast well-equipped whaling ships and oceangoing factory processing vessels. The activities of the shore based Japanese whalers hardly depleted the vast herds of passing rights, humpbacks, greys and sperm whales. Unlike today's methods fueled by commercial greed, with its shameful wasted by-catch, nothing was left to waste.

It is interesting to note that during this particular period of history, the relationship between human and whale held substantial spiritual significance. The killing of whales was not taken lightly in those seminal years and the whale was accorded a deep reverence and respect. Looking around the village, one is left with no doubt as to the strong sense of spirituality with which the great whales were once viewed. Memorials, temples and religious ceremonies still pay homage and respect to the great whales whose lives were taken to ensure the villagers' survival.

The taking of nursing mothers and calves was avoided to ensure the continuation of the great whale species. This was an era of subsistence whaling in its truest form. A small village collective would kill enough whales for the townspeople to eat, with enough left over to permit a small-scale trade with other locales for produce like vegetables and grains which were unable to be grown in the cramped confines of the little coastal towns. In the 1600's community-based subsistence whaling was reported to be in operation at four major locations in Japan with Taiji being one of the principal whaling villages. One observation that can be made from the formative years of whaling in Japan is that whilst claim may be made to whaling being a localized cultural tradition, it cannot be said to be a Japanese national tradition simply because the practice of eating whale meat was restricted to only four small coastal centers.

Today in addition to Japan's well publicized and controversial 'scientific whaling' program in the waters of the Southern Ocean, small-scale coastal whaling still takes place in five isolated locations in Japan, including Taiji's offshore waters. Here the targets are the smaller whale species–Minke whales, beaked and pilot whales–with government issued permits for their slaughter.

Somewhere along the way Taiji met with a fall from grace, not just economically but also spiritually. The ancient reverence for whales; tradition and ethics dissolved into a modern-day culture of greed and

Taiji

cruelty. Undoubtedly the influence of the whaling fleets of the Western world contributed to this decline. By the 1800's organized whaling fleets from the nations of America, Britain, Russia, France and Holland were plundering the oceans off Japan; greedily hunting the bounty of great whales for their oil. It is estimated that as many as six or seven hundred whaling ships had plied the waters and competed with Japan's land-based subsistence whalers for the passing whale herds. Western technology and sheer logistics proved to be overwhelming competition against the primitive hand lance and net method of Japan's whaling community. Several decades of this intensive pressure took its toll and whale populations slowly went into decline, placing an incredible pressure on the tiny local coastal industry.

By the late 1800's this pressure ultimately took its toll on Taiji, and the once flourishing local whaling industry went into decline and finally depression. Many whaling men abandoned the little town and took up residence in other countries, including Australia. Then in the 1900's, the influence of the West gave rise to Japan adopting the mechanized western approach to whaling, utilizing modern ships equipped with harpoon cannon. In 1934 the whalers ventured into the Antarctic with an ex-Norwegian factory vessel. A large number of the Taiji whaling men were amongst those that made that first foray into the dangerous waters of the Southern Ocean. A new chapter in Japan's whaling saga was commencing and the days of localized small-scale subsistence whaling were truly at an end.

The story of present-day Taiji is, by comparison, a rather salubrious tale of dolphin slaughter and captivity. Although it is generally the tales of mass slaughter that rise to public attention, it is in fact the lucrative live dolphin trade which financially sustains the drive hunt enterprise. As worldwide interest in captive dolphins for marine parks and aquariums increased, so Taiji came to the fore as a willing supplier of live specimens. Taiji rapidly established itself as the world's *principle* supplier of live dolphins.

TAIJI

In the year ending March 2010 the Japanese government estimated that seventy-nine dolphins were sold to the live export market, bringing in a total of ¥277 million yen (just over USD $3 million). With a steady increase in the numbers of dolphinariums and marine parks through Japan and Asian nations, the sales of live dolphins have similarly been increasing over recent years. Japan itself has approximately fifty dolphinariums which are supplied directly from Taiji. Internationally, China has emerged as a major buyer of dolphins and orders are also placed by the nations of Taiwan, the Philippines, Korea and Thailand as well as Iran, Turkey, the Ukraine and the United Arab Emirates. Sadly, this growing domestic and international demand has become the 'cash cow' for the dolphin hunters of Taiji.

There are elements of truth in the mayor of Taiji's 1994 address to the International Whaling Commission. But then there is also distortion, rationalization and justification in large doses. To refer to the activities of present-day Taiji as those of a subsistence industry is not unlike the directors of an open cut gold mine likening themselves to crusty old prospectors speculatively panning for gold on the banks of a creek.

An industry that has become the prime exporter of hundreds of live dolphins to the world's marine park industry can hardly be referred to as a business of subsistence. And then there is the well-worn reference to the traditions of the past. Present day Taiji sees the pride of regional heritage shamefully hidden from view behind a roughly built marquee of dirty tarpaulins and conducted in clandestine secrecy.

National park areas and adjacent public beaches are closed and roped with 'no-go' lines of roughly strewn fishing nets and festooned with hand painted 'No trespassing' signs. I know of no other cultural ceremony or tradition in the world that goes to such guilty lengths to shrink away from the glance of an outsider. The good mayor calls for us to *'trust the people of Taiji as rational and humane people'*. There was nothing rational or humane in fishermen physically drowning dolphins by holding them underwater to prevent them from drawing breath, as I witnessed on one occasion during my first visit. There was no humanity in the scenes of dolphins left to die a slow and agonizing death as they exsanguinated on the sharp rocks that ringed the Cove.

When I first saw the documentary 'The Cove' in 2010, I was drawn to learn more about what went on in Taiji. Set in a landscape and a culture of almost hypnotic beauty an annual tragedy was taking place. Of course, as an animal lover and a child of the ocean, I felt anger and outrage. If I was to be perfectly truthful, I took all of that outrage with me the first time that I went to Taiji, and no doubt some of it surfaces in my early writing. But the more that I saw, the more that I realized that there was more to the story; and the more I took on a preparedness to try to understand.

Having introduced you to the experience of a dolphin drive hunt, let me now take you back a step, to my first footsteps– the very first journey I made to Japan.

ଔ ❀ ଓ

TAIJI JOURNAL First arrival in Japan – Friday January 14th 2011

I finally arrive in the small town of Katsuura almost a full twenty-four hours after walking out the door of my house; lugging my bags to the waiting taxi under the harsh blaze of an Australian summer afternoon.

Flying to Japan involves a transit through the stale and oppressive swelter of Bali's Denpasar terminal and then on through the early hours of the morning to Kansai international airport, Osaka. By the time I step onto Japanese soil I have transitioned from my summer wear of t-shirt and khaki shorts to full black hoodie, layers of clothing and heavyweight jeans. Kansai is clean efficient and orderly, and sets the tone for my experience in Japan. I opted to travel the two hundred kilometers from there to Taiji by hire car and I'm really glad I did. Thank God for George, my trusty Garmin GPS which I carefully pre-programmed with the necessary road maps beforehand! The in-car GPS in the tiny Japanese hire car has no English option, and I very quickly give up trying to program it.

The motorway sweeps through numerous tiny villages, all quite industrial looking with banks of little houses painted a shabby earth red, or tan or grey, with somber grey roofs. The countryside consists of endless rolling hills which the motorway simply negotiates by ploughing through them via long stone tunnels. It is quite a culture shock, especially considering the majority of signs beyond the main motorways are in Japanese characters only. I am in wide-eyed awe of the beauty of the surrounding countryside broken by the sprawl of multiple towns and villages, each with banners and signs giving the towns something of a rustic anime cartoon feel. The russet greys and earth reds of the buildings, the deep olive greens of the surrounding hillsides are broken by bold splashes of primary color and cartoon caricatures.

One road sign that both perplexes and amuses me is a yellow diamond warning sign emblazoned with the black silhouette of a creature with a rotund catlike body and the widened tail of a beaver; its large crazed eye staring wildly as it waddles forwards on stumpy legs. The sign is repeated at intervals along the motorway giving me the impression that these demented four-legged ferals with wild zombie eyes could be anywhere–perhaps biding their time in the bushes by the motorway waiting to maul unsuspecting passing motorists. Or maybe it is just that exaggerated Japanese sense of cartoon melodrama? From the sign I can't be certain of the size or the scale of this creature and I'm equally unsure as to whether I will laugh or cry if I'm unfortunate enough to meet one crossing the motorway.

Taiji

'Welcome to Japan', I mutter to myself with a bemused grin as I wriggle into a relaxed slouch in the driver's seat, slowly growing more comfortable with each passing mile despite the unfamiliar surroundings. I later learnt that the animal depicted on this sign is a *tanuki* or Japanese raccoon dog, which is part of the evolutionary family that includes foxes, wolves and dogs. They inhabit the forest areas and resemble a large portly raccoon. In the richly magical mythology which typifies the mystical land of the rising sun, the tanuki is described as a shape shifter with supernatural abilities and possessing a wickedly mischievous personality.

According to Japanese folklore the tanuki gained notoriety in the ancient past by using their powers to trick passers-by; performing deceitful acts such as changing leaves into counterfeit money, and making horse manure appear to be a delicious dinner! (I kid you not– the Japanese have an almost comical sense of the bizarre!) Today they are often depicted wearing a jaunty peasant's straw hat and carrying a sake bottle in one hand (most likely purchased with a handful of leaves) and a promissory note in the other hand (a bill they have no intention of paying). It appears my first impression was correct. It would seem the tanuki is definitely well worth avoiding!

Winding its way southwards along the Kii peninsula, the motorway leaves behind the little inland villages to follow the scribble of the rocky coastline. I can't help but feel the restlessness and the promise of adventure whenever I breathe salt air, and the view here is both dramatic and picturesque. The broad expanse of the North Pacific Ocean extends to become the gentle curve of the horizon to the east and meets heavily treed hills and mountains here along the coast; the lush greens and rich earth tones of the mainland are now complemented by the breathtaking blues of saltwater and sky. Each little coastal town I pass through sports a harbor boasting fleets of small fishing boats; rows of white hulls bobbing at anchor in the calm safety of man-made stone sea walls. The air smells sharp and fresh with the heady aroma of the surrounding trees. I find myself wondering what type of trees they are; indeed, I know very little about Japan's geography and natural surrounds. I drive on in silent awe feeling a little humble and very much the ignorant foreigner. And it appears that I am in fact the *only* foreigner. The only other Westerners that I have so far encountered were a small group of Europeans in transit through Kansai airport. Outside of the major cities like Osaka, there are precious few tourists visiting rural Japan. I start to become more than a little self-conscious the closer I get to my destination. Signs bearing whale and dolphin effigies start to become more evident along the side of the road on the approach to the Taiji turn off. Despite the fact that many signs are in Japanese, there is no mistaking a huge billboard advertising the Taiji Whale Museum, its picture now seems darkly iconic with its huge mural of a massive black Right whale.

The images of angry dolphin hunters with knives come to mind, and I can't help but feel an air of uncertainty as to what might be awaiting me. Today however I will be bypassing Taiji and heading on to the neighboring town of Katsuura to find my hotel accommodation. It has been almost a four-hour drive from the airport and I've now been on the move for almost twenty-four hours since my departure from Oz. Five kilometers of winding road beyond Taiji, I reach the peaceful sprawl that is the seaside fishing village and resort town of Katsuura.

High above the dark rolling green hills that ring the bay, flights of coal brown hawks wheel and circle lazily in the weak thermals, feathers delicately spread like fingers on the tips of their outstretched wings. As a former pilot I am quietly impressed by the almost majestic sense of control and grace as they describe their slow orbits overhead, dotting a perfectly clear blue winter sky. The Westerner in me stands awestruck in the watery winter sun on the harbor's concrete dock walkway, absorbing unfamiliar sights and sounds in quiet fascination. That being said, there are some sights which are instantly recognizable from the documentary movie 'The Cove' and there is the occasional sense of having walked into a three-dimensional postcard.

Chugging its way across the harbor with a throaty baritone diesel throb is a passenger ferry gaudily decked out to look like a jaunty cartoon sea turtle; its head topped with a comical blue sailor's cap cranes forwards above the enclosed bow. This is the passenger ferry which connects guests with the exclusive Urashima Hotel which overlooks the bay from a long isolated spit of high land which neatly shrouds the harbor from the blue of the Pacific. I breathe the heady sea air deeply and it sends warm tingles down my spine. Winters are mild here, dry and bracing, and the air is fresh with the hint of ocean salt.

Opening directly onto the narrow concrete footpath little shops display their wares–I step around large concrete tanks full of shellfish and mussels, a constant stream of fresh water bubbling through the tanks and running away into the old storm drain on the side of the road. Alongside them an old wooden rack containing rows of squid hangs to dry. On the harbor side of the road, fisherman toil alongside their boats preparing equipment and carrying bait boxes on board, the smooth machine-like thrum of the fishing boats engines adding to the background noise. The fishing boat crews appear to be a mix of Japanese and Indonesians.

A morning walk to the Katsuura fish markets proves to be an eye-opening experience. Shortly after sunrise the fishing fleet returns to harbor and ties up along the docks in front of the fish market to disgorge their catch on to the broad expanse of concrete under-croft. The sheer scale of the catch leaves me stunned, and this is occurring every morning of each working day. Craning the catches out of each ship's hold, workers dressed in uniform overalls and white boots lay out the catch in neat rows. The Bluefin tuna (*maguro*) forms the largest portion of the catch. Row upon row of massive streamlined metallic blue bodies stretch the length of the warehouse floor like lines of plump bullets. The description is really quite apt as this species of fish are exceptionally powerful swimmers and well capable of speeds of up to 70 km/h in the open ocean. Many already have head and tail removed, but even so the sheer size of each fish is stunning. Mature Bluefin can weigh between 200-400kg on average. In one area, rows of majestic swordfish lie together, their long sword bills already removed. A school of giant orange-sided sunfish adorn another area, their bodies as large as my outstretched arms. The fish market is a seemingly chaotic flurry of noise and activity with white booted workers rushing purposefully in all directions. Forklifts attack the neat lines of laid out catch, carting away huge specimens in rough wooden packing crates filled with cracked ice.

The contents of a ship's hold are briskly hoisted out and swung onto the concrete dock. Other men stand waiting by the cranes, ready to drag the catch away with long metal gaff hooks. Another man walks the orderly rows with a brush and paints a large Japanese character in bold red paint on the bodies of some of the fish, presumably marking them in readiness for the morning auction. Off to one side of the dock is a growing pile of blue shark, all with fins removed. Many appear to be juvenile and undersize. Regulations here do not stipulate a minimum age or size for the catch–the requirement is simply that the shark bodies be presented for inspection. Adding to the flurry of activity, buyers are slowly filtering in to inspect the catch and place bids in an auction to the rear of the under-croft complex at the regular morning market (*asa ichi*). Standing watching the mêlée I begin to realize that what appears to be apparent chaos is in fact perfect order, with each player in the busy spectacle playing a specific role. My mind whirls with thoughts of sustainability and dwindling fish stocks. It is one thing to read about these issues, but to physically view the sheer scale and logistics of the fishing industry here is a sobering jolt to the system. How can this possibly be sustained day upon day? It is a short walk back around the periphery of Katsuura harbor from the fish market will to my hotel. Along the way I stop at one of the many street side vending machines to buy a can of Georgia café au lait and sit for a moment at one of the wooden benches lining the dock. Nearby to me stands an open public area, not unlike a long gazebo with a tiled roof. In it an old Japanese couple sit along a low stone wall, dangling their outstretched feet into the waters of a long rectangular trough. With my curiosity getting the better of me I wander over for a closer look. The couple sit peacefully, their bare legs immersed in the waters of a tiled foot spa. Catching my eye, they nod politely.

'*Ohayu gozaimasu*' ('Good morning') I venture, lowering my head respectfully in a courteous bow.

I've learned that a great deal of feeling and sentiment can be relayed in just one simple bow. The lower and more deliberate the gesture, the deeper the sense of respect and thoughtfulness you are trying to convey. I find there is a great power in that, and it can bridge the divide of the language barrier. The elderly couple smile amiably and mumble a quiet greeting before returning to their comfortable afternoon reverie, stoically gazing out across the busy harbor. Putting down my canned coffee on the low stone wall I remove my shoes and roll up my jeans, joining them at a polite distance along the wall of the foot spa. Cautiously I dip my bare feet into the water and relax. It is nicely and unexpectedly warm. My expression must have been telling, and the old couple meet my gaze briefly with beaming contented smiles.

We share no common ground nor language but the three of us sit together in quiet contemplation, each lost in our own private thoughts enjoying this shared moment. A group of Indonesian fishermen wander past, smoking casually. We are all but ignored except for one of the men, who steals a surreptitious sideways glance at this unlikely trio as he draws on the stub of his cigarette.

In the harbor the little white hulled fishing boats come and go endlessly. The afternoon takes on a timeless surreal quality under the dappled golden rays of a winter sun. The water that bubbles over my bare feet is comforting and warm.

CHAPTER THREE

Drive Hunt

Taiji in the picturesque Wakayama prefecture is presently the only Japanese locale where organized large-scale *oikomi* drive hunts take place. Some three hundred kilometers to the north-east along the island of Honshu's Pacific east coast, the town of Futo was also a proponent of drive hunt dolphin slaughters for many years. Over several decades the number of dolphins rounded up and slaughtered here numbered in their thousands. The last known drive hunt in Futo occurred in 2004.

Apart from Japan, drive hunts also occur in the South Pacific's Solomon Islands, the North Atlantic's Faroe Islands and also in South American Peru.

Unlike other fishing methods which use nets or hooks to catch their prey, the drive hunt technique exploits the whales' and dolphins' highly sensitive auditory systems. Toothed whales (including dolphins) possess a sophisticated sonar ability which they utilize to constantly assess their surrounds for navigation, hunting and social purposes. It is this advanced auditory system that sadly contributes to their downfall. A number of fishing boats are each equipped with a long metal pole which is flared at one end like a bell or the mouth of a trumpet. With the flared end placed in the water the pole is struck repeatedly with a hammer producing a sound wave which is then amplified and carried underwater, disrupting the dolphins' sensitive sonar and causing confusion and discomfort.

Possessing a highly cohesive social structure, the pod tends to turn and run as a group, away from the disorientation of the harsh sound.

With the fleet fanning out in a horseshoe formation around the fleeing pod, the dolphins are shepherded into an area of shallow enclosed water where their escape to open ocean is then prevented by the positioning of nets and boats.

In Taiji, an enclosed bay known locally as Hatajiri bay serves this grim purpose. These days, better known as the Cove, this bay has borne witness to the capture and cruel deaths of thousands of cetaceans; bottlenose, striped, Risso's and Pacific white sided dolphins as well their larger relatives, the short-finned pilot whales and false killer whales. With the distressed pod secured in the V-shaped bay, the fishermen move in past the nets in small outboard-motor driven skiffs to carry out the final slaughter. Officially the kill is carried out by driving a short metal spike or spear deep into the cetacean's body at a point just behind the blowhole, severing the spine. According to the government, death by this prescribed method is almost instantaneous. The truth of these killings, as I was to witness first hand, is both savage and cruel, and a far cry from the sanitized official government propaganda. The cold reality is that many of these dolphins will die a slow and agonizing death lasting many minutes. Even if the killing blow brings instantaneous death, these beautiful and placid creatures have already endured hours of distress and anxiety from the pursuit by a dozen powerboats, the acoustic disorientation of the banger poles and finally the agonizing trauma of swimming in waters staining red with the blood of their pod mates before being roped by the tail and dragged roughly into the shallows of the Cove.

TAIJI JOURNAL – Tuesday morning January 18th 2011
Tuesday dawned to cloudless skies and light winds. This unfortunately means potentially good conditions off-shore for the dolphin hunters and my uneasy feeling is confirmed as I follow the road past Taiji harbor.

The drive boats, or 'banger boats' as the activists refer to them, which are normally sitting white and gleaming in a long line around the harbor are notably absent from their berths. From the high point overlooking the harbor mouth, ten drive boats can be seen describing lazy circles about a mile and a half off-shore from the mouth of the harbor. The leisurely slow turns, with some of the fleet lying stationary in a ragged line, tells me that no pods have been sighted as yet. I pray a silent prayer that it remains that way. The fleet have adopted the routine of putting out to sea in the early morning, and returning to port by late morning if no passing pods are located.

With a few hours of watching and waiting ahead of me I park the hire car in the relative anonymity of the harbor car park just around the winding harbor road to seawards of the Fisheries Co-operative building and the squat white concrete slaughterhouse at the far end of the harbor. I want to have a closer look at the 'butcher's shop' facility and the floating pens lying directly across the harbor whilst the hunters are away. The slaughterhouse building looks much like an expansive warehouse with a long line of unpainted metal roller doors, all presently shut tight.

I glance across the narrow span of the harbor to where numbers of shabby yellow and green pontoons surmounted by lengths of rough wooden plank walkways form the long line of tiny holding pens where the captive dolphins are held and trained daily by their keepers. There must be about a dozen dolphins presently held in the cramped confines of the pens. They are not unlike a row of somber solitary confinement cells in a prisoner of war camp. Finding myself alone and exposed here, I feel a palpable anxious tension. There is no sign of life at the hunters' base. Occasionally a raucous 'air raid' type siren wails across the length of the harbor, causing sinister echoes in the surrounding hills. Sonically it completes the oppressive image of a concentration camp and puts me slightly on edge. Across the steely-grey waters, the holding pens occasionally burst into froth as one or two of their captives leap skywards from the cramped confines of their floating prison. My presence at the dock attracts the occasional wary glance from a passing local and I decide to move position and head off on foot up the sloping road that extends beyond the harbor mouth.

With my olive complexion and kitted out in baseball cap and sunglasses I almost pass as an oriental, and having carefully watched the locals over the past few days I can now easily adopt their characteristic shuffling gait as I walk expressionless looking fixedly ahead of me. This provides me with a half reasonable 'disguise' and thus affords me some degree of anonymity as I recce the harbor area each day. Off to the side of the road a small footpath winds its way up the side of the hill and following it I am quickly lost in dense bamboo and shrubbery, broken by sprays of stunning pink and red flowers. Again, I marvel at the natural beauty of this place. From my sheltered position on high ground I have a bird's eye view across the expanse of harbor from the slaughterhouse to my left at one extreme end, and the long stretch of weathered concrete sea wall running toward the navigation marker at the harbor mouth to my right. Craning around the dense shrubbery I can make out one of the white shapes of a banger boat bobbing gently in the current just off the coast. When I left the lookout, the remaining boats had fanned out into a ragged line relatively close in-shore; occasionally describing lazy unhurried circles in the current.

With the fleet out of sight beyond the rocky headland I return to the car and make my way by road back through the town site to the lookout point at the tip of the rocky peninsula. By the time I make my way on foot along the leafy walkway from the lookout car park, the drive boat fleet have already located a large herd of dolphins. Sometimes they will pick up a pod close in-shore; other days they may sit for some hours out toward the horizon, looking for their prey. Today chance has brought them an early catch. The fact that the banger boats have located themselves relatively close to shore might suggest that they have been tipped off by local fishermen as to the location of the large pod.

TAIJI

Over the past hour the movement of the boats has appeared leisurely and aimless. Now in an ominous and stark contrast the white hulls move rapidly and change course sharply with deft control, and in a thrashing of foam an enormous pod heaves into view, driven inshore by the line of boats. Metallic thuds ring out across the open expanse of water; the sound of a mallet on a metal pipe. Like a badly punctuated tympanic chorus the remaining drive boats take up the hammering, causing a wild stampede in the water. We estimate there must be almost one hundred striped dolphins running from the pursuing boats; breaching wildly the pod is clearly panicked as they run from the cacophony of sound behind them. Ahead of the drive boats there are occasional shards of silvered lightning; sub-groups are breaking off from the main pod and streaking away tangentially for the safety of the open ocean. Powerful tail flukes thrash the water into foam.

Like a cloud of angry wasps, the drive boats shift position with short bursts of speed, simultaneously blowing oily dark clouds of smoke from their funnels. With streamlined hulls approximately thirty feet long surmounted by a high central fly-bridge, these boats are fast and maneuverable. They move like a wolf pack as they desperately attempt to rope in the rogue elements of the pod making fast their escape. The ringing metallic blows continue. By the time the fleet approach the harbor mouth, they are shepherding a good forty to fifty panicked dolphins towards the nearby cove. Striped dolphins are a pelagic species; their natural habitat is deep water and open ocean, and rarely do they venture close to land unless the water is of sufficient depth. With the drive boats forcing them into unaccustomed rocky shallows they are clearly showing the signs of distress, their movements rapidly becoming skittish and feverish.

When striped dolphins travel they tend to leap energetically. The leaping, I have learned, actually helps to preserve their energy on long journeys. I love their sense of exuberance and free spirit, and now I feel the anger rising for the men who are taking it upon themselves to snatch that freedom away from such gentle majestic creatures. It is actually the striped dolphin that appears in the frescoes of ancient Greece, where they were held in such high regard that it was illegal to do them harm.

As the pod is shepherded towards its final destination I consider the harrowing fate that awaits them in that sad place. Unlike the bottlenose dolphins, this species does not 'take' to being trained in captivity and nor are they comfortable in the shallow waters so close to land. There can only be one grim outcome for this pod. I resign myself to standing vigil and simply being there for them in that last desperate hour. It seems a small gesture, but it is all I can do. It is five minutes by car from the harbor area to the parking area across the road from the cove. By the time I arrive, I can see the escort boats already hovering together in the mouth of the bay. From a small skiff manned by two fishermen, a heavy net is being deployed to seal off the exit back to open sea.

The tiered observation area is already a hive of activity and with over a dozen uniformed police and coast guard officials observing proceedings I pace across the bitumen and down the flight of concrete steps to the beach area. Today I am not really in the mood for exchanging polite pleasantries with the watchful officials. With the holding nets now positioned, the fishermen move into the crowded cove area in their small open boats. The surface of the water is churned by circling dorsal fins as the pod weave in tight frenzied circles. A marquee of blue tarpaulins has already been rigged over the waters right at the rear of the cove–testament to the fact that these brave fishermen are keen to keep proceedings hidden as much as possible from outside scrutiny, and carry out their cruel business away from prying eyes.

Today they are unable to hide everything though. In sheer blind panic several adult dolphins have thrown themselves onto rocks in a desperate attempt to escape. Torn and bleeding they are ignored by the fishermen who continue their sordid work under the cover of the tarpaulins. The days leading up to my arrival in Japan were marked by several days of similar large catches of striped dolphins. The activists present had reported similar occurrences where dolphins were left to die slowly in excruciating agony on the sharp grey rocks littering the shores of the cove. Representations and protests were made to the Fisherman's Union–it is one thing to catch and kill dolphins, but this was blatant animal cruelty. Perhaps stung into action by these complaints, the hunters have responded by instigating a number of precautionary measures. Extra nets are now being deployed over rocky outcrops and the drive boats have been decelerating significantly as they shepherd their catch around the jagged coastline, to avoid panicking them unnecessarily. Today a fisherman wearing a black wetsuit clambers across the rocks to push the terrorized and bloodied mammals back into the foamy water to await their turn for slaughter.

I make eye contact with the officials standing close by, only to be greeted with remote wary glances in return. Once again, I am left amazed by the size of the official contingent overseeing proceedings here at the beach. More than a dozen personnel, some uniformed and some in plainclothes, others with blue jackets and caps bearing Japan Coast Guard logos. And everywhere they have video cameras–mounted on fixed tripods, recording our presence; ever vigilant in case we Western miscreants go a step too far and attempt to disrupt proceedings.

There were further acts of cruelty witnessed that day. With so many dolphins crammed into the tight confines of the cove, several captives are roped by the tail flukes and dragged backwards through the water by the skiff to be deposited roughly in the shallows underneath the tarps to await the death blow. Here the waters are thrashed into blood red foam by the desperately panicked creatures. Other fishermen impale the creatures with a two-foot metal rod. I can tell you that death is most certainly not instantaneous. On the contrary it is agonizing and slow; precious minutes pass before those powerful tail flukes slow and finally thrash no more. The sounds recorded at the cove that day are disturbing; the muffled thrashing and vocalizing of the pod is punctuated by the blatting roar of outboard motors, and the workmanlike yells of the fishermen as they push the dolphins into the killing area. But even more chilling than that is the constant background sound which is not unlike the noise of a large washing machine. It is the sound of these striped dolphins thrashing their tail flukes wildly in a desperate fight for life, and it continues minute after agonizing minute. Amongst the last of the pod to face the spears are several juveniles. This leads to the speculation that the fishermen intend to spare the young and perhaps release them to the wild. Sadly, this does not eventuate and the youngsters meet the same cruel fate as their parents and pod members before them.

Of the hundred or so dolphins which the boats pursued through the morning's drive, approximately forty dolphins were corralled into the cove. None of them were spared. Today's dispatch took longer than usual; striped dolphins are strong by nature and will tend to resist and fight vigorously. There were no trainers present today to select specimens.

These beautiful ocean dwellers left the cove hidden from view under roughly thrown covers, or roped by their tails to the port side of the small skiffs which sat low in the water with the weight of their cargo. Up until late December the fishermen would tie the bodies to the starboard side of the skiffs; this being the side of the boat furthest away from the beach as they departed the killing cove. As of the New Year however, the dolphin hunters have taken to roping the dead on the nearside of the boats as if flaunting their handiwork in the faces of the watching activists. It appears a raw nerve has been struck. There have been signs of the hunters growing frustration at the constant scrutiny they have endured since the beginning of the season last September.

TAIJI

Today I leave the Cove feeling distressed and trying to process what I have witnessed. The weight of it seems to hit you afterwards. A friend of mine drew a parallel with an abattoir;

'Why aren't you protesting the treatment of cattle? Isn't that the same thing?'

Somehow, I can't see it as the same thing. These dolphins…these are highly intelligent, sentient beings.

'Pigs are intelligent creatures too,' my friend patiently replies.

All I know is this isn't right. We cannot treat a sentient being this way. I cannot think straight right now. I'm a hundred questions in search of an answer.

Drive Hunt

'Whaling'

On a night when the sea roars,
A winter's night,
With roasting chestnuts crackling, crackling,
I heard the tale told.
A tale of whaling, long, long ago
Here in the sea of Shizu-ga-ura.
The sea was wild in the wintertime
Blossoms of snow whirled mad on the wind
And across the flight of snow flew the rope of harpoons.
The crags and the pebbles are purple here.
And even the water of Shizu-ga-ura
But then it turned red, dyed red up to the shore.
In their thick winter coats the whaling men
Stood in the bow of the boat and looked on
And when the whale's strength was broken
They stripped down to their skin.
Below, the red eddies of ocean; without pausing they leapt in.
The tale of the whalers, long, long ago –
Just listening to the story
My heart dances within me.
The whales of those days do not come any more
And Shizu-ga-ura is now lonely and poor.
Outside the sea roars
On a winter's night
When the tale ends
When you stop to hear.

– Misuzu Kaneko - Japanese poet (b1903 d1930)

CHAPTER FOUR

A Fall from Grace

'Even in a dream, look not upon a right whale and her calf'
— LOCAL TAIJI SUPERSTITION

IT IS 1878 and a troubled year is ending in Taiji. The catch yield has been poor this season and now with late December pressing upon him, the beach-master feels the bleak desperation of the approaching winter.

December 24th is fast drawing to a close and as the afternoon drags on there has yet to be a whale brought to the beach. It is here in the dying hours of the day that the shore lookouts finally make a sighting. Three black and white pennants are raised, signifying to the whalers the presence of a female whale and calf.

Fishermen are a superstitious breed the world over and the whalers of Taiji are certainly no different in that respect. There is a saying here amongst the whalers:

'Even in a dream, look not upon a right whale and her calf.'

According to local superstition it was bad luck to hunt a mother whale and its calf. Japanese folklore suggests that these early whalers held the nursing mother whale in high regard, and to capture and kill a nursing mother was taboo. In truth of course, many superstitions have their basis rooted in cold hard fact. It is highly likely that the ancient fishermen were also well aware that a normally docile female

A Fall from Grace

right whale with calf was highly capable of fighting with fury to defend its young from the men in the sleek black lacquered whaling boats. And battling an angry ocean giant in a small open rowboat was a recipe for disaster.

Up until now it has been a time of bounty for the whalers of the Kii peninsula; the nutrient rich ocean current running just off-shore providing a perfect migratory route for the multitude of passing whale herds. For almost three centuries a technique of 'net whaling' known as *amitoriho* has been employed; heavy rope nets are deployed to slow a whale down sufficiently to allow harpooners to approach and dispatch their stricken quarry with long hand lances. The pickings are good and plentiful, and the whalers in their brightly painted open boats operate a perfectly sustainable industry amidst the vast populations of passing whales. Indeed, up until now there has been little reason for the men of Taiji to defy superstition and pursue the taboo 'mother and calf'.

But by that fateful December day in 1878 the winds of change were already blowing. The invaders had come to the waters off Japan to hunt the great travelers of the deep. By the mid-1800's whaling fleets from the nations of Russia, Britain, Holland, France and America were massing off the coast of Japan and slaughtering whales in great numbers, principally for their oil and baleen. Several hundred whaling vessels now competed hungrily for the ocean's bounty. The halcyon days of Taiji's net whaling harvest were fast drawing to a close, driven to the brink of collapse by greedy Western whaling fleets who were stripping the local waters of passing whales.

Sighting the three striped pennants the whalers draw back and relax. The taboo of pursuing a mother and calf is well known to all, and this afternoon's sighting is confirmed to be a female right whale shepherding her young offspring–the very stuff of superstition. Today in Taiji-cho, a small town looking out onto the azure expanse of the Pacific Ocean, a great tragedy is about to fall. The whaling operation here is headed by two hereditary leaders; Taiji Kakuemon, the chief of business operations, and Wada Kinemon the advisory head. On the beach in the dappled afternoon light the two leaders clash. No doubt burdened by the pressures of a poor season and faced with an imminent new year, Kakuemon insists that the village needs to land a whale. Kinemon disagrees, perhaps reminding his colleague of the implications of defying superstition and local custom. But it is Kakuemon who prevails and the hastily hoisted red signals indicating that the hunt is on surprise the whalers, who jump to and thrust the brightly painted boats seaward. It is already late in the day, and the conditions offshore are less than ideal. With a blustery cold wind blowing, the whale is eventually netted and harpooned and a fierce battle ensues. The sheer size and strength of the mother right whale defies the boat crews. Chilled to the bone and exhausted from the struggle with whale, the strong currents and fierce winds; the men fight on into the gathering darkness. Finally, a winter storm blows up and out of sheer desperation the boatmen are forced to cut the whale loose. To their horror they find themselves pitted against the forces of nature; lost on a wild sea in the heart of the storm.

In the morning the sunrise reveals the terrible aftermath. Swallowed by the storm, Taiji's *kujira-gumi* whaling fleet has been destroyed. The defiance of superstition has been met with tragedy and most of the whalers who went out that day never returned. Almost one hundred and thirty men meet a watery grave, dying either from drowning or exposure to the elements. The proud fleet's black lacquered boats are flung far out to sea and destroyed–turned into matchwood. In the months that follow, a grieving Taiji Kakuemon relinquishes his estate to the bereaved families and turns his back on the ill-fated coastal town. Taiji falls into a period of grim depression.

'Even in a dream, look not upon a right whale and her calf'.
The dream had become a nightmare.

A Fall from Grace

TAIJI JOURNAL – Thursday January 20th 2011

Sunrise always seems to sneak up suddenly here in Katsuura. As the sun rises, part of my morning routine is to check the weather from the hotel balcony as I drink my morning green tea. Today was a carbon copy of the past two days–clear skies with light winds. It's going to be another one of those days. I pack the gear and head down the road to collect Canadian activist Bob from his hotel before making the drive to Taiji in the chill morning air. Sitting peacefully in the dawn stillness, the harbor has scarcely a ripple on the still-dark waters and the long line of white-hulled drive boats which normally line the length of the dock nose to tail are conspicuous by their absence. The hills which fringe the harbor rise darkly like a steep protective shroud.

Up the road to the Point lookout out and we discover the fleet is already out to sea; perhaps a mile or two off shore, jockeying from position to position. Bob has dubbed the dozen drive boats the '12 Deadly Sins'. A very apt description I think to myself as ugly puffs of black smoke rise from their funnels as they methodically change position with an evil intent.

The surface of the water is calm and smooth and I scan the waters with binoculars for signs of dolphins breaching. Nothing. Let's hope it stays that way. I would love nothing more than to see the entire fleet parade back to harbor empty-handed just like they did yesterday.

'Today I want to wave to these jokers as they come in empty-handed', I tell Bob.

We are continually checking our watches. 9.30am. Still nothing. The standard drill is for the fleet to call it quits and return to port if they have had no luck by late morning.

At time ticks by I start to feel more confident that the day will again be a happy one. The fleet is slowly driving closer to the coast and still no sightings. I note that two boats seem to have what appear to be hydrophones in the water, listening for dolphins. *Bastards.* The boats hover for a while before shifting position. It's like watching some sinister ballet rehearsal out on the water.

TAIJI

Not long after ten o'clock the luck runs out. Fairly close in towards the harbor mouth I pick up the slow breaching of a small pod of dolphins. They are packed close together and breaching only very occasionally. Further out to sea, the banger boats appear not to have noticed them. Sweeping the binoculars back and forth, I scan between the grey falcate fins and the ominous fleet trolling to seaward some distance behind, hoping the small pod will escape their attention. Backwards and forwards I sweep between the pod and the fleet, as though I'm watching the ball in a tennis game.

Please don't notice. Please. In that moment my chest is tight and I realize that I've been holding my breath all this time. No such luck. Someone on board has finally spotted them. Suddenly, like a pack of hungry dogs, the drive boats home in. The staccato metallic clang of the banger poles commences. The sound hangs in distant echoes like the hammering of coffin nails.

This is a very quick drive, as the dolphins are very close to shore on this occasion, and the fleet is rapidly abeam our position on the high finger of land, pushing the pod back toward the harbor mouth. Down through the trees we can hear the faint blow of the dolphin's breath as the pod accelerates to escape the metallic pounding from the white hulled boats drawn up behind them. They are now panicking. Alongside them on our raised vantage point, we are running for the car with Bob yelling breathlessly to me:

'What kind of dolphins are they?'

Keeping pace with the pod he is snapping off camera shots on the fly. Images from the whale rescue training course run through my mind. I note the shaped falcate dorsal fins surfacing below us as the pod runs.

'From the dorsal fins they look like they might be bottlenoses or Risso's,' I counter as I scrabble in my pockets for the car keys.

A closer look at the high, light grey dorsal fins and the breaching of blunt snouts shows them to be a pod of twelve to fifteen Risso's dolphins. Bottlenoses are a deeper grey, and have a distinctive bottle-shaped snout or rostrum, as it is called.

Despite the harrying drive boats, a few of the pod manage to break free and run to open ocean. With only minutes before the fleet muster the remaining dolphins into the cove area, we are in the car and pulling seatbelts on as we accelerate through the suburban area of the town, along winding streets of endless old compact houses and then down the harbor road, threading our way past the Fisherman's Co-operative building and the slaughterhouse whilst trying not to draw attention to ourselves.

By the time we reach it, the Cove car park is already a hive of activity with the usual throng of police, officials and fishermen taking up position with video cameras at the ready to watch our every move. Bob and I decide to try the little used hill on the opposite side of the bay from Takababe Hill. Tsunami Hill, so named because it is the official safe point for the locals to muster in the event of a tsunami, separates the Taiji Whale Museum from the bay which leads into the cove. If we are able to get a suitable view, we will be able to look directly into the mouth of the cove and straight into the tarpaulined killing area.

A quick breathless climb up though the dense rainforest and we break out of filtered light into the naked glare of the sun. We very quickly realize why the hill is little used. The grassed parkland area here at the summit of Tsunami Hill is ringed with tall stands of dense shrubbery, denying us a view into the cove. The entire perimeter is netted off with fishing net, which is tied to the trees. We survey the makeshift barrier, designed to prevent anyone from scaling their way down the steep side of the hill to get that perfect view into the cove. Tied to the netting are a series of signs with warnings written in English and Japanese. The first of the English signs reads "No Entry Past This Point. Trespassers Will Be Prosecuted." We walk a little further along to find a similar sign, written in Japanese only. We look at each other.

'Can you read what this sign says?' asks Bob.

'Nope,' I reply, 'Haven't got a clue.'

Casting a discreet glance around the park, Bob lifts up the netting directly under the sign.

'Me either. So, let's go under here then,' he says with a mischievous shrug.

In a crouch, we make our way hastily down the steep incline through trees and dense shrubbery. Further down the side of the hill, the trees thin out, leaving us rather exposed in the waist deep tangle of coastal plants, vines and greenery. The view is spectacular, and across the mouth of the bay lies Takababe Hill and beneath it, the gaping mouth of the cove. Off to the right, I can clearly see the beach and the scattering of police, officials and activists milling on the grassy tiers. With their attention on the open bay, awaiting the arrival of the boats, it's unlikely they will be looking high up here on the hill. I can hear motor noise across the water, indicating the fleet is getting closer. We are still scoping out a decent position to tuck ourselves into when the fleet slowly rounds the rocky headland, in plain view.

My chest tightens as the pod heaves into view, clustered together and breaching slowly just ahead of the gleaming white hulls. The drive boats are near stationary now, lying just off the entrance to the bay. Our position, though hidden somewhat from the beach, is naked and plainly exposed to the drive boats immediately below us, and we hastily pull the shrubbery around ourselves. Peering out, I can plainly see a fisherman on the topmost fly-bridge of one of the three drive boats. He has a pair of high-powered binoculars, through which he is now scanning the hillside around us. It is only later, over a beer in the little restaurant we frequent in Katsuura that we learn they noticed activists taking photos from the cliff face some days ago, and the hunters are wary of a repeat performance.

'They've got binoculars on that last banger, mate! They're scanning the hill, so keep yourself down,' I call to Bob, who has been busying himself setting a telephoto lens on his camera.

A Fall from Grace

He has crawled into a neat little natural hide in a thick shrub, through which he now trains the dull black lens. I crawl a bit further from Bob's position seeking out a similar hide.

Down below in bay, the pod is not complying and they make a series of sudden stops and turns. The sea is perfectly calm and shimmering in the bright mid-morning sun, every move the dolphins make nakedly exposed to the hunters. The hunters must now shepherd the circling dolphins into the mouth of the cove. The three banger boats have taken up position across the broad entrance to the bay, cutting off the escape route. With the small skiffs jockeying around the wheeling dolphins, the pod makes a sudden unexpected run to seaward and I am physically and mentally willing them to dive under the bangers and head for the safety of the open ocean. I suspect the water is too shallow here for them to do that, and not being accustomed to being trapped in shallow water they are reluctant and confused.

From one of the big drive boats, the metallic hammering starts up, increasing in speed and intensity; the tempo picked up and echoed by other boats in the evil squadron hammering in staccato unison. Startled by the sudden onset of the wall of noise, the dolphins again turn landwards. The cove entrance is their only option now, and they glide through it.

A small skiff, outboard motor rasping like a buzz saw, briskly advances and positions the drop net with its floating white buoys in behind the pod, blocking their escape path. Netting into the killing cove, there can be no hope of an eleventh hour escape now. Slowly and excruciatingly the inevitable unfolds but what occurs next leaves me horrified. With the pod shepherded toward the rough marquee of blue tarpaulins at the back of the cove, the brutal killings begin and the water begins to take on an ominous crimson hue. A dolphin appears in the shallow water to one side of a skiff near the killing area. A fisherman wades out to the dolphin and grasping it on either side of its dorsal fin he holds the struggling form underneath the water, drowning it slowly. Feelings of anger and frustration well up in me. This is sick and unnecessary animal cruelty, pure and simple. There is no justification for such an inhumane act. As the Risso's becomes motionless, the hunter pushes the big dolphin up underneath the marquee.

A glint of white catches my eye, off the steep hill face on the ocean side. One of the banger boats has moved position, and I am now nakedly exposed in the bright sunlight. I scurry in a half crouch further up the cliff toward cover. *Shi-ii-t!* The undergrowth here is only knee high and thick with a crisscross of vines and creepers. In the messy scrabble to find a covered position, I lose my footing in the thick tangle of vines and fall back awkwardly into the dense undergrowth. My knee buckles sharply and I pull myself into the little cover the place offers.

Adrenaline and mild shock stop me from noticing the pain immediately and I grope for a comfortable position. With each passing minute I realize I can no longer crouch motionless, and I'm forced to roll from side to side to relieve the pain. Clearly stealth and subterfuge are not my strengths! Finally deciding on discretion as the better part of valor, I crawl my way back to the fish-net barrier; scanning the open parkland for police or Coast Guard officers before stumping painfully down the seemingly endless row of stone steps.

By the time I have limped my way back to the beach, the skiffs are departing the cove loaded with bodies hidden under tarps. Behind me, up on the footpath overlooking the beach, two of the fishermen are casually scrutinizing me; white booted and arms akimbo. I am fast developing that expressionless 'poker face' that characterizes the Japanese. Standing here on the beach bearing silent witness, I realize I have been biting my lip with the pain and the salt taste of blood is in my mouth.

☙❈❧

A Fall from Grace

Japan, as I am very quickly learning, is a country of contrasts and incongruities and Taiji is certainly representative of that. Indeed, the more that I have come to learn of the Japanese people and their culture, the more I have come to realize that they are a nation characterized by duality and paradox. That of itself is not necessarily a bad thing.

Yet there is a niggling sense of spiritual disconnect here around this former whaling village. Whales and dolphins are iconic in this little town and their imagery and symbolism can be seen everywhere; on signs, on multi-hued tiles set into the old concrete footpaths and on frescoes which decorate the hewn stone entrances of the many tunnels in the region. Nestled amongst the greenery on the side of the road into Taiji, visitors are greeted by the sight of an imposing full-size humpback whale mother and calf monument, rising high overhead. A little further beyond it on lies an old whaling vessel set into a pretty park. Standing proudly in front of it is a bronze sculpture of a traditional whaler, arching his back to hurl the long harpoon spear he holds one handed. Everywhere you go, it seems you are never far from a reminder of the town's heritage of whales and dolphins.

However, watching the actions of the dolphin hunters over the past few days I feel a damp cloying sensation–the vaguest feeling of moral bankruptcy. If there was a superstition about taking a nursing mother and calf, it appears those days are long gone. That is now the stuff of legend. What remains in Taiji now is a work-a-day commercial harvesting venture. And it is a crude commerce. The hunters seized upon the passing pods and they spared none; young and old alike. The juveniles were often left until last; witnessing the cruel deaths of their elders and their own mothers until they ultimately faced the cruel metal rod themselves.

TAIJI

So, what was the outcome of the Tsunami Hill incident? Having left the car in the public car park directly across from the Taiji Whale Museum, so that we weren't spotted by the police and Coast Guard officials further along at the Cove beach car park; I had wandered back as the crowd dissipated after the skiffs left the cove. Bob was nowhere in sight, and to my dismay, I watched two uniformed police descending the stone steps we had earlier climbed up to Tsunami Hill. They had been patrolling the hill. Hell…had they caught Bob?!

I bought a can of coffee from the nearby vending machine (there always seems to be a 'nearby vending machine' wherever you go in Japan), and waited. My knee was now throbbing angrily but I was too worried to be concerned. Forty-five minutes later, there was still no sign of Bob, and I began to fear the worst. I may likely have to make a trip to the local police station to plead for his release. Or perhaps he was still hidden out on the cliff face; lying low thinking that the police were still hovering around? I walked gingerly back up the road staying under cover of the trees which lined the footpath, before checking no officials were around and making my way slowly up the steep flight of stone steps.

On top of the Hill, the grassy public area was deserted; the nets still in place. I wandered around singling loudly to myself; hoping that Bob would hear my voice and realize the coast was clear. Still no Bob. Fearing the worst, I headed back down the long flight of steps for what seemed the umpteenth time that day. Reaching the footpath, I recognized two figures hurrying toward me from the direction of the cove. It was Leah and Peter. What were they still doing here? On seeing me, they paused and then appeared to recognize me.

'Did you know you look kinda Japanese from a distance?' asked Leah distractedly.

'Seriously?' Despite the gravity of the situation, I was quite chuffed that my disguise wasn't just imagined.

'Have you seen Bob? I can't find him.'

'I haven't seen him all morning,' replied Leah, 'Have you seen Lesley?'

We hastily traded stories. It appears Lesley, another Canadian activist, had being taking photos from the cliff face that morning also; unbeknownst to me and Bob. Great–it looked very much like a trip to the local police station was on the cards. We considered options and elected to take one last trip up the Hill just in case. Damn, said my knee. Another bloody flight of steps. We were no more than a dozen steps up when two figures appeared hurrying their way down the steps toward us like naughty schoolchildren. Bob and Lesley. *Relief!*

'Hell, you guys, you had us worried!' Leah breathed a noticeable sigh of relief.

'Let's scram,' urged Peter, throwing a nervous glance over his shoulder; 'There might still be cops around. We'll meet up and talk over dinner tonight.'

Back in the close warm of the car, Bob recounted the events as we wound our way leisurely back to Katsuura. It seems that just after I left the cliff face, a police patrol went through the area. In turn I recount my own reckoning of events, the drifting banger boat and my dirty dash for cover resulting in a very ungraceful fall.

'Lucky you headed back to the beach when you did, buddy,' Bob replied, 'A cop came down the hill searching for us. He walked down right alongside where I was hidden and then turned and headed back up towards me. I saw his blue cap coming back up the slope and I was getting ready to give myself up. Just when he was almost in sight of me, his phone rang. He stopped to answer it and then headed off in another direction!'

'You've gotta be kidding me!' I replied with a surprised chuckle.

'Seriously, it was like a Hollywood movie, brother! I hid myself in the foliage, wondering where you were. I thought he might have found you. Then later I heard someone singing in English.'

'That was me,' I said.

'What the hell were you singing?'
'Domo arrigato Mister Robarto!'

Later when we all compared notes, it transpired that Lesley had been tucked away further down the hill, even before Bob and I got there. Like Bob, she had been busy taking photos; up until a crashing through the shrubbery above her caused her to panic and cover herself in branches and foliage. I had to sheepishly admit that the crashing noise was most likely me as I tried to get out of line of sight of the banger boat!

For the record, photos and video footage taken that day reached government officials in Tokyo; causing some concern and embarrassment. It was a stern condemnation of the 'humane' slaughter methods which the Japanese claimed to employ, and the footage effectively undermined their recent claims and assurances that the new method they were employing resulted in almost instantaneous death.

Yes, there was video captured that day too. If Bob and I had flown a little under the radar that day, there were other activists who had been even stealthier. Hunkered down into the undergrowth right behind the tarped area at the rear of the cove, another party had managed to video the slaughter at close range. Their graphic close-up footage taken from directly behind the killing area showed conclusively that the new killing method was neither humane nor instantaneous.

So, the presence of activists on the ground here has counted for something. The first drive hunt season that I have witnessed has been characterized by large numbers of striped dolphins being mustered hastily into the cove, resulting in many of the panicked dolphins driving themselves onto rocks in their confusion. The barrage of cameras capturing this unnecessary cruelty resulted in the hunters taking extra precautions to ensure there was no repeat performance in the following season. The drive boats subsequently took extra care to slow the dolphins down as they approached the rocky coastline, and extra protective nets were deployed around rocky outcrops to spare the dolphins' unnecessary suffering.

It seems in the greater scheme of things to be a small mercy.

CHAPTER FIVE

'A Memorial for the Whales'

Held late in spring when flying fish are caught
When the temple bell travels across the bay's water
When fishermen dressed in their formal attire
And hurry to the temple
A lone whale child
Listening to the temple bell
Cries alone missing its mother and father
How far into the ocean
Would the temple bell resonate?

– **Misuzu Kaneko - Japanese poet (b1903 d1930)**

ෆ❁ඊ

Misuzu Kaneko was a young Japanese poet born and raised in the fishing village of Senzaki. Overlooking the Sea of Japan, the tiny village bears a long tradition of coastal whaling imbued with the deep Buddhist beliefs of reverence and respect. Just like the subsistence whaling village of Taiji; the whales were held sacred and prayers were offered up in respect of their souls. By age twenty, the strikingly pretty Misuzu was forging a career for herself in the writing of children's poetry and several of her poems were accepted for publication.

A Memorial for the Whales

Featuring heavily in her verse are references to the sea, fishing and whaling; the influences of her life growing up in a small coastal town. Her own tale is one of deep sadness and her tragically short life seemed to mirror the melancholy of the poems she wrote about whaling. Entering into an arranged marriage at age twenty-four, she found herself forbidden by her new husband to continue to write poetry or to maintain contact with the friends she had made from the magazines that she wrote for. Misuzu soon gave birth to a young daughter. Her husband spent long periods away from home and was known to frequent prostitutes, eventually catching a venereal disease which he passed on to the unsuspecting Misuzu. In 1930 she asked for a divorce; conditional upon her keeping custody of their daughter.

This was initially agreed upon; however, her husband later reneged and demanded that he be granted custody of the child. Such was the law at the time that Misuzu discovered she had no legal right to custody as a divorced woman. Perhaps this was the last straw for the young poet. She wrote a note asking that her mother take care of the child.

On 9th March 1930 Misuzu took her own life, dying as the result of an overdose of anti-depression medication that she had secretly hoarded. She was just twenty-six years old.

Her poem 'A Memorial for the Whales' refers to an annual memorial service (or *eko*) which is held in the Koganji Buddhist temple in Nagato, Yamaguchi Prefecture to honour the spirits of dead whales. In it she refers to a young whale calf left orphaned following the slaughter of its mother and father; asking the question of just how much comfort Man's ceremonial respect for the whales will actually be to the orphaned youngster left alone in the ocean to fend for itself.

TAIJI JOURNAL – Sunday January 23rd 2011

Today it was a pod of approximately fifteen Risso's dolphins that were driven in to their deaths. A number of townspeople including a family with young children are amongst the curious onlookers standing at the beach viewing area as the drive boats heave into view with their prize catch and prepare for the slaughter. On the run in from the sea, three of the pod had broken away, evading attempts by the pursuing fleet to recapture them. The trio were all but forgotten until it was discovered that one of them has found its way into the mouth of Taiji harbor. Following its ordeal and with the rest of its pod now split and decimated, the solitary Risso's dolphin is remaining close to the row of holding pens, obviously seeking the company of the bottlenose dolphins held captive there. Despite the fact that these dolphins are a completely different species to one another the communication between them can be clearly seen from the increased physical activity and vocalizations of the captive bottlenoses in the floating pens. In the wild, bottlenoses and Risso's have been known to travel together and occasionally interbreed.

Having witnessed the state of many creatures by the time they reach the shore, they are more often than not exhausted as a result of the sheer effort of trying to outrun the armada of drive boats pursuing them relentlessly; anxious and confused by the surrounding wall of noise. From the harbor wall, I can clearly see the lone Risso's surfacing slowly, displaying its beautifully tall curving 'surfboard skeg' dorsal fin, the steel-grey sides of its blocky body showing the characteristic long white scar marks that typify this species.

From the relatively sparse amount of scarring and darkening body color, the Risso's circling forlornly in the harbor appears to be an adolescent. Having returned through the harbor to the slaughterhouse with the bodies of its fellow pod members, the fishermen eventually turn their attention to the lone dorsal fin curving slowly through the water against the pens. Our concern is that the fisherman will complete their day's gruesome task by simply dispatching this lone survivor, and several of us have now taken up station on the wharf on the far side of the harbor with video and still cameras trained on the circling dolphin. It may very well be our presence that precipitates the next move by the fishermen. From the slaughterhouse end of the harbor the rasping buzz of outboard motors can be heard, growing steadily louder as two of the skiffs approach the pens. On each boat are three fishermen, one in a full black wet suit, swim fins and a weight belt. Watched closely by several pairs of activists' eyes, the hunters slowly and meticulously maneuver one of the skiffs against the pen wall to seaward of the steel grey dorsal fin, carefully playing out a mesh net in a slow circle so as not to frighten the creature.

Once positioned, the second skiff moves in and the snorkeler in the wet suit enters the water. It can be clearly seen that the small boat is carrying a long grey stretcher. So, it would appear that the intention is to capture this dolphin rather than slaughter it. After long minutes of careful maneuvering, the slick dark body is jockeyed onto the sling which is then secured against the side of the boat, at which point its small outboard powers up with a harsh nasal roar and drives out of the harbor entrance to sea. So, there it is. The lone dolphin has been spared death and capture. It is simply returned to the open ocean without its pod. Although still relatively young, perhaps it is mature enough and strong enough to have a fighting chance at survival; the Risso's is effectively a 'teenager'. What memories will it retain of its brush with humankind?

A great deal of effort was put in by the six fishermen in two boats to capture and return the lone dolphin back to the wild. I wonder if they would have got to all this trouble had there not been an audience of silent watchers?

Today fifteen were slaughtered. One solitary adolescent was set free–its future uncertain. The youngster's family lies dead on the rough concrete floor of the harbor slaughterhouse.

TAIJI

TAIJI JOURNAL – Sunday January 16th 2011

The drive boats have remained on their anchors in Taiji harbor for the past three days. Weather conditions have been unfavorable with strong winds gusting from the north. Sunday's skies are a clear watery blue and the wind chill factor is high. Despite the improving conditions there won't be a hunt on today. The hunters take the weekends off. I have opted to do a leisurely drive-by of the harbor and surrounds. Packing the gear in the morning sunshine I depart early from my hotel overlooking Katsuura harbor, the narrow street already busy with numerous little vans buzzing around the harbor road. Pulling my beanie down low over my ears, I smile and nod a polite greeting to the old lady across the road. She has spread out her wares of dried fish and vegetables in a quiet corner of the concrete harbor walkway. With a cheerful toothy grin, she waves a gloved hand and bows a return greeting before settling onto an old canvas deckchair she has set up alongside her makeshift market stall.

I coax the hire car out of the cramped parking lot alongside the hotel. The drive to Taiji is relaxed for once, and turning onto the road into the township I am once again amazed by the sheer number of whale and dolphin signs and effigies. The little traffic bridge is decorated with smiling dolphin statuettes at each corner and rising massive above the foliage by the roadside is suspended a lifelike full-scale statue of a humpback whale, tail flukes raised high with calf nuzzling alongside; their stunning gloss black bodies and white pleated bellies presenting a sharp contrast amongst the dappled greenery. A little further on, a large concrete fresco of a leaping killer whale adorns the roadside against the serene coastal backdrop. In front of it, water fountains spray across a large whale tail in a decorative stone pond. The sunlight filters easily through contented stands of dense greenery and I'm reminded of a peaceful English country road, basking timeless in winter sunshine. There is a poignant yet painful beauty about this place; indeed, this seems far too

A Memorial for the Whales

beautiful a place to be desecrated by what goes on here. It is hard however not to become tense as the roadway nears the cove. Looming menacingly on the ocean side of the road is the Taiji Whale Museum. Overshadowed by verdant Takababe Hill, the squat bulk of the museum has an ominous feel; rather like a sentient guard dog watching the roadway approaching the cove. Eyeing it warily I follow the sweep of the road past the dreaded bay. The Cove beach car park is eerily deserted as I pass by. After the chaos of the 'japarazzi circus' yesterday the cold expanse of water has an almost surreal feel to it.

Suddenly the car is swallowed by the dark closeness of the traffic tunnel, which spits me out abruptly into stark sunshine on the other side to negotiate the winding harbor road around the Fisherman's Co-operative with the long slaughterhouse alongside.

Taiji township is unnaturally quiet and still and I take the opportunity to have a good walk around the narrow streets surrounding the harbor. Save for the occasional passing car I am the only pedestrian out on the streets this morning. The banger boats sit nose to tail along the dock; pristine white with their array of radio aerials rising like thin whips. A gentle sea breeze sings prettily in their rigging wires and water laps gently against the hulls of numerous small fishing boats.

Out across the harbor, set against a long narrow seawall is the floating holding pen area–a cluster of small netted sea pens where the dolphins bound for captivity are held. This is the transition point from their free-spirited life in the wild to the sterile and unnatural surrounds of a life in captivity. I stand for the longest time watching them leap occasionally from their painfully cramped surrounds, describing perfect grey arcs through sunlit air before quickly disappearing again. Often the trainers can be seen around the pens; doling out fish from plastic buckets as they teach the dolphins their first basic tricks with shrill whistles and hand signals. Today there is nobody in sight.

Tracing my way back past the cove on the return home I cast a final glance across the dark waters of the bay; cold and still against the surrounding hills. In stark contrast the open water further out glistens a bright aquamarine blue with the reflected sunshine.

Out on the shadowy waters beyond the net with its white buoy markers, however, steady movement catches my eye. The surface is broken and churned by several shiny dorsal fins and the unmistakable misty blow of dolphins.

Being completely alone I'm a little wary of stopping, but I am curious as to what's going on. Have they penned some dolphins into the bay? Pulling quickly into the car park across the road, I make sure the car is secure and cross the narrow bitumen strip to the beach. My first thought is that a pod has been driven into the bay to await their slaughter the following day, as was the practice here in years past. There are just six dolphins turning in confused circles in close proximity to the cove mouth and the security net which bisects the little bay. But what is keeping them there? Their behavior is far from normal for a pod and I can now see there is no net holding them, to cause their erratic circling. As the bay area is actually a public beach, a protective security net forms a natural barrier preventing anyone from swimming out from the beach to the cove, whose entrance lies just beyond the line of floating white marker buoys forming the fishermen's self-appointed 'no-go' line. I can hear the unmistakable blow as the pods surfaces for breath; the staccato blast of exhaled air pumping a misty gossamer spray above the water's surface.

Then it occurs to me why they must be there, and tears involuntarily well up in my eyes. The past week had seen a series of horrific slaughters of striped dolphins at the cove. Being a pelagic or deep ocean dwelling species, striped dolphins very rarely venture close to land and their stress and anxiety levels thus increase markedly in shallow water. A series of incidents involving dolphins beaching themselves on the surrounding rocks had tragically marred the events of the past week. Three days ago, a pod of twenty-five dolphins had been driven in. In plain view of the watching activists, four adults and a small juvenile struggled to break free and dashed in a blind panic towards the rocky shoreline. Ignored by the fisherman these five slowly bled to death in the shallows against the jagged rocks; dying in a slow agony that lasted over an hour before the hunters returned to remove them.

There seems to be a sense of urgency about the sharp crisscross movements of the sleek dorsal fins breaking the distant waters beyond the barrier. They are skittish. Have these dolphins perhaps returned to seek out the missing members of their pod? Following a stranding it is not unusual that re-floated survivors will remain in the shallows nearby awaiting the remaining pod members to return. I know from my whale rescue training that you never return a beached pod to the sea in small numbers. The entire pod must be readied for return and released together. Such is the strength of their social bonds that they will return for the stranded or sick members of the pod.

In the eerie solitude of the cove there is a painful poignancy to the sight of them circling before running the length of the net barrier. This is my first experience of dolphins choosing to be near the cove of their own volition. The tranquility is broken only by the occasional breathy blow of the distant dolphins. A pastel blue sky and winter sunlight adds a final watercolor touch to the whole scene. After the craziness of the past days, I simply sit respectfully and share this one melancholy moment in a hushed reverie. For now, it is just me, the cove and the dolphins.

I realize that today I have been shown another dimension to the drive hunt–the pain of those who have been left behind.

CHAPTER SIX

Nami

*'God loved the birds and invented trees.
Man loved the birds and invented cages'*
– JACQUES DEVAL - 'Afin de Vivre Bel et Bien'

NAMI, A JAPANESE word meaning 'wave', was the name given to a young female orca captured off the coast of Taiji in October 1985. She was trapped and kidnapped by the dolphin hunters, together with a male orca who was given the name Goro. Nami was barely three years old at the time, and Goro even younger. Orcas, for those who are not familiar, are probably the most highly distinctive and iconic of all the whale species. They are toothed whales belonging to the oceanic dolphin family. Recognizable by their distinct black and white coloration and high peaked dorsal fin, they dwell in the coastal regions of most of the world's great oceans. It was a captive orca named Keiko who played the central role in the popular movie 'Free Willy'. But that is in itself another story.

Orcas, like other whales and dolphins, exist in an extremely close-knit social group and hence we can be certain that the two young orcas belonged to the same family clan, or pod. They may well have been brother and sister. It is this fact that makes the story all the more painfully poignant. The orca possesses a family bond even stronger than other species of whales. Family life for these imposing black and white mammals means that the offspring remain with their mothers in a travelling group for their entire lives.

Nami

With lifespans of up to eighty years, an orca pod is comprised of several family generations of the same family. Travelling vast distances as they feed and socialize, the pod is typically led by an elderly matriarch, with the older males taking up protective positions to the front, rear and flanks of the group safeguarding the mothers with their young in the center.

Sadly, on that October day off the Japanese Pacific coast, the hunters were able to split the pod and deliberately capture the two youngsters. Both juveniles were immediately pressed into a life of captivity in the confines of a shallow and cramped bay at a facility called the Taiji Whale Museum. The Museum occupies the natural bay immediately alongside the killing cove. Just a month later, the pair were separated when young Goro was sold and shipped to a marine park called Nanki Shirahama Adventure World in the city of Tanabe, approximately sixty kilometers to the north of Taiji village. Now alone, Nami became the solitary representative of her breed at the Museum, stolen from her pod off the coast of Taiji, and now separated from the young companion who was her only company, and the last remaining link to her family. And so Nami's connection with freedom and family came to an end. Her pod and her anxious mother may well have remained just off the coast for some time desperately awaiting her return with Goro.

For the next twenty-four long years Nami remained in captivity there before finally being sold and transported to the Port of Nagoya Public Aquarium in June 2010. She was lifted by crane onto a flat barge to make the twenty-three hour sea journey northeast to her new prison. It would be the first time in all those years that she could see the ocean where she once swam in the company of her mother and clan members. She would never see it again.

Her new keepers intended to use Nami in their captive breeding program. This plan was never to eventuate. The years of strain and depression in captivity had exacted a heavy toll on the once exuberant orca. According to the Nagoya Aquarium, Nami's health deteriorated badly just four months after her arrival. By late December 2010 she was being treated for a condition of ulcerative colitis, an inflammatory bowel disease. Suffering from loss of appetite, she dropped approximately three hundred kilos from her three-ton body weight. And so, on January 14th 2011 at 7:24pm, breathing abnormally and floating listlessly, she passed from life.

She was approximately twenty-eight years old at her death. Goro, the young male orca who had been captured with her had already passed on, almost exactly six years before; succumbing to pneumonia on January 21th 2005. He had spent nineteen years of his life in captivity.

On February 19th 2011, a month after Nami's death the Japanese newspaper *'The Mainichi Daily News'* ran the following article:

Autopsy shows killer whale swallowed 80 kilograms of stones before death at aquarium.
'NAGOYA - A popular killer whale that died at an aquarium here last month has been found to have lost its life apparently after swallowing more than 80 kilograms of stones over the course of many years, which led to it suffering from a stomach ulcer and pneumonia, the facility has announced.
According to the Port of Nagoya Public Aquarium, an autopsy has found that the female killer whale, named 'Nami,' had 491 stones–weighing 81.4 kilograms in total–stuck in her stomach.
One pocket of her stomach was reportedly sagging due to the weight of some 70 kilograms of pebbles stuffed in it, including the largest stone that measured 17 centimeters in length and weighed 2.1 kilograms.
Furthermore, an ulcer was found in another pocket of her stomach, and bleeding from the spleen and enteritis were also diagnosed. The ailments are thought to have put a strain on Nami's heart.
There are reportedly no study documents on killer whales that include reports of them swallowing stones. Nami is believed to have

Nami

repeatedly swallowed pebbles at the Taiji Whale Museum as whales at the facility are displayed in part of a natural cove. There are no stones in the pool where Nami was kept at the aquarium in Nagoya.'

Stones. Eighty kilos of stones and pebbles from the ocean floor in that tiny bay in Taiji where she was held prisoner for almost a quarter of a century. I know those pebbles so well. The first slaughter that I witnessed in Taiji was a pod of forty striped dolphins. I stood there that day feeling impotent and helpless. With the knot in my guts tightening and my throat constricted and dry. With so many dolphins penned into the tiny killing cove the dolphin hunters could not hide all of their acts of shameful cruelty from view. The sight of those beautiful deep-sea dwellers dashing themselves against rocks, torn and bloodied, to escape the fishermen's cruel knives was heart-wrenching. Hiding my disgust and upset from the throng of officials and fishermen standing nearby, I kneeled and picked up several of the smooth grey pebbles that cover the beach area. With my hands thrust deep in the pockets of my jacket to stave off the cold, I turned those smooth stones over and over in my hand.

The settled familiarity of my peaceful Aussie lifestyle had seemed worlds away. It was incredibly hard to stand by and simply watch what feels to be a cruel injustice. That handful of stones became comforting somehow, and I imagined them as something of a connection; to the water, and to the dolphins. I pictured those dolphins as they should be. Together in the open ocean. The amorphous shapes sleek and silvered, the foam ebbing and parting suddenly to explode into the viscous striped arcs of dolphins.

And so, standing there on the beach, the only thing that I could do was to stand in a silent vigil for them. I wondered if they knew that there were people here that truly cared. I still have those stones–kept safely in an ornate wooden box as a reminder of the Taiji dolphins.

When I first read the tragic story of Nami, I wondered what exactly drove her to swallow those stones. Video footage of Nami from her days at the Taiji Whale Museum clearly shows her floating listlessly and disconsolately in the shallow waters of her enclosed sea pen.

Maybe it was grief–how does a sentient being survive the years as a lone captive in the cramped confines of a shallow bay? Or was it anxiety? Or hunger. Or perhaps the mind-numbing boredom. Or maybe they were a reminder to her of the life and the family that she lost? Had she felt the same way I did when I held those stones, I wondered? In the wild, orcas are far ranging and will travel an average of seventy to one hundred miles a day, reaching speeds of up to thirty miles an hour and diving as deep as five hundred feet. Orcas are extremely socially creatures and this particular species are used to remaining with their family pod throughout their entire lives. Think for a while on what captivity in a small artificial pool, living in solitude and separated from family must mean to such a highly intelligent and self-aware creature.

In the open ocean, Nami would have had a life expectancy of as much as eighty years. She lived to age of just twenty-eight; spending twenty-four of those years in captivity before she finally found her release in a forlorn and painfully lonely death.

I would ask you to pause here for a moment and think back on the past twenty-four years of your life. Think back to all of the places that you've been in that quarter century of existence; the sights, the sounds. Consider the holidays and the trips that you took. The magic of twenty-four winters and summers. The time that you spent with your family, your friends. Perhaps that special person that you met and fell in love with. Or the children that you've raised and watched grow into adulthood. Think of all those things that you've seen and done. Nami, like so many of her kind, was cruelly denied all of this. The right of association with her family and her pod. The right to choose a mate. The right to navigate the length and depth of oceans, unfettered and unbound. The right to be free. The thing that we value the most here on this mortal coil is *freedom*. We fight for it. Some of us die for it.

We all are intimately aware of the importance of freedom. And yet so few of us stop and think that this same sense of freedom is similarly cherished by highly intelligent self-aware 'non-human persons' like whales and dolphins. I wonder how many people who have watched them perform in captivity, or who have participated in a 'swim with the dolphins' program have ever really stopped to consider this underlying truth. The fact is, I never really thought too much about this when I was younger. In truth, it never even occurred to me. So, I can understand perfectly how we can be led to believe that these dolphins actually enjoy their time in captivity. Putting it in the words of some of my fellow activists; *'Come and see the whales and dolphins, they are dying to entertain you'.*

The facility where Nami was held–the Taiji Whale Museum–is located immediately alongside the killing cove; tucked into lush foliage at the base of Tsunami Hill, which forms a natural mountain barrier between it and the cove. So, I decided that I needed to visit the Taiji Whale Museum and see it for myself.

CHAPTER SEVEN

Whale Museum

LIKE THE BELLE of the ball shirking off the unwanted advances of cloying over-eager suitors, Taiji in 2011 plays reluctant host to an international cadre of activists. Owned and operated by the township, the Taiji Whale Museum brokers deals with the Fisherman's Co-operative for the purchase of live specimens for dolphin shows. It is for this reason that several of the activists who have visited the village flatly refuse to patronize the town's Whale Museum. The museum complex includes an outdoor area built around a small lagoon which forms the natural setting where the show dolphins are forced to perform.

Shrouded by picturesque hills, this lagoon neighbors Hatajiri bay and the cove where we now know the dolphins which are not destined for a life of captivity are corralled and slaughtered. Forming a natural barrier between these two bays is a heavily forested hill atop which sits Tsunami Park–a verdant and lush national park area so named because in the event of a tsunami it would provide a safe area of high ground for the villagers. Ironically the cove on one side of Tsunami Park represents a death sentence whilst the bay on the other side means a life sentence for its occupants. Another example of the strange duality which seems to infuse everything here in Japan.

Over the past few days the weather conditions offshore have kept the fleet of twelve pristine white hunting boats in their line astern berths around the stone walled periphery of Taiji harbor. Tucked amongst scores of other fishing vessels they are remarkably clean, well-conditioned and imposing. Despite the conditions off the coast the day is picture perfect and the serenity of the lush landscape basking under the cold clear winter sky belies the evil that is done here. During this lull I decide that I need to see the Whale Museum for myself. There are only a scant few cars in the parking area across from the vast squarish concrete building when I arrive mid-morning. It is a weekday and the place is peaceful and still, which only adds to the eerily disconnected feeling which carries in the chill morning air.

I stand for a while at the car and survey the scene. The museum itself is a monolithic, white-blue concrete giant standing starkly against the backdrop of greenery. A huge effigy of a charcoal black Right whale set against a checkerboard geometric of pale blues and greys decorates one slab side of the building. The dated architecture and its almost ethereal surrounds instantly remind me of an old 1970's sci-fi thriller movie called 'Coma'. A high-tech white multi-storied Institute is the center point of the movie. Eerily devoid of life it is the holding place for scores of people deliberately placed in comas to have their organs harvested for commercial gain. I shiver as the image passes and I make the connection between the movie and real-life. I cannot shake the feeling that something is oddly jarring here–it is almost as though I am standing on a movie set, one step divorced from reality.

Even the weather adds to the sense of disconnect. When I left my home in Australia it was the height of summer; thirty-seven degrees of dry heat with little respite. Gum trees motionless in the heat; a uniform parched dry green. Here in the northern winter the mercury hovers around five degrees. A watery sun devoid of heat shines earthwards through a washed crystalline blue sky and paints everything with a cold beauty. I glance down the road towards the cove–all is quiet today. The stillness is complete and near-perfect, broken only by the passing of an occasional car. Not far from the museum building the moss-covered staircase of stone steps cut their way steeply upwards through the greenery to Tsunami Park, disappearing from view under an ancient canopy of trees. I cross the grey footpath to the cold slab of waiting concrete and glass, shivering now as its sumo bulk blocks out the sun, leaving the entry in shadow. Approaching the double glass doors at the front entrance I can't help but feel that the imposing size of the building matches the immensity of the problem that we are fighting to overcome here in Taiji. Finding a small glass windowed pay-booth alongside the entrance, I am eyed with reservation by the young attendant.

'Sumimasen, ikura desu ka?' ('Excuse me, how much does it cost?'), I venture.

The young lady types numbers on a hand-held calculator and warily maintaining my gaze she shows it to me. I bow politely, handing over the equivalent of twelve Australian dollars before thrusting the paper ticket into my pocket as the automatic doors slide open soundlessly.

Three stories of open museum stand in front of me in hushed library silence and I make my way past a gift shop amply stocked with trinkets and rows of colorful stuffed toys. Something amongst the splashes of color catches my eye and I wander over to investigate. A freezer similar to the supermarket frozen goods refrigerators back home occupies a prominent position in the gift shop. In it are trays of whale meat. I knew of this prior to coming here but the revelation still sets me back. Here at the Whale Museum you can watch a show of performing dolphins and then pay your respects by buying a tray of dolphin meat on the way out. I understand that many people patronizing dolphin shows do so in blissful ignorance of the devastation that captivity is causing these unfortunate creatures. Many will profess their motivation for attending as a love of whales and dolphins. I cannot however understand how those same people rationalize the fact that the dolphins that they love so dearly are obviously slaughtered to provide the meat adorning the gift shop freezer.

The parallel of the coma hospital is not far from the truth I think to myself as I explore the interior of the three-story museum. The

Whale Museum

building has a stark clinical atmosphere which is not helped by the fact that I am its sole occupant on this peaceful mid-week morning. The floors are gleaming and sterile, and I can't help but feel a little self-conscious as my footsteps echo around the vast cavernous interior. A display in a large glass case lining one wall attracts my attention. A long row of glass sample jars, their contents submersed in cloudy formaldehyde liquid presents a rather stark spectacle. Carefully arranged are a series of whale fetuses graduating from small to large, each carefully marked to show the advancement of age in months for each individual specimen. Knowing what I do of the cove next door, a sense of quiet despondency fills me as I gaze at the lifeless waxen forms. Were these the unborn young who never stood a chance, now displayed nakedly in undignified glass wombs? Were some of those slaughtered dolphins found to have been pregnant? Further similar displays line the walls; viscera and internal organs of various species of whales and dolphins.

I find myself struggling to reconcile the brutality of the drive hunt slaughters with the trappings of what appears to be a love of whales and dolphins. It is a contradiction which I cannot fully comprehend. The clinical and detached scientific display seems to be at total odds with the garish circus pageantry of the dolphin shows which run just outside. It seems something of a sick juxtaposition; macabre displays of viscera and whale meat for sale set alongside fluffy children's toys and live dolphin shows promising 'family entertainment'. My immediate impression is that Dr Hannibal Lecter seems alive and well and living here in the Wakayama prefecture. Perhaps I am over-dramatizing it? I remind myself that I am looking once again through the eyes of a Westerner, and this jarring paradox typifies the sense of duality I experience time and time again with the Japanese culture.

The central focal point of the museum is a display occupying the central open area and rising three floors high. A massive full-scale Right whale model occupies pride of place, hung in place by guy wires, its massive flukes raised and thrashing. Suspended alongside the gargantuan tail, a beautifully painted open whaling boat from the *amitori-ho* era completes the scene. It is perhaps a third of the size of the creature dwarfing it and I marvel at what it must have been like all those centuries ago in these fragile open boats battling whale, winds and an unforgiving ocean. The gloss black lacquer hull is over painted in blue and burgundy with intricate paintings of serpentine creatures decorating the length of each side, the bowsprit rising upward to a sharp conclusion like a curving scythe. Standing in the boat a dozen oarsmen wait expectantly with oars shipped whilst a harpooner standing at the bow prepares to deliver a harpoon blow to the flank of the hapless whale.

Something strikes me about this place. Suspended at the very heart of Taiji Whale Museum, the whale and pursuing whaling boat hang frozen and timeless; a snapshot of the past which perfectly portrays the roots of cultural tradition which gave birth to Taiji. And then, folded around this proud central focus is the grotesque evidence of what it has morphed into. Just a few hundred meters away is the killing Cove, its waters regularly turned a sickly blood red from the dispatch of hundreds of dolphins and small whales, hidden behind a rough erection of blue tarpaulins drawn shamefully tight around the killing area. In the museum grounds, the beautiful natural bay which it nestles in is now a prison for the chosen few dolphins and small whales which were spared the harsh spike through the spine; condemned to a captive life for the entertainment of spectators and museum patrons.

Let me address the argument of those who defend what goes on here in Taiji with the rationalization of 'proud cultural tradition'. The small-scale subsistence whaling that once existed here is a proud cultural tradition. The wholesale mechanized slaughter and the lucrative live capture industry which have flourished in recent decades are not. Greed and commercialism were not the way of the ancestors. And neither do they have a place in present-day society.

Whale Museum

Suddenly from outside the strains of amplified music can be heard. The library stillness is broken and it seems as though the carnival has come to town. A singsong female Japanese voice can be heard over the Tannoy; clear and bell. Even here inside, I can hear the slap-back echo from the surrounding hills around the lagoon outside. Finding an exit door, I make my way down a flight of concrete stairs to the rear of the building. Beyond a small concrete 'swimming pool' is the bay which neighbors the cove itself; lined at the museum end with long wooden bleachers which allow an audience to watch proceedings in the lagoon. Being a weekday however there is barely an audience for the scheduled show. Adding yet another layer to the unreality of today's expedition, I take a seat front row center, the only other audience members being a Japanese family comprising mum, dad and a young daughter who looks to be no more than ten years old.

Out on the water on a floating dock four trainers dressed in matching blue overalls hold four performing whales–three pseudo-orcas and a short-finned pilot whale–in check with curt hand signals, punctuated by bursts from a shrill whistle. The show has already started and the four charcoal black whales proceed through their choreographed routine, leaping, pectoral fin waving and vocalizing all on cue to the curt hand waves and staccato bursts of whistles. The routine is followed closely by the watching family sitting off to my left, who openly display their excitement with enthusiastic clapping.

Mixed emotions flow through me. Despite my best intentions I feel an overwhelming sense of shame and guilt to be sitting here like arrogant royalty watching the humiliating display being played out in front of me. The scene is heartbreaking and I find myself mentally apologizing over and over to the poor creatures, hoping that they may in some way understand my intent. I feel miserable. Then out of the corner of my eye I notice movement from the smaller pool on the other side of the bleachers that I hurriedly passed by. I had paid scant attention to the two bottlenose dolphins quietly circling the small pool when I had descended the steps from the museum. Now, turning to watch them I realize just what they were doing. Although the pair is not taking part in today's show, they are despondently mimicking the moves of the main performers in the bay in the hopes of being fed. But they are not a part of the show, and there are no trainers to feed them. Their gyrations are ignored by the trainers and the Japanese family sitting in the bleachers. I am grateful for the dark sunglasses I am wearing and I sit motionless.

The thing I notice the most is the noise; the singsong cadences of the Japanese commentator streaming a never-ending commentary across the bay which echoes in a sharp slap-back against the tight ring of hills. The blaring carnival music is a constant backdrop, jarringly out of place with the range of emotions running through me. My mind drifts to the plight of these whales and dolphins. Water is a far better medium than air for transmitting sound and these creatures use that to their advantage. Toothed whales, which include dolphins, utilize a highly acute echolocation system, receiving vibrations of reflected sound through a sensitive oil filled cavity in their lower jaw which is then conducted to their middle ear. This system is so sensitively tuned that rescuers at a stranding must avoid any extremes of noise and undue vibration by stepping quietly around the sensitive jaw region. How noisy and disorienting this artificial world must be for them. This rude wall of noise must be as annoying as the persistent buzz of a dentist's drill.

The four whales move dutifully through their choreographed routine performing high leaping breaches, coordinated jumps and slapping tail flukes before finishing in a 'lap of honor' waving one pectoral fin perfunctorily towards the gathered 'crowd'. The family standing nearby–the only audience members besides this oddly out of place Westerner–stand and applaud the finale with great enthusiasm.

It is one of the few times that I witness such a spontaneous outburst of emotion from the normally staid and controlled Japanese. I

Whale Museum

wonder if they even begin to realize that after the show they can go home whilst the entertainers sadly cannot.

As the show comes to an end the family filters away and a lone trainer feeds dead fish from a plastic bucket to one of the whales. I sit back and allow things to settle down. I am keen to see how these whales act when not being forced to put up the demeaning facade for the benefit of onlookers. Within minutes the trainers have drifted away to other parts of the museum complex and I am alone in the bleachers with the four whales. With their part in the morning's performance over, three of the whales immediately take to 'logging'– floating in a sleep like state on the surface of the water. Cetaceans are voluntary breathers which means that their breathing is not an automatic response like ours. This simply means that these complex marine mammals do not sleep in the same sense as humans–they simply shut down part of their brain in a 'cat napping' state whilst maintaining a minimal level of brain function in order to maintain breathing and to check for threats. The pseudo-orca remains active and describes slow circles around the 'display area'–the cordoned off portion of the bay. I sit quietly and make eye contact with it as passes by me, tracing its way in slow circles around the periphery of the bay. Time and again it passes with head raised, assessing me each time with heavy lidded eyes. The sensation that comes back with each passing circuit is one of dulled torpor, distracted by its constant search for food.

Perhaps satisfying itself that I am not able to provide it with sustenance, the sleek glistening body navigates off to the far end of the bay. The dulled look in his eye speaks of the futility of this place. Of the mind-numbing boredom and monotony. This was no way for them to live. The remainder of the bay is divided into separate subsections by floating pontoon walkways. Wandering down towards the seawards end of the bay, I pass the pens which hold a score of bottlenose dolphins which are currently being fed and tended to by the troupe of trainers.

Even here with no show in progress, the trainers coax the dolphins into performing various tricks with sharp whistle bursts, deft hand movements and the reward of dead fish from a number of blue plastic eskys which dot the wooden walkways around the pens. What fate befalls those who refuse to perform the demeaning acts for the reward of food, I think to myself grimly. I do not linger at the pens; instead making for the deserted ocean end of the bay, leaving the trainers to fuss over their captives.

Perhaps I will be able to spend more time with the dolphins later, away from the trainers' assessing glances. Standing in a waft of salt air as breakers hurl flecks of foam over the rocks, I find myself alone and take in the setting once again. The sweep of hills provides a near-perfect closure to the bay, completed by a man-made groyne of concrete and rock, effectively cutting it off from the open ocean to form this captive lagoon. Teasing glimpses of the Pacific can be seen through the hilly rock outcrops at the bottom of the bay, a freedom so tantalizingly close yet forever lost and out of reach.

Tucked into a corner at this far end of the lagoon a small squat concrete building catches my eye. On closer inspection, it carries a sign in Japanese and English which identifies it as the 'Dolphinarium'. Passing through the tinted glass entrance door, a clear-view Perspex tunnel carries a sloping walkway up through the depths of a large tank, which appears to be almost 2 stories high. The occupants of this tank are four bottlenose dolphins who appear in constant motion around the curved acrylic see-through walls of the viewing area.

The winter air has a cold edge to it even indoors, and my beanie is pulled down to keep the warmth around my ears. Overhead fluorescent lighting gives the deep water a diffuse glow. Despite the glare I have my sunglasses off so that the dolphins have a clear view of my eyes. When you catch the glance of a whale or dolphin; when it engages you with those deep eyes, you recognize there is a clear intellect behind them. This perhaps comes as no surprise to many.

Whale Museum

Dolphins are amongst the handful of species considered to be 'self-aware'–they recognize themselves as individuals. So, when dolphin and human regard other, a moment of recognition and acknowledgement passes from one self-aware being to another. As the gunmetal grey shapes steal past I am in awe of their sheer size.

The bottlenoses cleave the waters easily; with deft easy pulses of powerful tail flukes they weave in perpetual motion, restless, unceasingly threading over and around the Perspex umbilical I am standing in. I try standing motionless in the center of the tunnel, willing them to notice me. Their eyes catch mine but none of them hold my glance for more than a few seconds. The same impression strikes me as before–the distracted stares, perhaps dulled with boredom. Impartial to my presence and seeking food. And then suddenly they are gone, drawn overhead to the top of the tank where a trainer is doling out a supply of dead fish. Minutes pass and I continue to contemplate the scene, suspended static and artificial at the bottom of this false ocean.

Having been fed, the bottlenoses return to their ceaseless prowling, backwards and forwards in the relatively tight confines of the tank. I'm overwhelmed by the futility of it all–the sense of joylessness typifying the whales and dolphins captive here; held at a selfish whim. It is my recollection of the river dolphins back home and our playful interactions as I kayaked with them that throw this miserable scene into stark relief. There is no joy here. This is the last emotional straw for me and suddenly the tears come–thick, heavy saltwater tears, which I have been tightly bottling up each day at the cove. Today the lid on my emotional jar came loose. I sob breathlessly and it feels like I can't stop. There is no one around to hear me anyway, but that really doesn't matter anymore. I want their pain to stop and I feel so powerless to help them. I am ashamed and angered at how harsh and unfeeling we have become as a species. How unimportant life has become to us. How we are so caught up with ourselves and our own precious wants. And in that crystalline moment, a magic occurred that I still cannot really explain to this day. From high above at the top of the tank, the bottlenoses dive in a bomb-burst towards me. I suddenly find myself surrounded by a steel grey halo of four dolphins–the sheer size of the quartet is blocking out the harsh fluorescent light. They have all taken up station, perfectly spaced around the semicircle of Perspex tube, floating absolutely motionless in perfect suspension in the water around me; nose to tail. The shock of this sudden freezing of motion and the close proximity of these four large mammals in perfect formation hits me in the pit of my stomach. *Is this some sort of a trick? Have they been taught to do this?* Through teary eyes I make contact with each of them individually; they are each arranged side on to me and this time all four are now meeting my gaze and holding it purposefully with fixed intent. But more than that, I can feel them looking into me as if seeking out the very essence of who exactly I am.

The dulled torpor I witnessed in those dark eyes is now gone, replaced by keen intellect; inquiring obsidian pools of knowing which seem to be now connecting soul deep. Perhaps they had been watching me carefully this entire time, unbeknownst to me. Assessing me. Perhaps they knew more than they let on. Or perhaps I had passed some sort of test and I had been accepted.

PART II

DEEPER WATER

Beyond the dark rock
Water is lit from above
Shimmering brightly

CHAPTER EIGHT

Kumano

'Darkness reigns at the foot of the lighthouse'
—JAPANESE PROVERB

THERE IS A traditional Buddhist fable which tells the story of a meeting between an old monk and a young impetuous samurai warrior. I'm going to tell it to you here, because in hindsight I realize just how relevant its moral was to my own mindset when I first set foot in Taiji. The fable goes something like this:

An old monk sat by the side of the road. With his eyes closed, his legs crossed and his hands folded in his lap, he sat in deep meditation. Suddenly his *zazen* was interrupted by the harsh and demanding voice of a young samurai warrior.

'Old man! Teach me about heaven and hell!'

Seemingly oblivious to the brash intrusion, the monk remained unmoved; deep in his prayer. When he finally began to open his eyes, the faintest hint of a smile played around the corners of his mouth. The samurai stood there, waiting impatiently, growing more and more agitated with each passing second.

'You wish to know the secrets of Heaven and Hell?' replied the monk at last; 'You who are so unkempt. You whose hands and feet are covered with dirt. You whose hair is uncombed, whose breath is foul, whose sword is all rusty and neglected.

You who are ugly, and whose mother dresses you strangely. *You* would dare to ask me of Heaven and Hell?'

Taken aback by the unexpected tirade of abuse from the holy man, the samurai uttered a vile curse. He drew his sword and raised it high above his head. His face turned to crimson and the veins on his neck stood out in bold relief as he prepared to sever the monk's head from its shoulders.

'*That* is Hell' said the old monk, just as the sword began its descent. The young warrior realized the significance of the holy man's words. Understood his intent. And in that moment, the samurai felt overcome with awe, compassion and respect for this gentle soul who had dared to risk his very life to give him such a teaching. He stopped his sword in mid-flight and bowed reverently; his eyes filling with grateful tears.

'And *that*,' said the monk kindly, 'is Heaven.'

TAIJI JOURNAL – Tuesday afternoon January 18th 2011

Today I have learned something; there is indeed a Heaven and a Hell. And I can tell you that the distance between them is only a paltry fifteen kilometers, give or take one or two clicks. For today I truly feel like I have witnessed them both.

I knew what I was letting myself in for when I made the journey to Taiji, but then can you ever really be prepared for the emotions that run through you when you are confronted with a sight like this morning? Anger and spite ran through my veins in a bitter rush as forty striped dolphins were decimated in roughly as many minutes. It was not only the pure scale of this bloodbath but also the fact that there were juveniles amongst the pod members, some of whom were the last to die. They waited anxiously whilst the rest of the pod were cruelly slaughtered. Waiting and circling helplessly in water turned red with the blood of their family. The painful memory of the tiny dorsal fins of the young circling nervously is burned deep in my mind.

TAIJI

Today I want to sink all your evil boats, and send your godlessness to the bottom of Taiji harbor. What kind of person can allow the young to suffer such an agonizing fate? These are the acts of the spiritually bankrupt. I feel like there is no compassion here, and I have seen too much cruelty and suffering. By noon the carnage was all over and the fishermen departed the cove, returning to the slaughterhouse in Taiji harbor with the dead piled high and covered shamefully by crudely thrown tarpaulins, others tied with rope to the side of their skiffs.

I need to walk away. Just for now, I need to see beauty; to know that Japan is not all heartlessness and cruelty. Heading back to my tiny hotel room opposite Katsuura harbor, I stop by the little information office in the center of town. Like many places, the railway runs through the heart of the town, and the white wooden planked office sits alongside the station. The whole place has an atmospheric old feel to it, and I can easily see the old building as it was in the wartime era. I feel quite out of place here as a Westerner, and I always sense my presence as a vague intrusion on the quietly familiar bustle of village life.

The air has an ice chill despite the weak winter sun and the lightest flecks of snow are beginning to drift and dot the sky, dissolving as they touch the earth. In the welcoming warmth of the cramped timber floored office, I pick up a tourist map of the area (one of the very few in English) and note that a short drive from here in the mountains is a waterfall and a series of shrines. With the afternoon free, I decide that I am not yet ready to be cooped up alone in my tiny hotel room documenting this morning's proceedings. I need to offset the carnage of this morning's drive and regain a sense of mental balance. Without disturbing the elderly clerk at the information office desk, I take the free map and cram it into a jacket pocket before walking the few across the road into the shopping precinct to get some food and plan my trip.

Greeted like an old friend, I exchange smiles and respectful bows with the staff at the patisserie in Katsuura where I buy lunch. My spirits are lifted by the genuine warmth I feel from these wonderful people. The fresh bread and pastries here in Japan are absolutely mouth-watering too! One of the things that the Japanese excel in is taking a concept and raising it to the next level. I was surprised to find patisserie shops in the village which would fit perfectly into a Parisian boulevard; replicated perfectly and selling French patisseries easily as fine as the original.

With lunch over, I make the leisurely drive into the mountains, losing myself in the quiet beauty as the scenery unfolds around me and starts to wash away the sights and sounds of this morning's mêlée. With cedar forests starting to shroud the sunny winter afternoon in dappled shadow, light dustings of snow begin to fall. My first stop is at the Nachi waterfall and the closer I get to the destination I become aware that I've been holding my breath as the natural beauty of the forest envelops me. By the time I reach the parking area which overlooks the steep gradient that I have just travelled up, snow is falling in large gentle flakes which vanish by the time they touch the soil. I am all open-mouthed wonder as I stand at the car park railing. There is something unfathomable about this place, over and above the natural beauty of the mountains and forest. There is a serene energy here that pervades everything. *I feel it!* At this point I reach what I can only describe as an emotional overload; it is as if the spiritual beauty of this place is simply too much for the senses, indeed too much for the soul. My eyes are brimming with tears of joy and wonder. There is something magically powerful about this place and I am entranced.

Several minutes have passed and it is all I can do to simply stand and absorb the scene, suspended in the moment as though pinned to a rich tapestry. A parking attendant dressed in official uniform grey has abandoned the comfort of his warm tollbooth and trotted over to me, presumably mistaking my fixed stance for confusion. With a series of polite bows, he offers me a ticket and with a humble smile motions me to wait whilst he hurries back in a loping jog to fetch my change.

Across the other side of the valley, the mountaintops disappear behind a thin veil of fine mist. Cutting through the forest is a magnificent waterfall, fountains of water tumbling for what seems like hundreds of feet from three distinct mouths high up in rocks of granite greys and blacks. It is a truly imposing sight indeed. Tucked away into the forest a set of old stone steps leads up through a massive stone torii–the ceremonial gate which marks the passage to the sanctified ground of a Shinto shrine. You have probably seen images of the iconic torii before but not realized what it represents. The torii is usually made of wood–two upright poles supporting a curved wooden cross-member shaped like a crescent moon. This delineates the crossover from earth to a spiritual place.

Dotting the stone trail are elements evidencing the sanctity of this place; ancient stone monoliths resembling tombstones, carved with Japanese characters. Enclosed timber hutches filled with rows of white ceremonial candles covered in canopies of ferns. All around me is primeval forest with thick canopies filtering the sun. Tall straight trunks, rising from a dense understory of ferns and thick bracken intertwined with ancient looking gnarled roots anchoring it all to the forest floor. It looks and feels like Middle Earth.

The air here is fresh, bracing and thick with a serenity of spirit. Running water and moving air always tends to create a naturally fresh ionization and I feel a strong sense of humility walking in this place.

There is tangible sentient energy in this place and it seems to be everywhere, permeating everything. Reaching the foot of the waterfall the trail opens out onto a cobbled courtyard which overlooks a stream running through tumbled rocks. The heady scent of sandalwood incense hangs heavy in the air and another heavy wood torii marks this as a sacred place. It is all I can do to stand and contemplate the waterfall, letting the powerful feeling of this place wash in heavy waves around me. There is the lulling sound of water against stone. The heady aroma of incense, cedar and ancient forest. And I am just a leaf in the wind; having been carried to this beautiful place. The anger and bitterness of the morning is gone. And in its place, there is a comforting sense of embrace; that I am cared for and that I am not alone. That *we* are not alone. Thrust into the pockets of my windcheater, my hands are numb with the cold but it no longer matters. *What is this place?* Standing there with flecks of snow dancing lazily about me I simply feel alive. I am enough. *I am.*

೦ಽ✿ಽ೦

High up in the Kii Mountains which form the lofty verdant backdrop to the village of Taiji there lies a sacred mystery. And like the slivers of a fractured mirror reflecting glimpses of an ancient past, there is something that looms powerful in the cracks. Its essence can be found in the dense forests, the ancient rocks and the wellspring of cleansing water that runs in the rivers and streams. Rising steeply to heights of 1000 - 2000m the thickly forested mountains of the Kii peninsula present a rugged natural beauty.

Nestled atop this mountain sanctuary lays the area called the Kumano; bounded by three ancient sacred sites, and linked by pilgrimage routes which have been walked by worshippers for the past 1,200 years. In a unique fusion of Japan's traditional Shinto religion and the Buddhism faith which was introduced from China and the Korean peninsula in the sixth century, the region is marked by stunningly beautiful shrines and temples.

Shintoism is characterized by the worship our connection with nature, the heart of which centers around *kami*–spirits which are said to infuse and permeate all elements of the natural world. Thus, the trees, rivers, oceans, mountains and waterfalls all assume a mystical reverence.

TAIJI

A method of demonstrating respect for *kami* is through one's sensitivity towards the beauty and the flow of nature. Since times long past, Kumano has been held as one of the most powerful spiritual sanctuaries in all Japan. Kumano is said to be the entrance way to the land of Yomi–also referred to as the 'Otherworld'–the mythological Land of the Dead, to which the ancestral spirits were said to have ascended.

This is a place synonymous with rebirth, purification and healing. In ages past it was said to be visited by people who had reached their lowest ebb physically and spiritually. To visit Kumano and to make communion with nature as a pilgrim was the path to spiritual rebirth.

All were accepted here–the Kumano embodied both Shinto and Buddhist spirits and people from all walks of life walked its paths. Samurai warlords, the holy and the unholy, the common man.; even the Emperor made the pilgrimage to this mysterious place to seek rebirth and re-connection.

The three boundary points are marked by three grand shrines–Hongu-Taisha, Hayatoma-Taisha and Nachi-Taisha; and the area is symbolized by *Yatagarasu*, a black three-legged raven. In Japanese mythology, the appearance of *Yatagarasu* is thought to be an indication of the will of Heaven or a sign of divine intervention in human affairs.

Of the three grand shrines, the Nachi-Taisha nestles amongst ancient forest, perched on the mountainside just fifteen kilometers inland of the village of Taiji. A stunning complex of buildings with traditional slate grey curved roofs and striking glossy orange-red walls, it is located close to a stunning waterfall one hundred and thirty-three meters high. At the confluence of four river systems, the Nachi waterfall is as breathtaking in its raw natural beauty as it is imposing in its sheer size and dimension. Water cascades against rock from three separate and distinct mouths, framed by the twisted wizened trunks of the surrounding forest. It is said that the waterfall can be seen by ships far out at sea. In the tradition of the Shinto faith which worships nature elements, the waterfall itself is revered as a deity. The god of *Musubi* (cause and effect) is said to dwell here. His holy task is the unification of the people and god.

Today the area is listed as a UNESCO world heritage site and it continues to hold power as a place of high spiritualism. In present day, support groups continue to bring needy individuals to this area–the depressed and suicidal, the spiritually destitute–and work to reconnect them with nature. Scores of other visitors are drawn here to simply to walk the old pilgrimage trails and enjoy the immense beauty and serenity of the region. If my words here resonate with you, then I would urge you to make the journey to experience this mystical place.

When I wrote my journal observations that first day at Nachi-Taisha, I was perfectly oblivious to the magnitude of the Kumano triangle's power and its deep spiritual roots. Indeed, I had not even heard of Kumano until later that evening in my darkened hotel room, my laptop throwing a pale glow around the tiny room. I searched the internet for information on that mystical area, curious to find out more about the force which had held me so entranced. My reactions on that winter afternoon had been pure and spontaneous and in hindsight, I was grateful that I had made the journey almost naively; without fore-knowledge or expectation. To be bluntly honest I had been rocked by the experience.

I had descended the winding mountain road back to my Katsuura hotel lost in private thought; trying to process the depth of emotional catharsis that I had experienced high in the mountains above Taiji. It seemed easy enough to explain away logically–I had obviously carried a great deal of emotional stress borne out of bearing witness to the carnage at the cove that day, and that would certainly have contributed to my state of being that afternoon.

And yet, there was something more to it. There was something primitively elemental about the Kumano. Standing there in the ice chill at the base of the Nachi waterfall; warmed by the cedar wood blocks glowing in the old ceremonial cast iron burner, embers lifting and mingling with falling snow in the gentle waft of mountain air. Earth, wind, air, fire and water all found their representation here.

Even now I find that words cannot completely relay just what shifted in me that day. I was being shown something high up in the Kii Mountains that day at the sacred shrine. And here is that strange duality at work again. The ancient spirits of Kumano look down on Taiji from high atop the surrounding mountains; from a place of great sanctity and deep spirituality. It is hard for someone endowed with any sort of spiritual awareness not to be profoundly moved by the sheer power of the forces at work in this place.

Kumano is often called *'The Land of the Dead'*, in reference to the belief that ancient Shinto spirits and family ancestors dwell here after they die. Yet modern day Taiji no longer sees nor hears. Taiji is a town that looks out on to a vast ocean, and with her back bluntly turned away from the sacred mountains she hunches and fixes her singular gaze toward the waves, listening intently for the calls of the passing pods.

൱ ✤ ൵

Lying sleepless in my bed that night, allowing the darkness to cloak me like a warm blanket, in my mind's eye I saw myself standing dwarfed by that waterfall. All of that natural beauty and that all-pervading sense of serenity. The sight, the sounds, the smell and the feel of it seemed like a sensory overload that I was still unpacking and trying to process. The waterfall; a quietly persistent flow of water against rock. The movement of form and force in nature. I don't remember the last time that I was touched so perfectly, right down to my very core. I was just a leaf carried on the wind.

Standing there in quiet contemplation that afternoon I had been reminded of what it is to be at one with nature and Everything That Is. In the short time that I have spent here in Taiji I have sensed the magnitude of the disconnection here. Is this perhaps what the dolphins are showing us? Is this the connection that we have lost? And if so, then how can it be that such harsh and ungodly cruelties can take place literally at the doorstep of such sacred ground?

'The brightest light will always cast the darkest shadow' whispered the quiet voice.

TAIJI JOURNAL – Friday January 29th 2011

Today is a perfect summer's day in my hometown of Perth, on Australia's west coast. Perth holds the dubious honor of being the most remote capital city on the planet, and in that sense, it is the perfect complement for the emotions that I am experiencing. Late morning and it's already a somewhat muggy 33°C and a far cry from the brisk 7°C daily temperatures in Taiji. My washing line looks comically unusual for an Aussie mid-summer's day with its array of hoodies and winter gear baking in the bright sun. I smile to myself as I make the correlation. It is out of place like me.

I've now been back from Taiji for four days and I am disconnected, physically and emotionally. The physical side is perhaps a little self-inflicted. By the time I had returned to my little hotel room in Katsuura the afternoon of our sortie down the cliff face on Tsunami Hill, my knee had swollen badly and the pain had well and truly kicked in. I jury-rigged a tourniquet using the sash from the hotel issue kimono. I joked with a couple of the other activists; perhaps I should write a sternly worded letter to the Taiji town council!

Fortunately, I was due to fly out of Osaka a day later, and thankfully my hire car was an automatic. The five-hour trip from Wakayama prefecture back to Kansai airport working a manual clutch would have been hell.

TAIJI

A quick trip to the local doctor on my return to Australia and I'm advised I have suffered a small tear on the ligament. So, my knee is now strapped in a pressure bandage until the ligament damage heals. But that is a relatively trivial matter and the physical injury will pass. It is the emotional disconnect that concerns me more. On the day of my departure, I didn't want to leave either the dolphins or Japan. As my mid-morning flight climbed out of Kansai airport on a perfect winter morning I could only stare fixedly out past the mountains to the distant point where I knew Taiji lay, before the aircraft banked lazily and hid the coastline from view, as if closing the curtain on my adventure. I thought the sense of disconnection may pass as I re-adjust to 'normal life', but I find myself still processing everything that took place. The strange experience with the four bottlenoses at the Taiji Whale Museum. The spiritual mystery that is the Kumano. My trip and the discoveries I had made on it had left me with more questions than answers, and it put me on a path of enquiry and understanding.

Two months after I returned home, I quit my job. A job I had put heart and soul into for seven years with precious little by way of respect in return. I sold the house that I dearly loved and cherished; moving closer to my parents' home–knowing instinctively that my father did not have long to live. Family seemed powerfully important. I seemed to be reassessing and re-evaluating my life. Events in Japan had put a sense of perspective on things; on what I should value, and what I should place my energies in. I seemed to be viewing the world through different eyes.

One year later I returned to Japan.

CHAPTER NINE

The Squid

THREE HOURS DRIVE south from Perth, on Australia's west coast, is the small coastal town of Busselton. In the nineteen seventies it was a sleepy holiday village, dotted with small fibro and weatherboard beach shacks just meters from unspoiled stretches of golden-white sandy beach. The rugged rocky coastline further to the south of the town-site offered any number of hidden coves and outcrops which were perfect for a spot of fishing. My father was always an avid fisherman and a lover of the outdoors. Having a love of all things aquatic, as a young teenager I seemed to naturally fall into the same rhythm of fishing with a rod or reel whenever I was not out swimming or surfing.

So, it was down at a spot called Sugarloaf Rock, I walked out across the broad flat expanse of rock under a blazing summer sun. The craggy rock outcrop allowed you access to deep water if you carefully picked your way out along the rocks, watching carefully for 'king waves.' More than once, fishermen had been swept to their deaths after being washed off the rocks down here by a sudden freak wave. I think this is something about the ocean that attracts me; she can be as cruelly unforgiving as she is wildly beautiful.

A natural channel was formed through a gap in the rocky barrier, and the water which surged through it had that deep green-blue luminescence. Baiting up a hook, I cast my line out into the middle of the channel and waited; hoping to lure a deep-sea fish coming in on the swell. Perched on the rocks, I could see the bait trolling in steadily toward me as I worked the reel; glinting like a small fish as it caught the light. Within moments, a squirt of mottled brown appeared in the water behind it, tailing the bait before taking it neatly off the hook in a fluid movement. It was a squid.

I reeled in hastily, baited the bare hook again and cast the line back into the same spot. And once again the same thing happened. The slick tentacled shape surfaced behind the bait, enveloping it greedily. Seeing this, I flicked the rod back abruptly, hoping to jag a tentacle as it made a grab at the chunk of fish. Once again it neatly stripped the bait from the hook, before sinking back into the dark water. Heading back to our beach shack that night, I thought about that squid. I figured that perhaps it lived in the rocky crevices around the natural channel, picking off whatever food was carried in with the incessant surge of the tide.

The next day, following a morning of swimming and body surfing, I found myself back at Sugarloaf Rock with my fishing rod. This time I had come prepared. I had brought with me a squid jig–a plastic lure with a ring of barbs around its tail specifically designed to catch on a squid's tentacles. I cast into the same spot–the deeper water in the gap. Some minutes passed before the familiar brown shape showed itself and took to the 'bait.' With a quick flick of the rod at that precise moment, I snared the squid.

I hauled the squid onto the rocks and unhooked it as it lay there; fascinated with its streamlined shape, and the beautiful mottled tawny-brown of its body. And then a horrifying thing happened. As I watched it in quiet awe, the color slowly leached out of its body, as perfectly as water draining from a sponge. The vivid brown striping simply faded away and vanished, leaving the tentacle body a pallid grey-white. In that moment I realized that what I had witnessed was the life-force leaving the squid's body. And for what? I didn't catch it for food. I caught that squid for nothing other than the sport of it. Simply because it lived there; down in the deep green water, and

The Squid

because in my mind it had issued a challenge to me by chasing after my bait.

Something shifted in me that day I killed the squid. Many years later I can still vividly remember that moment; standing there on the rocks watching in horror as the color drained out it as its life quietly receded.

I have never fished again since that day.

CHAPTER TEN

Colors

TAIJI JOURNAL – February 2012
My second 'tour of duty' here in Taiji, Japan sees many happy reunions. Firstly, with a number of the activists I had the pleasure of meeting on my first trip in-country last year. More importantly, with the captive dolphins who have found a special place in my heart. There is bittersweet familiarity about the place now, and it re-kindles a broad swath of memories. During the dolphin drive hunt season, the days here are colored by such a range of emotions and feelings. If I could paint for you a typical palette of those colors, it would be something like this....

Anxious. Watching the drive boats suddenly all converge on a point beyond the small fishing boats in the distance. Have they located a pod? Scanning the grey blur of open water for the first sign of breaching dorsals. Holding breath deliberately so as not to shake the binoculars focused at distant range. Time passes slowly, watching a hunter stalking prey. *Wary.* I imagine roving sets of eyes on the flotilla of boats, watching and waiting. *Frustrated.* What chance do the passing dolphins have against them? The boats heave-to and circle lazily for long minutes before slowly motoring away toward the distant blurry arc of the horizon. Breathe out. *Relieved.* Another false alarm.

I smile to myself; obviously the hunters are having as hard a time as we are; trying to distinguish between the whitecaps dotting the choppy sea and the breaching of dolphins. *Joy.* Recalling the previous day when a pod of dolphins eluded capture by diving underneath the boats several times, causing mass confusion amongst the banger fleet. How we cheered for the home team! Japan Dolphins 1, Hunters Nil. I'm no follower of football but their neat evasive maneuvers had me punching air and willing them on like a fan in the bleachers. *Cold.* Briskly walking around the pretty little lookout area to stay warm. Idle talk easing the dull knot in the pit of my stomach. *Waiting.* An hour passes slowly, like a rainy Sunday afternoon. My eyes are tired.

Waiting. Drive boats disappear into distant anonymity amongst the clutch of boats transiting the shipping lanes out near the horizon. Banger boats forced to divert and split up. The passing commerce of tankers and container ships do not wait for mere dolphin hunters. The local bullies are merely small fry in the traffic lanes. I have often wondered if some of the other seafarers do not share the dolphin hunters' sentiments; on several occasions passing boats have driven across the bows of the banger boats, cutting them off from the pod they were driving. I like to think that there are at least some locals here who secretly disagree.

Hopeful. Regular glances at my watch confirm that mid-day is fast approaching. The hunters will usually break off and head for home by late morning if they fail to sight a pod. Then suddenly the tell-tale black oily puffs appear and seven blips in the distance move into the classic drive position. *Angry.* Not again. Boats resolve themselves into the classic drive positions, fanning out into side profile from our viewing point. Teeth clenching. Knot in solar plexus tightens. The deliberate movement in unison means that they have found a pod. It is an evil choreography. Holding breath again for what seems an eternity so as to keep the view in the binoculars steady; staring at a point in the water between the leading trio of boats, where they so often position the pod. *Tense.* Stomach sinks and body chills–a huge line of splashes blurs the water across a large stretch of ocean. So many of them that they are churning the water's surface into flying foam.

TAIJI

The pod is huge. Small sub-groups are breaking off from the periphery and dashing seawards, falling back to safety behind the line of boats. *Bitterly cold.* Everybody seems to report a sudden drop in temperature on days like these. I realize it's most likely our own internal shock and anxiety. Hearts and minds are out there in the steely-grey waters with the dolphins. *Thankful.* Grateful that there are still people who care, and understand the importance of protecting these beautiful sleek creatures. *Assessing.* Fast leaping, small dolphins in a huge pod. Looking for the tell-tale flash of color along their flanks. Most likely they are striped dolphins. Others call similar assessments, confirming the species. Striped dolphins, if caught, will suffer only one fate. *Grim.* Teeth now chattering as we gather up the gear and head for the cars to change position to the hill overlooking the cove. *Rushed.* A glum sense of hopelessness. Still hanging hopes on a death-row pardon. Praying for one rebel dolphin to take the lead, charge the boats and lead the herd away to freedom.

Several times in the past a pod has managed to elude capture at the last moment, in the 'funnel' toward Taiji harbor and the cove. *Driving.* Cold body hit with the smack of sudden warmth from the car heater.

Winding hill road; easing on the brakes down the steep gradient. Drive quickly, but not too quickly–don't want to draw too much attention to ourselves. Harbor. Slaughterhouse. Tunnel. Cove. *Queasy.* Car door slams, keys jangling. Blur of motion and color. Nodding a quick bow to Wakayama policeman in navy blue cap with gold trim. Stern unblinking eyes. A flash of white jacket. A blue scarf. Black shirts, white skull and cross bones of Sea Shepherd. Then legs numb and breathless, running up the stone steps cut through beautiful greenery. Thin air. *Worried.* Funereal walk through canopy of trees at the apex of the hill, emerging into stark sunlight and perfect blue sky. Hard breathing. *Wincing.* Bright light. Full sun on neatly manicured green grass. Oddly peaceful.

Cautious. Warily eyeing a cadre of police–a conspiratorial smile of cordial greeting from our friends the Police Special Task Force. In contrast, the local Wakayama police, sternly businesslike and watching like the brown hawks wheeling overhead on the thermals. A scattering of locals in plain clothes, identity unknown. Most likely undercover police. Taiji town officials, remaining aloof and carefully avoiding eye contact.

I always make a point of greeting them all politely and openly but I'm usually studiously ignored by Coast Guard and town officials. So be it. *Re-focusing.* Drive boats now in clear view in the sea below our vantage point; throat tightening as we hastily count the multiple dorsal fins circling slowly. Their movements appear confused and unsure. Striped dolphins divided into two sub-groups. One group already being gently nursed back out to sea from where they came. Small mercy–there are too many to be taken by the hunters. They don't want so many of this species. Focus on their freedom. An activist cheers, and then says she will deal with the grief for the others shortly. Celebrate the freedom of the ones re-joining their pod out at sea. Mouth dry. *Waiting.*

Rasping outboard motors play the accompaniment to the saddest symphony. *Listening.* From below, an all-pervading background noise like a laundromat full of busy washing machines. A hundred children paddling at the seaside. No. There is neither happiness nor contentment in the constant wet thrashing. It is the sound of steady fighting and of fear. The sound of thrashing fins, roped helpless under tarpaulin. Deep sea creatures confused at unfamiliar human intervention, noise, fear, confusion. Shallow water. No escape. On and on it goes; five…ten…fifteen. Twenty long minutes. *Numb.* A vague sense of hopelessness and futility. Mouth dry. Eyes stinging salt. Slowly the sound halves, then quarters; reducing progressively until it is gone. Evaporated. Fade to black. *Silent.* Reluctant to turn and leave; as though in some sense they are still down there. Calling.

TAIJI

Shattered. Thud of bodies, wet and lifeless. The last skiff leaves the cove and the peace returns.

A picture, as they say paints a thousand words. After today's episode with the striped dolphins, we made the short walk back from Takababe Hill to our cars in the Cove car park in almost reverent silence. Normally trading a joke and a laugh, today we were each lost in our own private thoughts. When we spoke, it was in lowered measured tones. With the ladies chatting quietly amongst themselves, I took up station behind them as we walked the pavement through the darkness of the tunnel that leads to the Cove beach. Though most Japanese prefer to avoid confrontation, there are still radical elements here who despise the presence of foreigners protesting on their home soil. There are so many unidentified bystanders in plain clothes, typically wearing the white surgical masks that further cloak their features that I never quite relax and drop my guard completely. I discreetly eyed each passing car as we exit the tunnel into broad daylight, looking down across the grass terraces to Hatajiri Bay and the cove on our right.

The poignant sight of Ric O'Barry standing forlornly alone on the pebbled beach right at the water's edge greets us. Shoulders stooped and gazing wistfully out to sea after the day's events; he perfectly characterizes the battle here. For those who are unfamiliar, Richard 'Ric' O'Barry is an ex-dolphin trainer turned activist and has now logged time on both sides of the dolphin pool. He spent ten years of his life working as part of the dolphin captivity industry, and the past thirty-odd years trying to tear it down. Working for Miami Seaquarium, and having captured and trained the bottlenose dolphins that starred in 'Flipper', the popular TV series of the 1960's, he reached a point of epiphany when one of the dolphins committed suicide in captivity. Now in his seventies, Ric has worked tirelessly to raise awareness for the plight of dolphins in captivity and has been actively involved in their release and rehabilitation, and the fight for their rights. As a person he is openly genuine and instantly likeable. Pointing to my Aussie surf hoodie on the day we first met, he asked me whether I was a surfer. His love for the ocean and its inhabitants is instantly clear. He has a fire in his belly and a sense of focus which is inspiring.

For me, Ric O'Barry has really been the quintessential human face of the struggle against the captivity industry of Taiji and its killing cove. He is a large part of my motivation to come here. Seemingly lost his own thoughts and hunched against the backdrop of angry grey ocean and forbiddingly steep rocky cliffs, his image personifies everything about how it feels to be here on the ground in Taiji. Sometimes it is the overwhelming sense of feeling insignificant and small. As though you are a feeble voice lost in the wild singing of the wind. There have been too many days like today, and I suspect Ric has seen too much of it, for far too long. Oftentimes, he appears to be a man haunted by his past; as though he shoulders a heavy burden of guilt for his perceived contribution toward raising the dolphin as an icon of popular culture. And if that is truly so, then it is an unjustified self-punishment. It is because of Ric's commitment and persistence that so many people, myself included, made the long journey to Taiji to stand up and be counted.

And what of today's events? How does one put perspective on all of this? If I appear to be repeating myself it is only because there are certain things which tend to become etched upon one's mind. Today the drive boats carefully maneuvered a large herd of striped dolphins towards land. Many made the break to open ocean on the long run in, however once again we painfully endured the passing of approximately forty of these sleekly beautiful ocean dwellers. The striped dolphins are fighters and it was sobering to realize that the constant background noise was not the sound of wild surf–it was the sound of tail flukes thrashing the water in their final moments.

I know that I will carry many of the sights and the sounds back home with me; but this one sound in particular drives me on. Many people that have been here say it is the metallic ringing of the banger poles that they remember hauntingly. For me it is that thrumming monotone sound of thrashing rising from the cove. When I cast my mind back it is the one sound that I can still hear as plain as day. It is the sound of death in shallow water. It is the sound of a final desperate struggle for freedom. It is the sound of forty roped tails. Thoughts of it surface unbidden in quiet unexpected moments. And yes, it still sometimes upsets and frustrates me. But most importantly it also raises a spirit of defiance in me.

The sound of forty roped tails is a poignant reminder that you never ever stop fighting for justice and fairness, no matter how badly the odds seem to be stacked against you.

CB✿BO

Blue skies and a blue cove today. After three days of slaughters, today the dolphin hunters returned by late morning empty-handed. Although the day started with perfect conditions favoring the banger boats, the winds picked up with the rising of the sun and the seas offshore grew increasingly choppy by mid-morning.

Our elation grows as we scan the far horizon and pick up first two, then four drive boats ploughing their way back through the rising swell towards us, heading in the direction of the harbor mouth. Our moods change and spirits lift. Jokes and banter steadily increase as we anticipate the return of all eleven boats that we earlier observed leaving the harbor in the pre-dawn light. We're sternly reminded not to 'count the chickens before they hatch' though. There have been occasions in the past when the fleet has all but entered the harbor mouth, only to turn and accelerate back to sea as a pod is sighted at the last moment by the rear-guard vessel.

Colors

Our watch does not end until all the bangers are berthed and locked down in Taiji harbor. Only then do we stand down for the day. Bear in mind that the return of a fleet numbering almost a dozen drive boats, from their positions miles out at sea is an extremely slow process. Often the reason for their return is inclement weather, and this means a long and chilly wait out on the exposed finger of land that juts from the mouth of Taiji harbor. With the boats fanned out across the horizon it can take as much as two hours from the time of recall, before all have finally returned to their harbor berths. With the confusion of passing traffic the headcount can become uncertain as the morning wears on. Several sets of eyes have been focused seaward, binoculars roving across the horizon in search of returning boats, each scanning different sectors of ocean. Leah and Tia of Save Japan Dolphins, and Scott of Sea Shepherd breaking every now and then from the long vigil, making intermittent updates to Twitter and Facebook to inform the on-line world of the current state of play.

Is this the sixth or the seventh drive boat we're looking at slowly making its way inbound? A count of the returning drive boats is maintained with a simple but effective method–a pebble placed on one of the lookout fence-posts marks the return of each banger boat. A quick glance by any of us at the fence-post with its growing circle of pebbles thus shows the number of boats returned and hence the number of boats yet to be accounted for. The wait is painfully long as one by one, each drive boat returns from their distant positions out in the *shiome* zone on the far horizon.

The last boat finally passes us on its way to the harbor mouth. The hunters steadfastly refuse to look at us as they motor past our elevated lookout position.

Today the color of the cove stays blue. Score one for the Taiji dolphins. *Hai, sughoi!* (Yes, awesome!)

CHAPTER ELEVEN

Faith & Hope

'Sometimes when I look at you, I feel I'm gazing at a distant star.
It's dazzling, but the light is from tens of thousands of years ago.
Maybe the star doesn't even exist anymore.
Yet sometimes that light seems more real to me than anything'.
—HARUKI MURAKAMI - 'South of the Border, West of the Sun'

TAIJI JOURNAL – February 2012
The Taiji Whale Museum is an ominously forbidding place. All places, including buildings have an innate energy about them, and the energy signature of this place always seems deathly cold despite the life forms held within its confines. Even the thin warmth of the sun and the cleansing breath of wind fail to counter and dissipate this low energy. Too much has happened here and, like the neighboring cove, the energy is faithfully recorded; absorbed into stone, rock and tree. It seems that the building's bulk lies permanently in the shadow of towering Tsunami Hill which flanks its southern wall. Within the Museum's expansive grounds, nestled alongside its natural lagoon, is a small seemingly insignificant white-walled building. To all intents and purposes, it appears to be little more than a tiny equipment shed or garage. A sign at the open door however bears the silhouette of a leaping dolphin, and standing bold above the Japanese kanji are the English words 'Pan-tropical Spotted Dolphin (*Stenella attenuata*).' Set into one wall of this small open building is a tank, or rather a small enclosed aquarium, not unlike a tank that you would keep tropical

fish in. On entering the building, my footsteps ring on the terracotta tiled floor. Inside the bare room, there is precious little to absorb the sound. It is stark, fluorescent-lit and nakedly harsh. It reminds me of a hospital ward. I feel a dull reflex of pain stab through the center of my chest and down through my internals. To look at this tank is to feel the pinpricks of heartbreak and I feel a heavy energy of despair. I have the faintest inkling that I have been somehow drawn here to witness this.

In the wild, the Pan-tropical spotted dolphin is a vibrant and energetic roamer of the open sea. Inhabiting both in-shore and pelagic (deep sea) habitats, these gregarious ocean dwellers will typically travel great distances in a single day. The Spotted dolphin is a species built for speed with a streamlined, torpedo-shaped body from its slim, elongated nose to a particularly strong set of tail flukes designed for both power and strong acceleration. Each of its fins is curved backward toward the tail to complement the streamlined shape and thus minimize drag through the water.

This slick body shape enables her to move quickly through the water, giving the advantage when hunting for fish and when traveling over long distances. Once this dolphin has built up speed, it will typically fire itself out of the water, repeatedly high breaching as it travels. This characteristic leaping motion actually assists the spotted dolphin in conserving energy during long travels. Air is less viscous than water, and offers less friction or resistance; permitting the dolphin to travel further on an airborne leap than it would through the water. Human swimmers mimic this technique with the butterfly stroke–a swimming style which requires strength and coordination. It is no coincidence that the powerful body movement used to execute it is referred to as a dolphin kick.

In large herds often numbering in the thousands, these fleet and nimble dolphins will spend the greater majority of daylight hours deep diving; plunging even deeper under cover of darkness in search of their favorite food. A beautiful creature born with all the perfect streamlining and inherent power to carry it scores of miles in a single day, pulsing its way through the dense ocean brine whilst diving to depths a hundred times its own body length before returning to the surface to draw breath.

Forgive me once again for laboring the facts and figures here. I want to give you these statistics because I want the scale of this injustice to soak in. This is a thoroughbred built for speed, endurance and performance.

Here in this dismally small tank at the Taiji Whale Museum, a pair of spotted dolphins languish as captives in a tank of chlorinated water barely seven meters in length and two meters deep. Allow me to do the math on that one for you. At a body length of just under two meters this means the unfortunate pair are forced to exist in an artificial enclosure which is less than four times their own body length, and just one body length deep.

The two souls held captive in the small aquarium at the Taiji Whale Museum are thus condemned to what is essentially a watery grave. Moreover, it is a grave without the benefit of the merciful release of death. For the record, the duo were originally given the names Faith and Hope by visiting activists who telegraphed their plight to the outside world. In more recent times however the pair were renamed as Sad and Lonely in view of the desperately poor state that they are presently in. This will be the only time that I will refer to them by these newly dubbed names. Our thoughts and words have an energy and an influence; hence I will never refer to these poor souls by negative names. I will only ever think of them as Faith and Hope. I hope that you the reader will appreciate my reasoning and choose to think of them in this way too.

Having witnessed the plight of the two spotted dolphins, we decided to take the gift of healing to them. We had to pick the day of our visit carefully. I did not want to visit the captive dolphins on a day where I had witnessed a slaughter in the neighboring Cove; I didn't want our presence there to be tainted with the energy and emotion of that particular event. And so, we made our trip on what we referred to as a 'Blue Day'–a day without killings or captures in the surrounding waters off the Taiji coast.

The waters of that small tank are a vivid blue; exactly like the artificial chlorinated waters of a public swimming pool. In fact, that is all this is–a glorified swimming pool–bereft of any of the trappings of their natural deep-water habitat. The thick pane of glass that forms the tank wall feels ice cold and unyielding to my touch. The tiled room feels both clinical and starkly impersonal, pungent with the astringent smell of chlorine and salts like a public swimming pool. If you were to imagine a hospital palliative care ward in your mind's eye, then you would have captured the essence of this place. I have never been truly comfortable in hospital buildings generally, with their confusion of energy, their disinfected starkness and their general sense of malaise. I am equally uneasy today in this small outhouse building in the grounds of the Taiji Whale Museum, with its two forlorn and docile inhabitants. The small of my back aches in the cold and the hardness of terracotta tiles does little to make my kneeling position comfortable. Today though, I push that sickly feeling of discomfort and unease to the back of my mind. Today I am here for Faith and Hope. Under the artificial lighting the waters of the tank glow nakedly, and there is nowhere for the occupants to hide.

The pair of spotted dolphins are floating motionless against the far corner of the tank, in a limp tail down position. A smaller species of dolphin, the close confines of the tank makes them appear relatively large. It is difficult to be here; in their current state they are pitiful to behold. The smaller of the two dolphins faces away from the front viewing pane of the tank; his head nestled into the far corner of the enclosure. Stationed protectively across the diminutive dolphin's tail flukes, his partner floats almost lifeless with eyes closed, only occasionally breaking station to rise to the surface to draw breath. The pair appears to be logging. Dolphins do not sleep in the same sense that humans do; they achieve a sleep-like state similar to a 'cat nap' by shutting down a hemisphere of their brain, remaining part conscious in order to maintain vital functions such as breathing.

Unlike land mammals which are involuntary breathers, cetaceans are voluntary breathers, and thus must retain a level of consciousness in order to breathe. Watching the pair in their dreamlike state though, I am also aware of reports that the two spotted dolphins have been spending extended periods of time in the tank with their eyes closed, as if they are blocking out the reality of their grim surroundings.

Here with me today is Kerry who, like me, is also a Reiki practitioner. You may recall that I described the spotted dolphins are the thoroughbreds of the dolphin fraternity. The small claustrophobic tank denies them every vital aspect of their natural lives. There is no room to accelerate and travel; they can neither dive nor breach the surface in airborne leaps. Indeed, there is no longer any sky. There is no sunlight or crisp sea breeze. In their cramped confines there is only artificial light and the stale breath of recirculated air. Nothing here is natural or familiar for the forlorn pair.

Now, kneeling at the tank corner across from the pair we both place our palms flat against the cold glass. I allow my breathing to slow and let my mind wander in space, seeking out the connection. The cold boundary separating us slowly heats and gives way to a definite warming against my palms. Minute condensation droplets are forming around the extremities of my fingertips. With our silent presence against the corner of the tank, the larger dolphin slowly opens one eye to study us. Making eye contact with her I continue to hold her gaze, breathing energy into the connection thus formed. Waking from her earlier sleep state, she is gradually becoming animated; slowly drawing her consciousness back into that facet of herself that resides captive in this small space. We are none of us perfectly confined by physical form, and dolphins are possibly far more aware of this than we humans are. As she draws back slowly into wakefulness, both Kerry and I remain passively focused on her.

It is at this point that something quite amazing happens; a gesture and an intent that demonstrates for me the beautiful nature of these creatures. Slowly at first, and then with movements becoming more deliberate, the larger dolphin has begun nudging at the tail flukes of her smaller counterpart with her beak and rostrum. Holding our attention, she exaggerates the motion with almost theatrical gestures. Despite the grim situation I smile broadly as I recognize her intent. *She wants me to focus my attention on her partner!*

With my eyes locked on hers I nod my understanding and with equal exaggeration I then deliberately break eye contact with her before swinging to refocus on her smaller companion, nestled into the far corner of the tank. Drawing a deep centering breath, I close the larger dolphin out of my mind for the time being and settle into a passive focus on the other quiet form huddled in the corner. Mentally I seek out and find the 'straddle point' between two worlds, as I refer to it. The silent minutes pass and I passively observe the start of the nagging ache around my wrists which for a Reiki practitioner characterizes the heavy presence of negative energy associated with disease. (This can be brought on by physical, mental or emotional disease).

This tiny dolphin is not in a good way. Typically, when drawing away heavier 'bad' energy, I sense it collecting around my hands like a dense glove before insinuating itself as a dull aching pain around my wrists. I find myself regularly flicking both hands briskly to alleviate the growing pain. A large amount of negative energy is being drawn out of the tank.

An extraordinary amount in fact; more than I have drawn from an average human patient in the past. Taking a deliberate and measured breath, I allow myself to slip deeper beneath the surface of consciousness. It does not feel healthy here. The image of a deep well forms in my mind's eye and I find myself pouring energy into the dark mouth of the well, down into the darkness below where a little

TAIJI

dolphin lies, lost and alone. He is a long way down. And he is far from home.

Satisfied that my attention is focused on her young mate, the protective dolphin leaves the placid form and locks her gaze onto Kerry; rearing her head above water as if poised to leap. Once again, her body language is clear:

'OK I'm ready, let's play'!

Obligingly Kerry waves to her and proceeds to run the length of the tank. With a splash that spawns multiple ripples across the small surface area of the aquarium, the dolphin pulses into life, easily keeping pace with Kerry along the small run of tank. She clearly recognized her human playmate from our visit yesterday. With the tank only four times its body length, one lap is run in the space of a few seconds, before an eager flick roll sends the slick little dolphin accelerating fast in the other direction. It is hard to contain your joy when you see that spark of life returning in such desolate circumstances.

The ring of laughter and the splashing of water echoes off the white tiled walls of the room. Keen to add to the dolphin's enjoyment I leave my crouch at the end of the tank and join Kerry in running across the front of the tank to the far wall. No sooner do I leave my station then the playful dolphin quickly returns to her earlier position, her flank nestled protectively up against the tail flukes of her partner. And once again she returns to a repetition of her earlier overture; nudging her beak emphatically against the smaller dolphin's tail and holding my gaze once again. As if her earlier message to me hadn't sunk in, she is slowly and insistently explaining it again for me:

'Look...I <u>need</u> you to look after this little one for me. Take care of him and <u>keep him company</u> while I go play!'

Feeling just the slightest bit sheepish at being chastised by the little dolphin, I quickly return to my kneeling position at the far corner of the tank. In all this time, despite the commotion in the water as his sister turns lap after lap in cramped but joyous play with Kerry, the little one nestled into the corner has not moved at all. He seemed distant; a small lost soul looking for the light. So, once again I slow my breathing and re-place my hands at a shoulder width apart, palms flat against the pane of glass. A brief minute passes and my mind stills as I extend the energetic connection.

Satisfied with my renewed vigil, the larger dolphin again turns and rears whilst catching Kerry's gaze. And again, the game is on, the two of them chasing each other endlessly backwards and forwards along the painfully short run of tank. Now and then Kerry stops short and swings into a sudden unexpected turn the other way, much to the delight of Hope who mimics her every move. From my kneeling position close against the glass, I begin to notice something else that the playful dolphin is doing. As the realization of her intentions dawn on me, I once again feel the pang of raw emotion tug at my heart strings. Executing a flick turn at the far end of the aquarium, the excited dolphin pulses its way energetically through the water back towards where I am kneeling at the far corner of the tank.

As she approaches each time however, she gauges her turn just before reaching the point at which my hands are making contact with the tank glass. She is very carefully ensuring that her body doesn't encroach between me and her companion floating across from my huddled crouch in the far corner. Could it be that she is aware of what I am doing? Can she sense or see the energy flowing through the waters in the tank? I already suspect from their behaviors and reactions that dolphins are energy sensitive in the same way that I am. Perhaps it is a function of their finely tuned echolocation system to 'see' the energy fields of other beings. There is nothing mysterious about this–we all generate a weal electromagnetic energy field, and I believe that dolphins are particularly sensitive to it.

She has gone to great lengths to indicate that I should focus myself on her smaller companion. Not once but twice; firstly, before she allowed herself the self-indulgence of playing games with Kerry. And then again when I briefly left my post and joined in the game that the two of them were enjoying. And now, satisfied in the knowledge that I am 'baby-sitting' her smaller partner, she is deliberately going to great lengths to ensure that she is not disturbing the connection between me and the tiny form in the corner, despite the cramped confines of the tank.

Every single time she makes the turn at my end of the tank, she carefully ensures no part of her body to interrupts my connection with her companion. I am hard-bitten by such an intelligent and deeply selfless act. Bear in mind that the span of this small tank is just slightly less than four times the body length of these spotted dolphins. With my hands positioned on the glass at shoulder length distance apart, I am effectively reducing the length of the tank even further. To this day I am in awe of that small dolphin's care for her partner.

Here in the smallest dolphin tank in the world, in faraway Taiji, I have been taught a lesson in loyalty and love by these amazing dolphins.

ೞ✾ಐ

Watching the boats in Katsuura harbor blend into the filtered half-light of late afternoon I thought more about the Japanese Reiki connection. To undergo a Reiki attunement means that one is initiated into a lineage that traces back to its origins source in Japanese Buddhism. It can only be passed down from master to master; I felt a quiet sense of honor that I was able to return that healing gift to the land of its origin. Moreover, to be able to use that gift to assist in the healing of a rift between human and non-human was to me a very satisfying and fitting outcome. I feel duty bound to give something back to these creatures, in recompense for the acts of

Faith & Hope

those who have visited so much unnecessary anguish and suffering upon them. And in the case of Faith and Hope, to what end?

In the hours that we spent in the company of the two small dolphins, several patrons passed through the small building. Not a single one of them gave the sad pair more than a passing glance. Not one single person. Floating somnambulistically in the far corner of the aquarium, they are flaccid and lifeless, and paying customers clearly seek vibrancy, life and entertainment. Ironically the Museum does itself a disservice by keeping the duo in such desolate conditions. The Taiji Whale Museum proudly boasts the claim that they are the only Japanese facility that successfully maintains an exhibit of Pantropical spotted dolphins. They point to the difficulties involved in successfully keeping this particular species in captivity. It is cold statistical fact that every single species of dolphin kept in captivity suffers a greatly foreshortened lifespan. For these two forlorn dolphins the additional stress of being held in the unduly cramped confines of a tiny aquarium means the odds of their successful survival are further stacked against them. Regardless of whether you agree with my anti-captivity stance or not, there is no place for acts of animal cruelty such as this.

I find myself constantly trying to understand the Japanese perspective on the keeping of these wild creatures. To try to look at the world through their eyes. But there is a vast difference between looking and seeing. I cannot help but think that if the director of this museum complex was to truly 'see' these beautiful creatures, the way that we have seen them today, he would not be able to condemn them to this cruel predicament. I suggest that an element of what I call 'species-ism' is at play here—we humans inherently see ourselves as unrivalled in terms of our intellect and sophistication. So, we see other creatures as something less than us. We see them as incapable of possessing the same levels of intelligence, of love and of social interaction. Perhaps is it us who have something to learn.

TAIJI

Walking briskly towards the exit door and away from that small tank, I try my hardest to think only positive thoughts for their sake. Our footsteps echo against the glazed sterility of ceramic tiled walls. Once outside the small building I squint and fumble for sunglasses, unaccustomed to the bright sunlight after the artificially lit neutrality of the tiny room. The sea air blows fresh, sensuously alive with the now familiar smell of cedar and the taste of Pacific salt. I have taken less than a dozen paces to stand under the wild blue dome of sky, but it may as well be a hundred miles away for Faith and Hope.

Tomorrow morning, as the sun throws its first furtive rays of gold across this beautiful stretch of rocky coastline I will be leaving Taiji, bound for Osaka's Kansai airport. I cast one last glance back over my shoulder in a begrudging farewell. Traced in a blurred oily condensation, the outlines of our outstretched hand prints remain on the glass tank wall; a legacy of our all too brief communion.

Before I leave the Taiji Whale Museum however; I have four more friends I must visit....

CHAPTER TWELVE

The Four

*'Some people talk to animals.
Not many listen though. That's the problem.'*
–AA MILNE - 'The House at Pooh Corner'

TAIJI JOURNAL – February 2012
One of the first things that strikes me about the Four is their sheer size. I have seen bottlenoses out on the river before, but never so intimately and up close. These are big dolphins. Powerful and slab sided, they are reminiscent of bulky steel grey battleships, effortlessly cleaving the waters with deceptively casual flicks of strong peduncles. They possess an understated power and charisma that commands attention and respect; I have already sensed however, that this is more than simply a function of their imposing mass. It has been said that dolphins are capable of 'seeing' us physically; possessed of sophisticated sonar they are able to assess us internally. They can see into our physical form, our innards; they are able to see if we are pregnant and with child. This is rather more scientific than mystical; they possess an incredible bio-sonar mechanism which permits them to 'see' great detail. With it they hunt and they navigate, and they assess other oceanic life.

I would further contend that they are also capable of 'seeing' us psychically and spiritually. I'm trying to pick my words very carefully here. Dolphins seem adept at navigating dimensions, and making passage between them. Indeed, there is far more at work here than sheer intellect and self-awareness. I feel myself strongly drawn to them at a far deeper level. They, in turn, seem to be well aware of who I am.

As I've previously mentioned, I have seen many bottlenose dolphins in the wild; a group of approximately twenty-five bottlenoses live permanently in the river system back home in Perth. They share the near pristine waters of the Swan River with the city's growing boating fraternity and have become a common sight; quietly navigating the snaking coil of waterway alongside the busy pleasure boat traffic. At the mouth of the river, looking out onto the sun-dappled Indian Ocean, lies the port of Fremantle; a quirky and atmospheric harbor town with enough history to remind me that we are the descendants of convict stock. The pearl blue waters along the west coast of Australia are well known as the 'humpback highway'– so named because it is the migration route for humpback and Right whales making the long and arduous journey southward in our summer months to the rich feeding grounds of the Antarctic. Their smaller relatives, the bottlenose dolphins, are a common sight in the coastal waters around the capital city. The two dozen bottlenose dolphins living in the river system are particularly special to me as I spend a lot of time in and around the beautifully picturesque waters of the Swan River, either kayaking the quiet meandering stretches of wilderness upriver, or cycling the miles of cycle paths that casually trace its shady periphery. I see them on numerous occasions fishing together in the shallows, or lazily plying the placid in-land waters, often shepherding their young; the small dorsal fins cutting playful arcs around their mothers as they explore their new world. I recall once sitting enthralled on the shore, watching two mothers hovering patiently mid-river whilst their youngsters made clumsy and uncoordinated dashes in their first attempts at catching fish. They are often to be seen playing in the murky waters around the massive wooden bridge pylons, in the shadows of the old traffic bridge; their steely grey flanks blending and flashing in the dappled green-grey

The Four

waters of the Swan. The river dwellers are Indo Pacific bottlenose dolphins (*Tursiops aduncus*), and they are somewhat smaller in stature compared to the four common bottlenose dolphins (*Tursiops truncatus*) held in the Perspex walled Dolphinarium at the Taiji Whale Museum.

'The Four', as I have come to know them, are the quartet of dolphins that share the sterile confines of the Museum's Dolphinarium enclosure. It is my special pleasure to be able to share a few insights about them with you now. You might recall these four bottlenose dolphins from my previous trip a year ago, when they had left me intrigued by their odd behavior, deliberately forming a 'halo' around me as I stood in stunned awe. But did I in fact witness it, or did I imagine it? The whole experience was imbued with a sense of the surreal; a dreamlike quality. When I first wrote of my experience with them, I played down the powerful impact that meeting had on me. I tried to find words to explain what I had experienced but fell short of the mark. To be perfectly honest, I am still confused by what I witnessed and what I felt. I will simply say that their influence played a very large part in my desire to return again to Taiji. At the risk of repeating myself I would like to recount that incident with some deeper detail.

It was with a sense of cautious reserve that I first visited the daunting institute that is the Taiji Whale Museum on my first visit in the winter of 2011. Given its complicity in the local drive hunt industry, many activists were openly vocal in denouncing the Museum and boycotting it with firm resolve. Despite this I was still left with the overriding feeling that I must see this establishment for myself, as an important part of understanding the background of the Taiji drive hunts. Despite the good nature of my intentions, I was still not immune to the deep sting of guilt as I sat alone in the rows of empty bleachers, watching the group of jet-black pseudo-orcas performing their routine in the sunlit lagoon to the coarse backdrop of gaudy carnival music and the singsong voice of the Japanese commentator. To further needle at my sensibilities, I recalled the dolphins swimming alone in the adjoining pool; desperately performing the same routine as they listened to the commentary booming across the complex in the hope of reward.

By the time that I had followed the bitumen pathway around the natural lagoon and entered the double glass doors to the Dolphinarium, I was at a painfully low ebb. Once inside and free from the brilliant glare of the morning sun, I stood momentarily to take in the scene, a little unsure of what I might expect. Reminiscent of the beachfront oceanarium at the local marina back home in Australia, a walkway stretches upwards through the innards of the complex, enclosed in domed clear view Perspex. Just like the wall mounted tank that houses Faith and Hope, just a couple of hundred meters away beyond the lagoon, this Dolphinarium is also little more than a deep concrete swimming pool. Anti-captivity advocates often draw a parallel between keeping a human being captive in the confines of a prison cell and holding a cetacean in the artificial sterility of a tank or a pool. I would add the further damning observation that a prison cell bears far more resemblance to our home living quarters than these coldly featureless tanks resemble the natural environment of the dolphins' ocean home. This then was my first introduction to the Four. I remember those first impressions well. They were big; like the orbits of four streaky grey planets locked in constant motion.

Mentally and emotionally drained I had stood passively at the center of the tank and simply allowed the quartet to revolve about me. Aware of my presence, they avoided contact. Their reaction to me remained cool and off-hand. Time passed by and food was doled out by a trainer standing at the top of the tank far above the walkway in which I stood. As well as sustenance, the feeding routine was probably also a welcome break from the sheer monotony of the dismal confines; a sliver of mental stimulation for the four bottlenoses. How difficult it was to see so noble and intelligent a

The Four

creature reduced to little more than a beggar, reliant on a human captor for the next meal. It was at that very moment that I felt it; the immense weight of this cloistered world. This Dolphinarium. The Whale Museum. Taiji. *All of it.* Standing at the bottom of that sterile well, gazing upwards at the four darting shadows, it was as if the very walls of the Perspex tank collapsed inwards and the sheer tonnage of that water prison bore down on me. I felt the weight of it all. I felt microscopic. Lost in a world of problems that seemed too big for a handful of people to change. I have said this before; our thoughts and our emotions possess a tangible energy that is capable of reaching out and touching others. Perhaps that is why they suddenly became aware of me.

Maybe they had been quietly assessing me from the moment I set foot inside the Dolphinarium. Whatever the reason, it was at that precise moment that a sudden swing shift of awareness took place inside the tank. In an instant there was a quiver of complimentary motion, as though driven by a single thought. The energy of movement within the tank switched from random and haphazard to intentional and deliberate. Harmonious.

Four gunmetal grey torpedoes cleaved the waters in unison and broke off to take up stations around me. The precision of this synchronous maneuver left me stunned; their sheer physical size and sudden intimate proximity awe-inspiring. Coming down at me like bullets, only to come to a sudden stop in a seemingly choreographed display. The Four aligned themselves neatly, snout to tail around curved Perspex tunnel that separated us. Each was positioned precisely; side on so as to observe me with one eye. A halo of greyish white bottlenose dolphins surrounded me–the scruffy wayfarer. Four eyes each held my gaze with a deliberate and measured intent. As motion ceased so too, it seemed, did time. Like a momentary suspension of breath. Thinking back, I would describe that moment as an odd feeling of 'lost time'. *I lost the sense of time.* Publicly, this is all I will say on the matter–just as water ripples, so too does time.

TAIJI

Perhaps one day, I will share more in another telling. In another book.

A year has now passed since that first introduction. Since setting foot on Japanese soil once again I have been quietly anticipating meeting the Four again. What could I expect of our second encounter? Would they remember me? To say that I was excited at the prospect of visiting them again was an understatement.

I simply want to be there for them, and more importantly I want them to be in the presence of someone who sees them for what they truly are; not as a curiosity or an exhibit for selfish entertainment. I have decided that it is far better for me to be joyful for them. It is more important that they see us in shared moments of happiness rather than in bleak moments of sorrow. A year ago, I would have felt the pang of guilt had I expressed any modicum of happiness and joy in their presence. My feelings have well and truly changed on this matter. For a dolphin, the stimulation of play and joyful interaction is an important aspect of their lives in the wild, and this is an important element glaringly absent from their confinement in captivity. And so, it was with that mindset that I again sent out to visit them.

The Dolphinarium complex where the Four are housed lies adjacent to the deep natural lagoon that lies in the deceptively peaceful seclusion of the Whale Museum grounds. Standing at the entrance, one can gaze through pretty grottoes and natural caves dotting the beautifully exquisite volcanic stone cliff which creates a natural barrier between the lagoon and the Pacific Ocean. It is a sad feeling of whimsy that envelops me as I stand there, consciously and deliberately breathing in deeply. The air coming off the rolling blue of the Pacific is an invigorating salt zephyr that sings of freedom and challenge. It marks a sad duality as I now enter the vacuum-close sterility of the Dolphinarium, before sealing it shut. Bright rays of mid-morning sunlight throw a warm glow across the tiled entrance foyer; stretching ahead into the semi-darkness, the viewing walkway disappears into the watery bowels of the building.

Deserted, the Dolphinarium is enveloped in a hushed library silence. A spark of memory floods back and I stand in silence momentarily, feeling butterflies in the pit of my stomach. I make a mental note to myself; despite the cultural tendency towards small cars, small streets and bonsai trees, Japanese butterflies of anxiety feel every bit as large as those back home! The first of four mottled grey submarines slides across the top of the Perspex viewing dome; I feel as though I'm laughing and crying simultaneously, a strange mix of contrasting emotions overtaking me. And then suddenly I am greeting old friends! Advancing into the middle of the walkway I allow them to descend from the top of the tank before running childlike to press myself up against the cold Perspex.

Studiously ignoring the metal plaques embossed in Japanese and English requesting that we do not touch the glass, both Kerry and I instantly have our palms smudgy-flat against the Perspex in joyous greeting. The dolphins are quick to respond, perhaps in conspiratorial bliss at our deliberate ignorance of the rules. There is a distinct rebel streak to their lively energy and their body language which I instantly respond to and revel in. The lyrics of one of my favorite Warren Zevon songs play in my head;

'I am a renegade; I'll be a rebel all my days.'

All at once I am the long-haired teenager again. Jubilation. We joyfully smear the glass with our hand prints and I cannot help but grin broadly and cheekily at the overtones of shared defiance. The twelve months since my initial meeting with the quartet have flown past; my first trip was a life changing journey, and my encounter with the Four has played on my mind ever since. What exactly had passed between us that day? Maybe, just maybe, today I will learn a little more. Already I note there is a difference in the dolphins' level of interest in us and the keen level of awareness they radiate; a quantum jump in comparison to my first encounter with them. There is still an assessment phase as the quartet checks us out, making several runs past us along the length of the tank, but this passes quickly. I note that they are returning briskly and lingering a little bit longer around us each time, until they are deliberately nudging each other playfully out of the way to remain close to us. The animated jostling for the best position in the waters directly in front of me prompts Kerry to teasingly remark about the 'fans' fighting for my attention! Eye contact is deliberate and lingering; those beautiful dark eyes bear a measure of deep serenity and wisdom. The often misunderstood 'dolphin smile' however, cannot mask the fleeting glimmer of sadness that I sense portrayed in those deep obsidian orbs.

Splitting up and moving from point to point along the walkway, we allow the dolphins to traverse backwards and forwards between us. The morning's contact with the quartet has engaged me to the point that I have scarcely noticed that we have largely had the Dolphinarium and its occupants' attention completely to ourselves. Over the course of the past half hour, I notice one dolphin who appears to be the appointed leader of the captive pod, spending more and more time in my immediate vicinity. She like the others has been basking in our presence, pushing up hard against the glass wall to 'rub' against our outstretched palms; closing her eyes in a dreamy lethargy not unlike a purring and contented house cat.

All of a sudden, from the corner of my eye I notice another human figure making her way up the viewing ramp in my direction. Resting against the glass as I am, my eye is no more than a few centimeters distant from that of the dolphin hugging itself up close against the Perspex wall in front of me. Almost in the same instant that I notice the woman approaching, so also does 'One of Four'. The reaction is both curious and amazing; in that instant of awareness, she draws back almost imperceptibly from the glass and a quick ripple of energy telegraphs her distrust. Fully alert now, she watches the young woman pass us by through dark heavy-lidded eyes. Similarly, I find myself doing the same, wondering if the Japanese woman passing along the walkway is in fact one of the Museum staff. Mutually engaged as we are in observing the intruder, I cannot help but sense the strong feeling of camaraderie that has quickly grown between me and the beautiful bottlenose on the other side of the glass. We can both clearly read what the other is feeling. It is very interesting to note the distinct difference in the dolphins' demeanor and reactions to other passers-by in comparison to the joyous reception that the Four have extended to us. As the day passes we are largely left to our own devices, enjoying the run of the Dolphinarium complex with its four inhabitants.

No more than half a dozen patrons pass through the viewing tank over the course of the morning. Each time they pass though, the contrast between the dolphins' cool indifference towards them, compared to the intimate and joyful connection they have established with me and Kerry becomes patently obvious. As others pass through the viewing area, the quartet pull back from the glass and maintain a discreet distance; following the same pattern as before, they quickly return to close intimacy with us as soon as they are satisfied that the 'intruders' have left.

An adult bottlenose positioning itself at such close range, pressed tight against the glass, is a striking sight and I reach for my camera to capture the moment. The dolphins however do not miss a trick. Despite its compact size, the bottlenoses quickly catch sight of the camera; in a flash they retreat and demurely continue to give us a wide berth, sliding past but refusing to seek closer contact up against the glass. Time and again I try to catch a quick photograph of them as they flash by, but regardless of whether I am holding a video camera or a still camera the routine remains the same. Feeling slightly ashamed of myself for seizing a photo opportunity I tuck the cameras back into their carry bags, but not before I manage to capture a few fleeting still shots; standing discreetly in the background whilst Kerry interacts with the dolphins up against the glass. Even then I noted, on reviewing the camera footage in my hotel room later that day that in each shot the dolphins were watching me very closely whilst I took the photographs.

This morning's visit had revealed a little bit more of the quartet's personalities. I pondered the reason for the bottlenoses' distinct reaction to the other patrons who stopped to watch them. Why exactly did they often react with annoyance and a sense of distrust? Were they reminded of the men and women who had separated them from their families, denied them their freedom and coerced them to perform on cue in return for food and sustenance? The more obvious answer, I decided, was that they simply despised being reduced to little more than a display or a curiosity for people to gawk and stare at. Surely any intelligent, self-aware being would feel exactly the same way. This may well also explain their obvious dislike of our cameras. Maybe they simply didn't like the camera flash. Or perhaps the act of taking their photos represented everything that they despised. Perhaps for them it was an unwelcome intrusion into their privacy.

Sitting here by the harbor at the end of the day, my mind wanders as I process everything. I am comfortable here. I realize that I am compellingly drawn to water, for solace; for a sense of balance. Perhaps as mammals there remains within us the dull shards of the memory of our own birth; our physical beginnings in the dark water of the womb. In synchronicity with the tides, we are each of us drawn subtly by the persuasive magnetic beckoning of the moon. In esoteric teachings, water signifies the unconscious mind and the world of spirit. Though our body's destiny is to return to the dust of the Earth from which it came, it seems to me that there remains at our spiritual core a deeply ingrained connection with water.

Land dwellers though we be, our physical body is almost seventy per-cent water. It is interesting to note that this is a commonality we share with mother Earth–seventy percent of the Earth's surface is covered by water. For me, this proximity to water is cleansing; the dying embers of afternoon sun find me sitting here on a rough wooden bench on the dockside at Katsuura harbor, idly gazing across the water at everything and nothing in particular. Despite the lower vibrations of thrumming diesels staining the air with oily smoke, and the passing white hulled fishing boats, the sea air rolling in off the Pacific is salted and enticingly fresh.

One thing that I notice about the waters of the Dolphinarium and the small tank which houses Faith and Hope is that they are so tainted by chemicals and affected by artificial filtration systems that they lose the natural healing energies of the water. Psychically the water has become a dead and sterile medium, in much the same way that preserved and processed food differs in its energy to natural fresh food. And if I am able to sense that by simply standing nearby, I wonder at the effect that it must be having on the inhabitants who have been forced to adjust to living in it.

The inhabitants. I can see them now in my mind's eye, in fine focus. The Four. They remain as enigmatic today as they did when I first met them a year ago. Standing in the Dolphinarium earlier this morning, playing and interacting with the four bottlenoses, I again wondered if the event of twelve months ago was just imagined. The odd sense of 'missing time' had played on my mind ever since. The surreal quality of that one unguarded moment. I have only a day left with them now–the Four, and Faith and Hope–before I must leave Japan once again.

ೡ⚜ೞ

On the day prior to our departure from Taiji, Kerry and I make a final visit to the Taiji Whale Museum to say our goodbyes. Following the events of our earlier visit, we resolve to leave our camera equipment behind this time; having witnessed the dolphins' adverse reaction to our camera equipment. This will be our 'quality' time with them,

TAIJI

perhaps at least for another year. Waking early that morning we find, to our great delight, that Mother Nature has again won out over the dolphin hunters. Strong offshore winds are already churning the coastal waters into angry rows of whitecaps, making it impossible for the banger crews to spot the breaching of dorsal fins. We celebrate and warm ourselves with coffee in one of Katsuura's quaint little cafes before making the short drive back to Taiji for a final visit to the Museum's dolphins.

The earlier chill has given way to another beautiful winter morning, with the coastal scenery taking on the warm palette of a watercolor painting. The earlier bluster of angry wind which had hurled sea-spray and foam at the banger boats, has given way to the gentlest zephyr of breeze. The softer face of Taiji presents itself, welcoming and timeless under a pastel yellow sun.

The lazy morning sunlight and postcard-pretty scenery are a welcome delight after the bitter chill of the exposed lookout, rugged up in several layers of clothing for warmth. Hot coffee and a delicious *egg-u toast-u* (Japanese for egg toast!) in the close inviting warmth of the quaint timber walled café have put paid nicely to any last vestiges of the day's earlier bone numbing cold.

Making the familiar drive back to the Whale Museum, the reality of once again turning my back on Taiji and its dolphins for another year confronts me. A wave of melancholy settles on me as we navigate the narrow winding road in perfect silence.

Back inside the Dolphinarium, any initial traces of wariness on the part of the Four has vanished; we are greeted enthusiastically upon our arrival like old friends. Once again, as before, Kerry and I have the run of the complex to ourselves. Finding ourselves different positions along the viewing walkway, we again allow the dolphins to shuttle between the two of us. A sense of exuberance quickly builds and it seems that both factions, humans and dolphins, are encouraging each other. The energy in the tank is a pure joy to behold as the bottlenoses playfully chase one another like rogue torpedoes.

The Four

A series of acrobatic breaches high up above us at the surface of the tank brings the watery silhouette of a trainer into our view, leaning over the tank's surface to see what all the commotion is about. We smile conspiratorially and I have the sense that the dolphins are doing exactly the same. That old familiar sense of jubilation, of rebellion and *joie de vivre* courses through me. Be bold and sing it from the rooftops! I love my friends the dolphins all the more for this timely reminder–*Rejoice!* Life is a precious gift.

As the morning progresses, the pod leader singles me out and spends an extended period of time in my company, in the same manner as our earlier visit. Despite the thick slab of Plexiglass which separates the two of us, I can clearly hear the muffled clicks, creaks and buzzes as she vocalizes in an animated manner. Then to my surprise–facing me directly and intently holding eye contact with me– she makes a series of exaggerated nodding movements with her head whilst moving closer; delicately placing her head in contact with the glass. It is clear from the theatrical motions that she is beckoning me to similarly place my head up against a transparent barrier of Plexiglass. I'm confounded. What is she up to? As I follow her lead she neatly maneuvers herself into a tail up position, carefully positioning her melon–the area of her head between blowhole and rostrum–directly against the glass so that we are now 'forehead to forehead'. No longer vocalizing, I can now distinctly hear the buzzing of her echolocation system, vibrating directly through the separating layer of glass where our foreheads meet. She is examining me with echolocation, though I'm not exactly sure what she is seeking to find.

All I know is that she was keen to connect at my forehead or 'third eye' position. The clicking becomes faster until it sounds rather like the extended sound of a creaking door; the noise slowly rising in pitch up until the point where I can no longer hear it. I can however most definitely feel it, as the glass continues to vibrate against my forehead even though all sound has now vanished. Dolphins are able to hear sound, and also produce it at frequencies well beyond the more limited range of human hearing. The motivation behind the bottlenose's deliberate actions has me intrigued. The focused beam of sound that a dolphin projects from its melon is a part of a highly complex sonar system which is used primarily for hunting, navigating and assessing surrounding objects and threats. The full capability of a cetacean's echolocation system still remains something of a mystery. What is known is that the dolphin's natural sonar rivals and indeed exceeds the capabilities of man-made sonar equipment. All of this goes through my mind as I relax into the gentle buzz vibrating through my forehead. Standing directly in front of the stationary beam of an aircraft's weather radar can actually sterilize a human being. What the hell then, I wonder to myself, am I doing here with my head nuzzled cozily up against the full force of the beam from the world's most sophisticated sonar system! Somehow though, I have an inherent trust and complete faith in the system's non-human operator. *Is she trying to 'reach' me, or is she sending me something?*

This then becomes my goodbye to the Four for yet another year. I feel as though I have been given a very special gift. An acknowledgement. And now it is time for me to leave. Closing my eyes, I visualise the dolphins swimming free in the wild blue of their ocean home. Mentally I say my goodbyes and, summoning all the happiness I can muster, I tell 'One of Four' that I will be back. *I promise.* As the streamlined grey bottlenose disengages contact and effortlessly rises to the top of the tank to draw breath, I stand back from the Perspex dome and catch Kerry's pained glance. We have to go. I feel the lump tightening in my throat as we hastily stride towards the exit. Once again, the morning sun is welcoming and bright.

I make stridently for the exit, not daring to look back.

The Four

After recounting my experience of the Four to you, I felt it worthwhile to give you some further insight into just how uniquely intelligent bottlenose dolphins are. In 2006 the Scotland University of St Andrews' Sea Mammal Unit conducted a series of tests on bottlenose dolphins in Sarasota Bay off the west coast of Florida. The whistles emitted by members of a pod were recorded by the group and loaded onto a computer. When the recordings were played back through a set of underwater speakers, individual dolphins seemed to respond to specific recorded calls.

'I think it is a very exciting discovery because it means that these animals have evolved the same abilities as humans,' Vincent Janik of the Sea Mammal Unit remarked. 'Now we know they have names for each other, like we do.'

The dolphins were recognizing specific vocalization patterns in precisely the same way that human beings recognize names. Let me paraphrase that in simple terms. Dolphins have individual names for each other, just as humans do! Scientists say that this is the first recorded evidence of wild animals referring to each other by name.

It was found that a dolphin creates for itself a unique 'signature whistle' as an infant; in effect it decides upon a 'name' for itself. Its trademark whistle appears to be created as it listens to the unique calls of others within its social group and then forms a personalized whistle of its own. A pod member's signature whistle differs from the others, but has often been found to be a blending of the sounds of the names of others in the pod. Once created the dolphin appears to use this name permanently. If an individual is lost or in distress it has also been noted that it will call out its own name, presumably in the hope that relatives or pod members will recognize it and come to its aid. Dolphins have also been recorded using those names to refer to another dolphin in the third person. So, they talk about each other! Gossip appears to be rife in dolphin social circles! And this is just the tip of the iceberg; we've learned that the dolphin vocabulary is extremely large and scientists can only speculate as to what all these sounds stand for.

'Their repertoire of calls probably numbers in the hundreds,' Janik stated. 'Some of them are food calls, but for most of them we have no idea what they're for.'

We now know that they have names and they possess a language. And just like humans, they have shown themselves to have unique personalities. They are sentient beings like us; living in a highly structured society. Should we really be putting these amazing beings into tanks?

Of all that I have written about the plight of the Taiji dolphins, this particular chapter has been one of the hardest for me to write. The encounters with the bottlenose dolphins of the Taiji Whale Museum may always remain enigmatic and mysterious. Will I see them again? And if so, what will that meeting reveal to me?

For now, I will finish this chapter in what I think to be the words of the Four. Because they, in their own inimitable way, have demanded it to be so.

Sing me your name and I in turn will sing you mine
Just as days gone by when I would move timeless
And you in your laughter would follow
Sing me your name and I will sing you all this and more
Listen! Beyond the shallows
Where fear holds limit over the cast of your line
Listen, do you hear? Do you dare? My music begins
Beyond the divide of breakers and wild surf
Where the hue of your heaven meets the blue of my sea
Let go the seeds of your doubt
On carefully charted shores leave them scatter and blow
My music begins in deeper water…

CHAPTER THIRTEEN

Blue Day

TAIJI JOURNAL – March 2012
Changes in Taiji. Those three simple words have an almost magical ring to them. Could it be possible? We have been hearing the first rumblings of it recently, and today we are witnessing some promising signs! Over the last couple of days, local sources have been advising us of a drop in demand for dolphin meat. If this is correct, then it would mean that the dolphin hunters will not want to actively target species such as the striped dolphins which are butchered and sold for their meat. Striped dolphins will typically travel in large pods or herds, and hence they are caught in relatively large numbers. A glut of dolphin meat flooding the local market will only drive prices down as a result of the relative over-supply. Presuming that the information is accurate, what is behind the change in demand? Is it something as innocuous as a seasonal variation; or perhaps a fleeting change in customer tastes? Or is there a more compellingly sinister concern keeping the shoppers away from the shelves? We have all known for some time about the dangers of the excessive mercury levels in dolphin meat. This is a rapidly becoming a major concern with marine life, and it accumulates progressively as fish eats fish, and so on up the food chain. The mercury concentration is therefore dangerously high in the top predators of the food chain as they have effectively consumed the aggregate from all the species below them. And this is putting dolphins and many of the game fish such as tuna

at risk. Is it possible that some of the dire warnings about the effects of mercury poisoning are finally filtering through to Japanese consumers?

Following the devastating Tohoku earthquake and tsunami disaster to the north in March last year, concerns have also been raised about the elevated radiation levels discovered in fish and other marine life in the wake of the Fukushima nuclear plant meltdown. Bluefin tuna, which are a migratory fish, were found to have radiation levels as much as ten times higher than normal. Perhaps the sheer scale of this disaster has served to heighten the local awareness with regards to the concerns of contamination?

Whilst the reasons behind the unexpected change remain something of a mystery, today's events do seem to confirm that the feedback we have been receiving is accurate. The banger fleet had carefully shepherded a large pod of striped dolphins in from the coastal waters this morning. Typically, when driving such large pods, many dolphins will break away and escape on the long run in towards the coast. Even with the fleet of a dozen banger boats taking up their classic 'horseshoe' positions behind the panicking dolphins, a pod of more than a hundred nimble striped dolphins spreads across a broad swathe of ocean, and many sub-groups will break away and elude the pursuing boats.

Bringing the pod carefully down the 'funnel' the banger boats take special care to decelerate and slow the stressed and flighty dolphins down. They must negotiate a hard 90-degree right hand turn to drive the pod parallel to the rocky coastline and in towards the cove. The striped dolphins are out of their comfort zone in the shallow waters and panicking them overly at this stage can spell unnecessary suffering and cruel disaster should they beach themselves against the rocky coastline in their blind panic. This year we are yet to see a repeat of such incidents. We are thankful for this small mercy at least; it is another of the changes that we have witnessed this year.

Blue Day

It is at least heartening that our voicing of concern for these acts of animal cruelty appears to have been acknowledged and heeded. Today, with the drive boats and attendant skiffs slowed to almost a walking pace, another unusual event occurred. Motoring cautiously through the slickly wet dorsal fins which are turning in confused circles, an open skiff divided the captured pod roughly into two. The group furthest away from the mouth of the cove were then slowly shepherded back the way they came, along the length of the peninsula which points the way back to open ocean. Curious about this new development, we carefully observed the lone banger boat patiently corralling the group of approximately twenty dolphins back to sea. Despite the presence of the boat behind them the group attempted to turn back towards the coast several times in a vain bid to re-join the remainder of their pod now captive at the mouth of the cove.

Even though there is some measure of joy in seeing at least a few given their freedom, it is equally heartbreaking to witness the depth of their familial bond. How many more times must they demonstrate this before we finally respect their right to freedom? Ric later observed that this was the first time that he had witnessed such an event here. Perhaps it's a portent of things to come. Most likely it is just another minor win on a long hard road. A chill wind howls and calls around my hotel room window as I write this entry. When will the winds of change truly start to blow in Taiji?

ଓ ✤ ଚ

TAIJI JOURNAL – March 2012

Today Mother Nature once again speaks the final word in Taiji. In a stony silence we witness the imposing sight of an eleven strong drive boat fleet depart the harbor mouth, line astern in the twilight. Proud, confident and haughty, their navigation lights glow like ominous fireflies chasing each other out to sea under a bleak overcast. I curse the still conditions under my breath and cast a weather eye to seaward. Where is that forecast wind? The limp black tri-sails of the fishing boats out in the mid-distance tell the story; the offshore winds are still, favoring the banger fleet. The morning drags by uneventfully until, out beyond the lookout things start to turn in the dolphins' favor. The temperature suddenly plummets from 'damn cold' to 'brass monkey cold'. We shiver, stamp feet and rug up as we watch the fleet vanishing into a misty grey fug which has started to blow up on the curve of the far horizon. Whitecaps begin to make their appearance in the sea lanes and the surrounding air becomes sharp with the fine taste of sea salt–the wind is up! A divine wind. Two and a half hours later it happens and our moods lighten exponentially.

A white blip slowly grows in size to become the outline of an inbound banger boat. Then another. And another. Our job is not complete until all eleven boats are confirmed as returned and the wait seems agonizingly slow in the growing cold. Several boats linger off-shore in a lazy 'fart-arsing' maneuver. Have they sighted something? The other day, much to our amusement and joy we watched a pod of Risso's skillfully evading the hunters by diving under the boats, causing the orderly ranks of bangers to split and turn erratically in an obvious confusion. It's hard to stay fashionable after a nautical cock-up like that!

    Collectively we hold our breaths, speculating that the remaining trio of drive boats may have sighted a pod surfacing in the confusion of foam and chop. The eyes start to play tricks in the deteriorating conditions; is that dorsal fins breaking the surface of the blue-grey waters, or just whitecaps stirred up by a blustery offshore wind? I know that on the decks of the banger boats the hunters must be asking the same question. They circle lazily and seemingly rudderless for long minutes before breaking off and ploughing deftly through the swell toward us. The mission is scrubbed for the day.

Blue Day

I'm suddenly aware of tension starting to drain from my neck and shoulders. The count-in continues. Three still unaccounted for. Where are they? Scanning the horizon, we spot three distinct plumes of spray in the mid-distance, converging on the harbor mouth. Banger boats, all three of them. They approach, rolling heavily on the swell to port and starboard, their high bows making hard work of cleaving the rising seas. Their approach through the harbor mouth is a study in slow motion, with wind and waves working against their homeward passage. A forlorn and bedraggled group of sea birds lazily watch their approach from the chill vantage point of a large rock jutting from the sea. Even the birds are grounded.

'Give it away! Take up melon farming!' yells Leah at the skipper of a passing banger boat–her voice snatched away by the growing fury of a wind which is now angrily rattling at rocks and trees on the lookout.

Sometimes the forces of nature call the shots in Taiji. We're done here. For today. I pick up one of the counting stones from the circle on the fencepost for good luck and we make the walk back along the pretty little promontory path towards the car park. Placing the small rounded stone respectfully at the wayside Buddhist shrine nestled under its protective canopy of trees and shrubbery; I nod a quiet word of thanks to the spirits of Kumano. The steady roar of a banshee wind buffets and moans through the disturbed canopy of trees.

Mother Nature speaks on a frosty breath – 'Return to your huts and your hearths. The dolphins are not yours today. They navigate my oceans together, free and wild. It is as it should be'.

Domo arrigato gozaimasu Poseidon! (Thank you very much Poseidon).

CHAPTER FOURTEEN

Breathe

'We don't see things as they are. We see them as we are'
—ANAÏS NIN

TODAY I KNOW the silence and the stillness in Taiji's pre-dawn light. No ominous throb of diesels as the drive boat fleet stridently follows each other out of the harbor in line-astern formation. The incessant hammering of the banger poles is silent for at least another day. Today it is Mother Nature who once more lays claim to Taiji, and she embraces her prize to an icy bosom.

> *Snow falls on distant mountain tops.*
> *Waves crescendo against rocks.*
> *A chill banshee wind howls and calls.*
> *My stomach doesn't knot.*

TAIJI JOURNAL – February 2012
Following the scrubbing of this morning's drive hunt, and with a good part of the day still remaining; I decided that I would visit the second point of the Kumano triangle–the Hongu-Taisha shrine. Leah and Kerry gladly joined me and together we set off on our pilgrimage to the mountains. Despite my preparations and with a hand-drawn mud

map to assist me (the GPS map didn't cover this region), we set off from Katsuura.

Wrong turns and backtracks marked our journey. First off, we missed the turn-off which led into the mountains. Re-tracing our steps, I stopped at a homely little *ryokan*–the Japanese equivalent of a bed and breakfast lodging–to ask directions. Peeking inside I found a family sitting together at a small bar; drinking and chatting together. It felt and looked rather like a home. I sheepishly excused myself in Japanese and attempted to converse. With friendly smiles they watched patiently and somewhat quizzically as I produced a crumpled hand-drawn map and proceeded to explain my motives with the few Japanese phrases that I knew (which were largely irrelevant to the situation), the word 'Kumano', hand gestures and broken English. After a few shambling attempts, a breakthrough was made when the older gentleman recognised the two petrol stations which, as it turns out, marked the turn-off into the mountains.

'ESSO?' the old man asks, stabbing a stubby nicotine stained finger at my hand-drawn petrol station.

'Hai, ESSO. Petrol!' I reply jubilantly, sensing a small breakthrough.

'Pet-lol! Ahhh...hai!'

Bingo. Much rejoicing, toothy grins and the raising of the odd sake glass ensued! The old man spoke animatedly in Japanese to the others; presumably explaining the whacky Westerner's conundrum, and together they motioned me to follow them outside.

Back outside, Leah and Kerry are wide-eyed at the spectacle. One slightly perplexed Westerner and two generations of Japanese family, all talking excitedly. The ladies had chosen to wait for me outside in the car whilst I, the humble driver, negotiated with the locals. What a sight we must be–me and a lively Japanese family each pointing animatedly down the road and speaking all at once. Satisfied they have helped the lost wayfarers we bow to each other multiple times, as is the custom. As I drive away, I see them in my rear-view mirror, waving at us. There is a simplicity to life here which endears itself to me.

TAIJI

'We were stating to worry about you. You were in there for ages,' said Kerry.

'Yeah, it was like a weird version of Pictionary. I was desperately trying to explain with the sketch map where we were going and how we missed the turn-off.'

'So, what did they say?' quizzed Leah.

'I can't say for sure, but I think they said turn left at the rock that looks like a bear, then turn right at the bear that looks like a rock.'

We scooted back up the main road, immediately sighting the signs for the two petrol stations hoisted high over the clutter of buildings lining the busy streets. Perfect! I'm surprised we didn't notice them the first time. Taking the turn-off, we made our way out of civilisation, to be progressively met with near deserted winding country road. An hour or later; switching to a tourist map of the region around the holy shrine, we start trying to pick up landmarks. My excitement grew–at last I will make the journey to the second holy shrine! Unlike my first naïve visit to the Nachi shrine last year, I now have an expectation and I scour the area looking for the tell-tale signs of spirituality and reverence. We find nothing.

Once again, we passed from civilisation into rural wilderness. At a fork in the road we made an educated guess and took the mountain path, disappearing almost immediately into the semi-darkness of thick forest. Another half an hour passes as we journey on through the heart of the Kumano; picking up the markings of pilgrimage trails dotting the woods. Yet no sign of the holy shrine. Stopping to re-assess our situation, we scrutinise the tourist map. We were definitely in the right spot...there's the river course which we passed. And that tourist centre which sold ice-cream is right near the shrine area! We all seemed to recall the ice-cream shop!

Doubling back and re-tracing our steps for the second time this afternoon, we find our destination. After stopping in at that ice-cream shop. The massive torii gate which towers over the landscape is in plain view. *How could we have missed it?!* We park the car in a nearby parking lot and pick our way towards the towering marker.

Breathe

The torii gate stands in a deceptively bland open field on a broad flat flood plain. Perhaps it is for this reason that its location completely eluded us, and we simply drove straight past; spending the better part of an hour heading in the wrong direction, before doubling back in our search for the holy marker.

When we finally walked beneath it; the sheer immensity was overwhelming. There is only the hushed whisper of the breeze through low foliage. The gate rises a full thirty feet above our heads; imposing dimension speaking of its great spiritual significance. The symbolic three-legged black raven is emblazoned high across the very top of the gate, sternly reminding us that the will of Heaven infuses this place. Once we found the grand shrine, its sheer majesty did not fail to impress. Located high on ridge, it nestles amongst giant cedar and cypress trees and is accessed by a large stone staircase of 158 steps. Traditional architecture with high curving roofs of cypress bark typify the four massive shrine buildings. The atmosphere is solemn and imposing. Lionesque stone statutes stand guard; purging the place of evil spirits. As I ring the huge ceremonial bell and clap my hands twice in the customary worship, I feel a pervading sense of humility which remains with me for the rest of the day.

CB ❀ ED

Looking back on the day's events, I suspect there is a lesson here for me. For all of us. It was a day of 'losing our way'. Firstly, in missing the turn-off from busy Shingu town and then being shown the way by a kindly Japanese family. Then looking for the gateway to the holy shrine, but not seeing it. Despite the fact that it is the largest torii gate in the world and towers 100 feet over the landscape; in an area which I didn't think would hold a sacred entranceway.

TAIJI

We must put away our preconceptions and simply learn to see things for what they are. To look with humility and to see what is there. My oversight perhaps even betrayed some vague sense of prejudice and scorn on my part. Surely a humble rural rice field couldn't host a doorway to the land of high spirituality! And yet, here on a modest agricultural flood plain stood the second doorway to the holiest of places in Japan. I think I'm guilty of setting off today with the notion of finding majesty, of high spirituality; which is of itself a noble thing. And in truth I did find it; hidden away in rather innocuous surroundings. Not in a lofty mountain nook. Not nestling against a mighty waterfall. The gateway to Hongu-Taisha shrine was to be found in a simple rural floodplain; in a rice field.

And therein lies my failing. I had decided that high spirituality did not belong in such a workaday, agricultural place. In the same way I would not expect to find a King wearing the clothes of a workman. How judgmental of me! In truth, is not the humble rice paddy worthy of nobility; having loyally fed and nourished those who lived around it year upon year?

So, today I have journeyed to the second of three Grand Shrines which mark the boundaries of the sacred Kumano. Twice lost, I eventually found my way. A humble Japanese family kindly helped to show me the path. And a simple rice paddy was host to the entranceway to the holy ground.

The eyes are useless when the mind is blind. I pray that I have passed the test.

PART III

THE NAIL

The tree which stands tall
Rising high above the rest
The cutter seeks out

CHAPTER FIFTEEN

Divine Wind

"Cherished from Mandate of Heaven, the Great Mongol emperor sends this letter to the King of Japan. The sovereigns of small countries, sharing borders with each other, have for a long time been concerned to communicate with each other and become friendly. Especially since my ancestor governed at Heaven's command, innumerable countries from afar disputed our power and slighted our virtue. Japan has never dispatched ambassadors since my ascending the throne. It is horrifying to think that your Kingdom is yet to do this.
Hence, we dispatched a mission with our letter particularly expressing our wishes. To enter into friendly relations with each other from now on. We think all countries belong to one family. How are we in the right, unless we comprehend this? Nobody would wish to resort to arms."
–KUBLAI KHAN - Mongol ruler of China to the Emperor of Japan (1266)

IN THE MID-1200s the empire of Japan faced the threat of an invasion by a foreign power for the first time in its history. After sweeping eastwards across China, the Mongol ruler Kublai Khan dispatched advance emissaries to Japan bearing a letter addressed to the Emperor. The letter was essentially a cached threat from the Khan, strongly advising that Imperial Japan should pay homage to the mighty warlord or suffer the consequences. The infamous Mongol hordes had swept every opposing army from their path. Born of a nomadic tribe, the military might of the expanding Mongol Empire was legend from Salesia and Hungary in Central Europe, to the Adriatic Sea in the south. Kublai Khan, grandson of the renowned general Genghis Khan, had carved out his own fearful reputation as a conqueror. Despite this; faced with a veiled threat in the barbarian's

Divine Wind

pompous and self-assured letter, the Japanese emperor chose silence, not even gracing it with the courtesy of a response.

Six times over the following years Kublai Khan's envoys were dispatched to Japan. And six times the emissaries were turned back before they could set foot on Japanese soil. But Japan's measured resistance was in no way indicative of their confidence in the face of the foreign threat. Quite the contrary. Fearful of the prospect of a waterborne invasion, Japan's military leaders hurriedly set about strengthening their defenses along the north-west coast of Kyushu. In the meantime, having conquered China and declaring himself Emperor in 1271; Kublai Khan, incensed by the insult to his omnipotence, set about gathering an armada of vessels with which he planned to bring Japan to its knees.

In 1274–eight years after his first letter–the first assault was launched upon Japan. Putting to sea from south-east Korea, a massive invasion force comprising thousands of Mongol and Chinese soldiers together with eight thousand Korean warriors sailed southwards. The fleet of three hundred large vessels and hundreds of smaller craft made landfall on Japan's southern island of Kyushu. The armada pillaged the off-shore islands of Tsushima and Iki before arriving at the place called Hakata Bay on November 18th. In an ominous display of savage brutality, they pierced the hands of women captives and hung them from their boats with thick ropes.

Japanese samurais silently gathered at the bay; grimly prepared to defend their nation against the barbarian force. On the following day, the invaders landed a short distance from Dazaifu, the ancient administrative capital of the island of Kyushu at a place called Hakata. The Japanese forces proved to be no match against the Mongol onslaught. Faced with unfamiliar cavalry tactics and methods, the regimented samurai who were used to traditional man to man combat, were forced to the beat a hasty retreat to a fortress near Dazaifu. Here the Japanese warriors considered the looming prospect of a bloody defeat. Under the mantle of darkness, the

Mongol forces retired to their ships, confident of an impending victory. However, the gods of ancient Nihon were about to make their presence known.

Shortly after nightfall, a typhoon approached and devastated the bay. Such was its fury that the panicked captains made the hurried decision to put the sailing vessels to sea rather than run the risk of being run aground on Japanese soil. By daybreak, only a few ships had not set out to sea. Those that had were totally destroyed by the deadly storm. As many as 13,000 soldiers and two hundred Mongol ships were lost that night. The Japanese small boats, far swifter and more maneuverable, seized the opportunity and gave chase. Japanese warriors boarded the remaining Mongol ships as they pulled back towards Korea, beleaguered and decimated.

To the superstitious Japanese the massive hammer blow that struck down their oppressors so violently and so completely that night at Hakata Bay could only be attributed to divine intervention. They referred to that miraculous wind as *kamikaze*, literally meaning 'divine wind'. They firmly believed that their homeland was under the protection of the gods.

It is highly unlikely that this mystical slant on events was shared by the enraged Kublai Khan. The conqueror of nations was not yet finished with the impetuous land of the rising sun. In the spring of 1281, in a last-ditch effort to overthrow imperial Japan, he assembled and launched what was to be the mother of all seaborne assaults. It was in fact the largest naval invasion force in recorded history, surpassed only in more recent times by the Allied invasion of the Normandy beachheads on D-Day during World War II. More specifically, Kublai Khan flung two separate naval spearheads at Japan. An impressive flotilla of 900 ships containing some 40,000 Korean, Chinese and Mongol troops departed from Masan in South Korea, whilst an even larger force of soldiers, estimated to be between 100,000 and 140,000 set sail from southern China aboard a mighty fleet of almost 4,000 ships. The overlord's plan called for an

Divine Wind

overwhelming coordinated attack by the two combined imperial Yuan fleets. However, hampered by the sheer logistics of mobilizing such a massive armada, the Chinese fleet found themselves delayed due to difficulties in provisioning and manning the war ships. The Korean fleet set sail first, suffering heavy losses in skirmishes with a now better prepared Japanese army at Tsushima Island, just off the mainland. In the summer, the combined Korean/Chinese fleet again over-ran the island of Iki-shima, before sailing for the Japanese mainland.

Finding suitable landing points to disembark their troops proved to be a major problem. In the intervening years following that first fateful battle in 1274, the Japanese prudently constructed a 'great wall' of stone some two meters high to stave off possible future attacks. And so, a number of minor individual skirmishes took place, known collectively as the Battle of Kōan, or the Second Battle of Hakata Bay. Although greatly outnumbered, the heavily fortified coastal line worked in the Japanese army's favor and for the second time in history the Mongol forces were driven back to their ships.

And once again the unexpected happened! The now-famous kamikaze, in the form of yet another massive typhoon once again assaulted the shores of Kyushu. Over two straight days it laid waste to much of the Mongol fleet. Much of the Chinese invasion contingent consisted of flat-bottomed Chinese river boats, hastily pressed into service and totally inadequate for operations on the high seas, let alone for withstanding the powerful might of the typhoon winds. Yet again a mortal blow was struck. And so, for the second time in recent history, Japan was saved from invasion by the mystical kamikaze. The Mongols fled, never again to return.

So why am I telling you all of this? Please do not misunderstand my intentions here–I do not seek to paint the Japanese as a race without their own history of callous brutality. But what does the story of a failed invasion by the Mongol hordes have to do with our tale of Taiji and the dolphins? I have recounted this history to give you an insight into the Japanese cultural. You see, the Japanese are a race that have existed in almost splendid isolation. Unlike so many other nations, they have never had their homeland invaded by a conquering force. A very large part of that pedigree can be attributed to *water*.

We live on a water planet. A full two-thirds of the surface of our home is covered in water, and it is because of this that life in all its diversity thrives. Wherever we choose to make our home on planet Earth, our surrounding environment has a major effect on our lifestyle and in the shaping of our culture. And so here in Japan, the element of water has an all-pervasive influence on life, culture and tradition. She is comprised of four separate islands which therefore means that Japan finds herself completely surrounded by ocean. Four oceans in fact, one at each cardinal point.

Japan's eastern seaboard looks out onto the vastness of Pacific Ocean. To the far north is the Sea of Okhotsk, the coldest of the East Asian seas. To the west, the Sea of Japan provides the buffer to China and Korea on the Asian continent. To the south lies the East China Sea. Thus, Japan's history, culture and traditions are inexorably linked to water. It is that water which has in the past afforded Japan a virtual safety barrier against invasion by foreign powers; firstly, in the 1200s with the threat of ransack by the vast battle fleet of the Mongol hordes. And then again in 1945 when faced with potential homeland invasion by the Allied forces; 'island hopping' northwards through the Pacific in World War II.

Most people equate the term 'kamikaze' with the Japanese suicide pilots who, in the dying years of the Second world War, were desperately pressed into service to fend off the impending invasion of their country by the advancing Allied forces. The concept of kamikaze, or 'divine wind' saw its origins in the 13th century typhoon which saved Japan from occupation by the Mongol invaders. Spirituality and splendid isolation gave rise to the notion that the gods, in the form of a divine wind from Heaven, would protect Japan from her foes. It is not surprising that the only other time in history in which Japan has faced invasion by a foreign force–the treat of occupation by the Allies in 1945–saw the resurrection of the kamikaze in the form of suicide pilots to defend her shores.

As much as water means protection, for Japan it has also meant *isolation*. Japanese culture has grown up in seclusion and unlike many other nations which over time become a cultural melting pot of ideas; she is proudly insular and to this day retains a wary aloofness to outside attitudes and customs.

CHAPTER SIXTEEN

The Nail That Sticks Up

Deru kui wa utareru.
'The nail that sticks up will be hammered down'
—JAPANESE PROVERB

A FUNDAMENTAL aspect of Japanese social custom is what is termed *'uchisoto' (uchi* meaning inside and *soto* meaning outside). This is the cultural ethic of separating people into 'in-groups' and 'out-groups'. Once this division is established one would then relate to those in each group in a different manner. Let me explain how this works. I'll take the example of an office workplace. Employees directly under the control of a department manager would be considered part of that manager's in-group. They would be spoken to in relatively casual or familiar terms. The company directors and upper management becomes the departmental manager's out-group. They are accorded an honorific status and are thus extended a higher level of politeness and respect when spoken to.

On a broader scale, the custom of *uchisoto* is also applied in the case of foreign visitors and tourists in Japan. Visitors are universally viewed as a *soto* or outside group and are thus treated with due politeness and respect. They have a word for the non-Japanese foreigner here–*gaijin*. The literal meaning of this word is 'outsider' (*gai* meaning outside, *jin* meaning person). This custom may not seem that far removed from social etiquette in Western society, however

The Nail That Sticks Up

here in Japan it is exceptionally difficult for an outsider to be accepted openly into Japanese society. They are always inherently recognized as an outsider. In other words, there is always an implicit sense of division between the Japanese (the 'in-group') and the non-Japanese (the 'out-group').

As we have already observed, the Japanese are a very insular race. The national *uchisoto* mindset might be summarized like this–there is Japan and then there is Everyone Else. Thus, the concept of *uchisoto* can also be thought of as 'us and them' and the gulf separating the two becomes patently obvious when we consider things like the controversial Japanese whaling industry. It is true of every culture in the world that we naturally take umbrage to outsiders telling us what to do. That is human nature, and in that fundamental the Japanese are no different. And indeed, why should they be? Nobody likes a complete stranger telling them what to do. Despite their demeanor of cool reserve, the Japanese are in reality extremely sensitive to what outsiders may think of them. There is strong evidence of this acute sensitivity here in Taiji where the dolphin hunters have taken great pains to cover their handiwork with tarpaulins and covered marquees to avoid the scrutiny of the outsiders.

Japanese society tends to be extremely group centric–everyone is part of some sort of group and the group comes first. Inside this collective, each individual is expected to have more or less the same understanding and be possessed of the same attitudes. From birth the Japanese perceive themselves as being members of multiple sub-sets–family, work groups, various organizations they may belong to, and over and above these the Japanese nation itself. Acceptance within a group therefore is considered extremely important, and there is an almost inherent fear of being ostracized.

Individuality can be seen as a potential for disharmony. Decisions tend to be made by group consensus and the rogue individual or 'lone wolf' personality is strongly discouraged. Here it is conformity and order that are prized and any tendencies towards unconventionality and attention seeking behavior are quickly curbed and quashed. This is the complete polar opposite of many Western societies where unconventionality and independent free thinking are feted and accorded an innate respect.

The conservative older generation view that nonconformity is an unacceptable social behavior still holds true in present-day Japanese society. This will undoubtedly change as the younger generation of Japanese, possessed of more worldly cosmopolitan views, slowly progress to occupy positions of power in lieu of their more traditionally conservative elders. The gulf between East and West is slowly narrowing in current times. The surrounding waters which afforded Japan a splendid isolation in the past cannot stop the cross flow of cultural exchange and ideas over the ether. The internet and ease of access to international mass media is slowly breaking down the traditional barriers of the past. In Taiji the first seeds of this breakaway from traditional cultural norms was witnessed when six young Japanese girls travelled from Tokyo and Osaka to the controversial village to visit the place for themselves and to voice their concerns. The weight of this cannot be underestimated; hopefully this one seemingly simple act will pave the way for others to stand up and express their views. It will be a ground swell of local support for the anti-whaling camp that will become the spearhead that will ultimately force the hand of Taiji's dolphin drive hunt industry.

Having spearheaded the raising of awareness of the issue; we now need to be asking ourselves just what role we *gaijin* are best suited to play in the ongoing dynamic of the drive hunts.

TAIJI JOURNAL – Saturday January 15th 2011

The Nail That Sticks Up

The Japanese are lovers of order and conformity. Perhaps it is born out of their innate desire to be accepted; to 'fit in' with the group. Whatever the motivation, it is a cultural trait which presents as pedantic at best and almost bordering on obsessive compulsive at its extreme. As a Virgoan I am certainly sensitive to this. It's been pointed out to me on more than one occasion that I exhibit all the neurotic traits which typify my star sign. The obsession with perfection, order and routine. I cannot walk into a room without straightening a crooked picture. At work, my desk always remains painfully tidy–*there is a place for everything and everything in its place!*' I am also on the Asperger's spectrum, which makes me heavily reliant on extreme routine. This all adds to the delight of my workmates, and they know full well that the best way to rattle me is to take something off my desk and hide it, or better still simply move it to an ever so slightly different spot. And yet even I am left astounded by the Japanese sense of a meticulousness which borders on neurotic.

My first brush with this comes within minutes of collecting my hire car and departing Osaka airport terminal. Missing a turnoff road almost as soon as I depart the parking area, I find myself at a security checkpoint blocked by a heavy striped barrier.

Pulling up to where a uniformed guard stands alongside a glass booth, I am hastily waved forwards by another white gloved guard. I have not pulled up close enough to the white roadway marker for his satisfaction. I move forwards, quite literally no more than two feet as he painstakingly guides me forwards with impatient movements of one gloved hand, his gaze flicking rapidly between the white 'Stop' line and the bumper of my car. I am as flustered as I am amazed at this demonstration of unnecessary precision. Even more so when, still unsatisfied, he then gestures for me to now reverse the car back a few inches! If only my workmates could be here to witness this–for once in my life I'm not the neurotically pedantic one! Despite being somewhat off-put by the severe expressions of the uniformed officers,

I feel smugly liberated by the fact that I have now met people far more obsessive than me!

What occurs next gives me an early insight into the Japanese psyche. Whenever there is discord or dis-harmony, the Japanese tend to become somewhat unsettled and edgy. There is almost a sense that they cannot completely relax until the anomaly is rectified. I have found myself on a feeder road into the airport's cargo complex which requires a security clearance to transit. I clearly don't have the required pass, and equally clearly had arrived there mistakenly. With my limited Japanese and by using hand signals I indicate my intention had been to turn back on to the main exit road to Osaka, which is in plain sight just meters away. A simple matter, you say? Over the next few minutes I'm questioned by no less than *four* uniformed guards. I am asked to fill out an A4 questionnaire handed to me on a clipboard. It is all in Japanese. I use three simple words repeatedly–Osaka, *hoteru* (hotel), tourist. C'mon, guys…a child could join up those dots! I'm a tourist in a hire car, leaving the airport with a suitcase. *Seriously dudes, this isn't rocket science!*

A good ten minutes pass by with a great deal of gesticulating and group discussion amongst the quartet of officers. Finally, after much consultation they appear to collectively arrive at a decision. Once again, the white gloved hand waves at me; motioning me to wind my window down and in halting English blurts out the command 'U-turn, U-turn!' indicating a turnoff just a few car lengths down the road. With the situation now in control, and not having been put on the spot to make the bold decision personally, the guard is all smiles and clearly relieved. *Jeez…seriously?!* One slightly flustered and bemused foreigner departs Osaka airport. Four Japanese security guards scurry back to their stations. Harmony and order reigns once again!

I particularly notice the innate sense of order while I am driving. Despite the fact I'm in a new place, in a foreign land; I'm more relaxed driving here than in Australia. No-one speeds or drives

The Nail That Sticks Up

erratically, and I can anticipate every move. For someone as meticulous and precise as me this is seventh heaven! I bet there is no road rage in Japan. As the miles roll on I study car upon car as they pass me by–each one with drivers sitting in a perfect straight-backed posture with eyes fixed straight ahead. The motorway is a neat production line of Zen-like order and harmony.

I include these anecdotes for a reason–they give you some further important insights into the Japanese mentality. Time and again over the next few days I will see these cultural elements surface in the way that the Japanese authorities and the dolphin hunters grapple to deal with an invasion of international activists; of *gaijin*, who are witnessing and documenting their activities. And today, unbeknownst to me a far more powerful protest is taking place in the form of the arrival of six young Japanese nationals. It has definitely upset the natural balance and order of things as far as the authorities are concerned.

There is a saying here in Japan: *"The nail that sticks up will be hammered down."* Today I witnessed the hammer at the cove. The drive boats have been in harbor the past two days; the inclement weather conditions providing some respite after the bloody events of the previous two days. A new arrival at the harbor is the sturdy grey bulk of a Japanese Coast Guard cutter. The small warship dominates the dock area and sticks out like an ominous steel slab amongst the workman-like rows of white fishing vessels. A number of blue uniformed Guardsmen have been spotted disembarking. Despite the drive fleet lying idle and with no sign of movement at the Taiji Fisheries Co-operative building, the parking lot at the cove is a hive of flustered activity as I pull in on my way back from the harbor. At least two dozen cars and as many officials are congregated in the roadside parking area.

Two groups of officers stand guard at the entrances at each end of the parking lot, some in navy blue official uniforms identifying them as Japanese police and Coast Guard. Several others wander the area, looking to all intents and purposes like a group of tourists, cameras and steady cams on display. These however are not curious onlookers or protesters, and nor are they passing tourists. A police car trawls its way through the car park, pausing momentarily across the back of my vehicle, presumably to record my car's registration number and to scrutinize me carefully. The nervous tension in the air is palpable. This isn't normal. *What's going on here?* Always present in large numbers whilst a drive hunt is in progress, the Japanese officials are usually wary but polite. Today however there appears to be an uncharacteristic edge of aggression to their demeanor which puts me slightly on edge. Bear in mind that I am not here to protest. Or to willingly break laws. And neither do I wear the colors of any particular organization.

I am here to observe and document; however, there is no doubt in the minds of these local officials as to what my personal sentiments are with respect to dolphin slaughter and captivity. Deciding that discretion is the better part of valor, I take the time to quietly observe the scene from the safety of the hire car. I lose count of the officials milling about. Noticeable in their body language is that subtle anxious edge; they are clearly rattled and don't seem to know what to expect here. Neither do I. Recently an activist group calling themselves 'The Blackfish' infiltrated Taiji harbor and cut the nets of the dolphin holding pens. I'm left wondering if a similar act has been committed, occasioning the anxious flurry of officials here at the cove today. This is definitely not normal.

Minutes of close scrutiny pass as several sets of eyes warily assess my presence and then suddenly my car is descended upon by six officers. Three of them stand behind the car, peering through the back window; each filming the car and contents with video cameras, a little like an angry Japanese paparazzi. (Or is that japarazzi?!). They are all dressed in plain clothes, two with faces covered in white surgical masks, making their rank and official standing, if indeed they have

The Nail That Sticks Up

one, a little difficult to determine. Their intentions and their sentiments however are patently clear though–they really don't want me to be there at all.

Now three uniformed officers hastily squeeze their way to the driver's side window and one attempts some broken English as I exit the car to meet him. When I bow politely and greet him in Japanese he takes a short back step of surprise and then fires off a rapid stream of Japanese at me. He seems aggressive and impatient. I'm hard pushed to pick even a solitary word so I interject in Japanese:

'Sumimasen. Eigo. Wakarimasen ('Please excuse me. I'm English. I don't understand.') Undaunted he continues to talk in rapid fire sentences. Another uniform steps forward to take his place. This one speaks reasonable English, though I respectfully answer as many of his questions as I possibly can in my limited Japanese. Swamped by blue uniforms, I now notice the three plain clothes remain in the background, pouting and continuing to film the exchange from every angle. Now I see that one is wearing the white boots of a dolphin hunter. He occasionally interjects a stream of rushed Japanese which is ignored by both me and my uniformed questioners. I begin to realize that the officers are as concerned about the aggressive hunters as they are about me. Pushing a camcorder overly close to my face I flash a cheeky grin at him, refusing to be fazed by their aggressive overtones.

'Now, you guys do know I'm not Brad Pitt don't you'? I venture, with a cheeky grin.

I wonder what they will make of that when they review the tapes later with an English translator.

In contrast to his uniformed cohorts the English-speaking officer's demeanor is somewhat more measured and polite as he interrogates me. The questions are fairly standard but quite intrusive in light of the fact that my only 'crime' thus far has been to park in a public car park.

Where am I from? How long am I here for? Where am I staying? He notes the dates of my flight arrival and departure, translating each of my responses for the benefit of his partners. The aggressive one appears to be in charge and occasionally presses me for more information. Using the mild English-speaking officer as a translator he asks 'Why have I come here? Am I with an organization?' There are many conservation organizations with representatives here at the current time, however I suspect he seeks to determine whether I am in fact aligned with Sea Shepherd, who the Japanese view as a terrorist organization. I have no group affiliations and I act independently; however, the Japanese cultural mindset is that everybody belongs to some sort of group. He presses me on the point. I must belong to an organization! I simply tell him that I take an active interest in the welfare of whales and dolphins; that I am indeed a member of several international marine conservation organizations as well as being a volunteer member of ORRCA, an Australian marine mammal rescue group. *Mammal rescue!* These words are something of a red rag to a bull and he digs a little further, asking me what exactly this involves. It is then I realize that he suspects I might be planning a different kind of 'dolphin rescue' here in Taiji! When asked for my passport, I proffer it two handed, with a bow; adopting the etiquette of respect in Japan. He continues to note my comments and details them in his notepad.

'How did you learn about this place?' he asks.

'From television and newspapers in Australia,' I reply earnestly, 'Most people who read the newspaper know about this place.'

There is a quick flash of interest on his face, his eyes opening wider in astonishment before returning to the controlled pokerfaced demeanor. Asian races are not as quick as Westerners to show facial expression, so I know that his involuntary look is one of genuine surprise. I smile inwardly, not wanting to give away my knowledge of this succinct revelation. He translates for the others, and I see similar flashes of surprise. They are a little on the back foot now and I subtly rise to the occasion and take the upper hand in this hitherto one-way interrogation.

The Nail That Sticks Up

Now it is the interrogator's turn to be a little rattled. In truth, the first I ever saw of Taiji was a six-page color spread in the local Sunday newspaper. I still have the copy of it at home. I decide to explain this to him and he relays the details to his companions who listen with interest. It really does seem as though it matters what we outsiders think. To authenticate my story, I politely offer to send him a copy when I return home if he would be willing to provide me with a forwarding address. I sense the blue coats have heard enough. He thanks me for my answers and tells me that this won't be necessary. I return his thanks and tell him that he can expect to see me around as I will be passing by each day to check on the well-being of the whales and dolphins, but I have no intention of showing disrespect to Japan. I politely hand him my business card with a curt bow, letting him know that he can contact me in Australia if he decides he ever wants more information. He bows his thanks and they depart, leaving me to go about my business.

By this time a small group of Japanese media and journalists have joined the throng. I am left amazed by the human circus I have just witnessed; more than a dozen authorities and as many cars. A small warship is docked in the harbor. I have an image of the human body; when an infection enters the bloodstream, hundreds of white blood cells mill around until the threat is neutralized. This appears to be the culture of threat management here in Japan.

It is only later that I learned the reason for the tensions here at the cove today. In an unprecedented move, six young Japanese ladies made their way to Taiji from as far away as Tokyo and Osaka. Having heard of the atrocities committed here they decided to make a journey to see for themselves and to voice their concerns.

This relatively simple act carries a great importance here. As much as the Japanese are somewhat embarrassed and concerned at outsiders witnessing and documenting what goes on here, it carries a far greater weight when Japanese nationals speak out in condemnation of their own countrymen. And this is an important key. Today perhaps marks the beginning of real national discontent with the crude actions of the dolphin hunters, albeit in a small way by six brave young ladies who have taken it upon themselves to come here and voice to their disagreement.

The nail that sticks up will be hammered down. And so, for the six petite nails who boldly decided to stand up and speak out, the authorities mustered a troop of Japanese Coast Guardsmen, a Coast Guard ship and a huge squad of local police. The pressure to conform here in Japan is simply immense!

After the morning's tension at the cove I drive the five kilometers of picturesque winding road back to my hotel in Katsuura and go for my late afternoon walk through the town. I am greeted by smiles of recognition and polite bows from these lovely people that I have only known for a couple of days. I find myself enjoying their company. As I stand politely out of the way of scampering workers with long gaff hooks and wooden crates, a fisherman at the Katsuura fish market recognizes my quiet curiosity and waves me closer to allow me a better look at the day's tuna catch. I smile my thanks to him but he is already busying himself with gaffing and loading the plump silver fish. There is no guilt or suspicion. He doesn't ask to see my passport. Or stick a camera in my face.

CHAPTER SEVENTEEN

Pest Control

IT IS INTERESTING to note that a place called Iki Island features heavily in both accounts of the Mongols invasion attempts. You see, Iki Island has a history of dolphin massacre and atrocity which far outweighs that of Taiji. In point of fact, the fishermen of Iki completely wiped out their local dolphin population.

Standing between the countries of Korea and Japan is the stretch of ocean known as the Korea Strait. Sitting about 50 kilometers from the center of the Strait. Is the small island of Iki. This little island found itself overrun by the barbarian invaders on two occasions. The irony of this is that just as the Iki islanders faced the brutality of the invaders in those latter years of the 13th century, they themselves eked out a gruesome and bloody revenge on the perpetrators of another waterborne 'invasion' in the 20th century. In more recent times the diminutive island bore a dark and sordid history of mass slaughter. In the early 1970's, changes to the prevailing currents occurred around the island. Running its way north from the Philippines, the Kuroshio Current which plays such a key role in bringing the pods of dolphins to the waters around Taiji also flows past Iki Island. Rich in nutrients, this super-highway of warm water acts as a fertile breeding ground for several fish species. A shift in a branch of the current in the 1970's led to an increase in the local fish schools and thus attracted pods of dolphins by the hundreds to the waters surrounding Iki. By mid-decade, the population numbers of the migratory pods were becoming cause for concern amongst the local fishermen. Average fish catch numbers had been dropping largely due to overfishing–a phenomenon typical of many of the world's fishing grounds. The fishermen however placed blame squarely on competition from the increased dolphin population and, fearing the threat to their livelihoods, they started randomly shooting and harpooning the unwanted visitors.

Word spread amongst the Iki fishermen about the drive hunt techniques employed in Taiji. And so, in 1978 the first organized mass slaughter of dolphins took place on the island. Utilizing the *oikomi* drive techniques, a fleet of hunting boats equipped themselves with the long flared metal poles; surrounding a passing herd in the typical 'horseshoe' pattern they drove the dolphins into the shallows and set upon them with long handled broad metal spears. Over the next few years the hunters openly conducted regular drives, slaughtering dolphins in their hundreds. In one recorded hunt, approximately two thousand dolphins were killed in a savage and bloody melee.

Unlike the shamed secrecy of the slaughters at the cove, the Iki dolphin hunters openly welcomed the publicizing and reporting of their kills and welcomed journalists to document the ensuing blood bath. By exposing the sheer numbers of dolphins feeding in local waters, their plan was to curry favor with the government in the hopes of gaining support in the form of assistance or a bounty for the slaughter of the cetaceans.

There have been propositions put forward in recent times to explain the motivation behind the mass dolphin slaughters of Japan.

Foremost amongst these theories is the claim of cultural tradition–the notion that these slaughters have their basis rooted in the region's cultural heritage and traditions. This is the preferred view of the Japanese pro-whaling faction. As we have already seen; subsistence whaling was limited to just a handful of rural locales and was not a national tradition. Moreover, it was a small localized subsistence industry and a far cry from the mechanized commercial organization that has replaced it.

Next there is the notion of monetary gain–primarily from the sale of live specimens to the aquarium industry and the secondary sale of dolphin meat. Money, as they say, makes the world go around. This certainly appears to be a primary motivation in Taiji.

And then there is a third theory, which I would suggest underscores the Japanese fishing industry's present-day relationship with whales and dolphins. This is the concept of *'pest control'*. In other words, mass slaughters are being driven by the perception that migratory dolphin pods are largely responsible for the serious decline in local fish stocks, and therefore threaten the livelihood of the local fishing community.

In the case of the Iki Island mass dolphin slaughters, we can clearly see that the latter concept of 'pest control' was the sole motivation. Iki Island had no rich cultural tradition to speak of as far whales and dolphins were concerned. Indeed, the dolphin pods were only drawn to the area in more recent times as a result of the change in marine species caused by the shift in the prevailing current. And neither was there any evidence that any monetary gain was to be made from the massacre itself. The local fishing industry expressed their greatest concern as being the potential loss of revenue from their usual fishing activities. It was reported at the time that the local fishermen had even engaged the services of a marine mammal expert to assess the impact that the feeding dolphins were having on local fish populations.

In short, they felt that the dolphins were literally eating their profits! Once again, it falls to the perception that *"those pesky whales are eating all our fish!"*

ೡ❀ೢ

TAIJI JOURNAL – March 2012

On returning home after my second trip, the old feelings of disconnect rose up; albeit somewhat more diffuse that my first experience last year. My father's health was in steady decline and this took much of my attention and energy. The lesson of the importance of family which I took away from my first trip burned powerfully. Nonetheless, the plight of the two spotted dolphins plagued me.

I had a great deal of trouble comprehending the mindset of the people who captured Faith and Hope only to confine them to a lonely existence in this small tank. The Taiji Whale Museum boasts the fact that it is particularly difficult to maintain this species in captivity. And yet the pair languishes in a most hostile and alien environment; floating forlornly in a chlorinated tank, denied of all the comforts of their natural environment. Denied the foods that they would hunt and eat in the wild. Denied the all-important social bond of their family pod. Consequently, they face a greatly foreshortened lifespan. In the context of a marine park, the lifeless pair were neither entertaining nor captivating to the passers-by, making their fate seem all the more futile. It seemed their presence in the small tank was simply for curiosity value, to be viewed in much the same way as one would view a solitary goldfish in a tiny bowl.

In the harshest of prisons, the odds were stacked severely against these two pitiful dolphins.

So, the dilemma of the two spotted dolphins continued to play on my mind long after I left Taiji. It was an injustice that I simply couldn't walk past. I found myself waking in the early hours of the morning and drafting e-mails to international authorities, canvassing their intervention. Whilst it was not my intention to make commentary about dolphin captivity, there was a clear and evident case of animal cruelty with respect of these two dolphins and the poor living conditions which they were being subjected to. I posed the question to several international bodies as to whether it would be possible to open a dialogue with the Taiji Whale Museum.

Given the sensitivity of the situation I decided that the best option was to petition for a 'middle ground' solution; a resolution that would benefit the Whale Museum and at the same time alleviate the two dolphins' immediate suffering. It seemed the ideal solution was the option that Ric O'Barry and Save Japan Dolphins were promoting; the relocation of the two small dolphins to a larger environment such as the pre-existing lagoon area at the museum facility. It wasn't freedom but it was certainly the next best thing; release from their present distress.

One thing I've learnt in dealing with the Japanese is that it often becomes very difficult to identify who exactly is pulling the strings, and just who is the dictating authority; if indeed there is one. The elements of cultural sensitivity and the inherent wariness towards outsiders all add to the mix, making it extremely difficult to establish an open two-way communication. Sadly, the rights and well-being of animals in Japan are not as well protected as in some other nations.

Generally speaking, issues of animal welfare and animal cruelty are left to individual countries to address with their own domestic laws.

Unless a country has laws governing care and maintenance of captive wildlife, there is no legal basis for international action against a situation like this. In the case of Faith and Hope, Japan has no specific regulations in place to protect the welfare of captive marine mammals, making the situation extremely hard to address through authorities. One key international body is the World Association of Zoos and Aquariums (WAZA). The stated goal of the World Association of Zoos and Aquariums is *'to guide, encourage and support the zoos, aquariums and like-minded organizations of the world in animal care and welfare, environmental education and global conservation'*. Whilst WAZA have benchmark guidelines and welfare standards in place, affiliation with their Association is purely voluntary.

The Taiji Whale Museum is in fact a respondent member, through their national affiliated body Japan Association of Zoos and Aquariums (JAZA). The World Association in the past have maintained a 'softly softly' approach with regards to the censure of its members for breaches of their recommended welfare standards. One school of thought with regards to this is that the Association should take a hard line with respondent members and strictly enforce their standards, strongly censuring those members found to be in breach of the guidelines. Given that WAZA are an *advisory body* rather than an enforcement organization, the sad fact of the matter is that they cannot legally intervene in order to ensure compliance with standards. It seems the only hard line course of action available is to simply expel those members who refuse to meet laid down welfare standards and guidelines. Of course, the downside to this is that the 'rogue' organization potentially continues with its activities, whilst virtually severing any pre-existing line of communication with the Association. And with it goes any chance of fostering further education and change. It is clear with this kind of dynamic that there is no simple solution to the problem.

All of this talk does not remedy the immediate plight of Faith and Hope. While we trade words and discuss what should and shouldn't be, they continue to suffer in silence. Their discomfort is real. And it is happening now. Can we continue to walk past extreme cases like this, without losing something of ourselves morally and ethically? I'm afraid that I cannot. All but two of the addressees that I reached out to were thoughtful enough to respond to my plea. The Japanese ambassador to Australia declined to respond.

E-mails to several high-ranking members of IMATA, the International Marine Animal Trainers Association equally elicited no response or acknowledgement whatsoever. Go figure.

The Japan Association of Zoos and Aquariums (JAZA) acknowledged in quick order and relayed a letter addressed to me from the director of the Taiji Whale Museum. The text of this letter read:

Letter from the Director, Taiji Whale Museum dated January 26th 2012:
"Thank you for your concern. Here is our official answer that we sent out to WAZA and others. I hope it can help you.

1. The tiny tank in which the live dolphins are kept on display seems to be in violation of the WAZA Code of Ethics. (Even though the same dolphins do not stay in the tank for very long, before they are processed and sold as meat.)
The tank you mentioned is the one for two individuals of Pantropical Spotted Dolphin *(Stenella attenuate)*. The tank size is 7m x 4m x 1.7m (L x

W x H). Additionally, we have 10m² with 0.3m depth, and total volume is about 50 m³.

We have kept Pantropical Spotted Dolphin for 3 years and 4 months. The husbandry of this species is difficult and we are the only one institution that holds this species among JAZA members. At first their body length was 1.7m, and they grow to 1.9m in captivity. By our training, we can measure their body temperature every day and blood sampling regularly.

The husbandry care runs smoothly. We can see them swim very quickly and jump in the tank. If we evaluate that this tank is not suitable for them by observation and examination, we will move them to other facility immediately, but in current situation we don't think it is needed. Our goal for this species is the long-term husbandry in captivity and they will never be edible. This is not only for this species, but also other every individual in our facility will never be edible.

2. In the outside tanks, the dolphins have no protection against the at times very strong sun. We don't recognize that we need the shade for keeping dolphins in captivity.

3. Although hygiene is of course very important for the dolphins, the chlorine concentration in the tanks is unusually high and can be smelled strongly by the visitors. As a consequence, the dolphins mainly have their eyes closed. We use chlorine for sterilization. The concentration is 0.2–0.4ppm. We also use chlorine at the stage and the passage for keeper. The smell of chlorine can be felt with the low concentration and we sometimes use the higher concentration landlubberly, and this might be smelled.

It is not true the dolphins have closed their eyes in consequence of chlorine.

4. Finally, the proximity of where the dolphins are harvested to the whale museum seems problematic, because one of the museum's main goals is to teach the public about these animals, so that they can be preserved.

TAIJI

Taiji is the town that has lived together with dolphin, and it has long history. The way to treat dolphin has been varied according to times, but our relationships with dolphin is deeply ingrained.
Our museum is one of the very few institutions that visitors can learn about dolphin from its fishing history to living animals with all kinds of view. The animal for husbandry and the animal for food are seemed as contradictory aspects, we never turn our back on both side and introduce both of them. We do our best to keep animals in our facility as long as possible with our greatest love, all possible effort and the best care technique. And we will bring forward the unique exhibits that Taiji can have.

We are proud of our facility that is located in Taiji."

ଊଊ❀ଌ

You may well need to read through this letter several times as did I. The Japanese attempt to communicate ideas and explanations in English has resulted in a commentary which at times seems contradictory and its logic fragmented. No doubt there will be those who read this letter and react with anger. As dire as the situation is for Faith and Hope I cannot feel a great measure of anger for the author of this letter, only a gnawing sense of deep frustration. It tells me that we have not yet reached a meeting of the minds. Whilst it appears that Mr. Hayashi is seeking to defend and justify the poor standards and facilities at the Whale Museum, what I take away from this letter is that the good Director does not quite grasp exactly what all the upset is about.

His reaction is typical of the general Japanese reaction; the misconception that Westerners are principally reacting to the fact that dolphins are being slaughtered for food. Automatically assuming that this is the motivation for the complaint against the small tank, the TWM Director attempts to placate us with what to him seems the well-intentioned assurance that *'every individual in our facility will never be edible'*.

In other words, he is saying: *'It's OK, we're not going to eat them; all we're doing is keeping them!'*

I was however heartened to note that the Director actually observed that the proximity of the Museum–a perceived place of education and learning–to the killing Cove, was "problematic" to use his words. Just what the Director proposes to do to resolve this paradox is unclear.

In my letter to the Taiji Whale Museum I made the point that whilst I disagreed with the issue of dolphin captivity, it was not my intention to make comment on that topic or to challenge their decision to engage in the practice. The principal issue that I wished to see addressed with regards to Faith and Hope was their removal from the small holding tank. I contended that maintaining them in their present living conditions really amounted to an act of animal cruelty.

To begin to understand how such a cruel fate fails to raise the concern of the Japanese, I really tried to look at the situation through their eyes. Plainly evident here in Japan is what I would call a 'bonsai mentality.' The nation of Japan is really a network of small islands dominated by rugged mountain landscapes. Derived from the need for compact living spaces on a densely populated mountainous island, the first impression that many travelers have of Japan is just how small and crowded the country is. Borne of sheer necessity, Japanese houses by Western standards are tiny and cramped, as are the vehicles, appliances and of course even the Japanese people themselves, the majority of whom are of slight build and relatively small in stature. And so, by virtue of geography, the country's 127 million-strong population find themselves shoehorned into a relatively small area, not unlike the much-adored bonsai trees which grow in miniature in very limited space and soil.

The most widely appreciated of Japan's design sensibilities is their inherent genius for making small beautiful items–it requires no great stretch of the imagination to thus understand this seeming lack of concern for keeping two dolphins, which ordinarily are accustomed to ranging far and wide in open ocean, in an overly small and cramped enclosure. Sadly this 'bonsai mentality' renders the Japanese somewhat incapable of appreciating the severity of the problem in the same way that we Westerners do.

⊂3❀8⊃

Weeks passed. And then, when the news began to filter through I was cautiously optimistic. Faith and Hope were to be released from the small tank! The plan was to relocate the two Pantropical spotted dolphins to an outside location in the Whale Museum grounds. That meant either the natural lagoon or one of the artificial pools. If that were true and it did come about, it would be a wonderful outcome. But could this be possible, or was it just another false alarm?

It turned out to be true. Faith and Hope's salvation came in the powerful form of Enson Inoue, Hawaiian born Japanese-American martial arts star. Enson had recently become aware of the plight of the Taiji dolphins and had made several trips to the small fishing village to learn more about the situation, speaking to both activists and dolphin hunters. It was not his first campaign for animals in need. Known for his brutal reputation in the ring, the man is also possessed of a softer side when it comes to animals in distress. In 2011, shortly before his visit to Taiji, Inoue had travelled to northeast Japan to lend his assistance and support to the earthquake and tsunami victims in the badly affected areas around Fukushima.

To help the thousands of domestic dogs abandoned in the wake of the massive disaster, he had entered the lethal eighteen-mile evacuation zone around Fukushima, putting his personal safety aside in order to get food to the region's starving dogs. Paying a visit to the municipal offices of Taiji, Enson was able to convince the Mayor to make a visit to the Taiji Whale Museum to view and assess the small tank which held Faith and Hope. Mayor Kazutaka Sangen did just that, and agreed that their present living conditions were less than ideal. He promised to negotiate their relocation to the Museum's outside pool.

True to his word, Faith and Hope were moved a couple of weeks later. When video footage of the two small dolphins in their new home was released, it was a moving sight that filled me with the deepest satisfaction–their demeanors had changed completely from the forlorn pair who had floated lifeless in that tiny fish-tank.

And now, here they were; frolicking and leaping together, silver flashes chasing each other through the waters. Life was returning. Yes, it was still captivity but here they had sunshine and fresh air. They had survived the soul-destroying ordeal of the small tank.

CHAPTER EIGHTEEN

Rock Paper Scissors

"Vision without action is a daydream. Action without vision is a nightmare."
— JAPANESE PROVERB

ONE SIMPLE YET powerful memory that still remains with me is the sight of one solitary Japanese student at the cove following a drive hunt in 2011. The young lad sat quietly at a nearby bus stop, not wanting to draw attention to himself yet discreetly watching all that went on. His discreet and low-key presence had gone completely unnoticed by the throng of Japanese police and Coast Guard officials who milled about at the beach area; so obsessed with the troupe of western activists that the young local wasn't given so much as a sideways glance. This quiet and humble young man waited until the commotion died down. Until all but one or two of us activists remained at the cove car park. Only then did he self-consciously cross the road to join us. With a bow of greeting, he proceeded to ask questions of us in badly broken English.

Despite our cultural differences he seemed to be really no different at heart from the average Aussie student; he was clearly curious and had a thirst for knowledge. He believed that what was going on at the cove was fundamentally wrong. With words and gestures he tried to make this point known. Satisfied with the simple act of voicing his feelings and making contact with us, he said a polite goodbye and walked away. Then it dawned on me– he had waited there until it was safe enough for him to join us and make that one simple statement of disagreement. In that earnest exchange I saw bravery and commitment. And in that gesture, I realized the solution, and the ultimate way forward.

The real work of the westerners in Taiji has been to show by their example that it is possible to speak your truth; to air your views without fear of ostracism and abuse. The way forward for Japan's dolphins is in the voices of the youth of Japan.

Not all people were supportive of the actions of activists in Taiji. Many felt that reporting and bearing witness was simply not enough and nothing short of direct action was sufficient. To those people I would say this–try playing a game of 'Rock Paper Scissors' some time and use the following tactic. Choose the rock every single time. I can guarantee you your result will be this–you will win a percentage of the time at first. However, once your opponent figures out your strategy (and even the least intellectually gifted opponent will figure this one out pretty quickly!) you will then lose every single time. Strategy on Japanese soil, subject to the laws of that country, calls for a different game plan compared to the direct action campaign against a whaling fleet on the high seas in international waters. There is no sheriff on the high seas. Open aggression on the ground in Japan simply means a one-way ticket out of the country for the transgressor. After that there is no chance of return. Game over.

This was exactly what the dolphin hunters were hoping for. We refused to play into their hands despite occasionally being goaded. In 1961, President John F Kennedy warned of 'another type of war, new in its intensity, ancient in its origin–war by guerrillas, subversives, insurgents, assassins, war by ambush instead of by combat, by infiltration instead of aggression, seeking victory by evading and exhausting the enemy instead of engaging him.' Ambush instead of combat. Infiltration instead of aggression. President Kennedy

TAIJI

intuitively foresaw a new face of warfare requiring a new set of strategies. Prior to the Vietnam War the US armed forces were geared towards a particular style of warfare. Put quite simply they historically dealt with their enemies by 'throwing the rock.' Massive rocks in most cases. The basic strategy up until the Vietnam war had been to pour massive firepower on an enemy. And so, totally ill-prepared for guerrilla warfare, the old techniques backfired on the frustrated ground forces in 'Nam.

'Winning the hearts and minds' was the catch-cry of the Vietnam campaign as the Americans strategized to win the popular support of the Vietnamese people in the face of the Communist invaders. Frustrated by an enemy they couldn't see, who chose to infiltrate and booby-trap rather than stand up and 'shoot it out', the US Forces lashed out blindly in growing anger and frustration at virtual shadows. They burned villages and killed innocents in an attempt to hit back at the Viet Cong. And in acts like these they ironically turned the 'hearts and minds' against the US, progressively putting the local populace off-side. The Vietnam war was a painful lesson for the United States–the strategy of throwing the rock didn't always work.

In the same way, effective activism is not all about simply throwing the rock. There will come a time to pick up the paper and equally there will be a time to use the scissors. And then there is the need for wisdom to know which to choose in any given situation. There is an old Japanese proverb that is worthy of our consideration:

"Vision without action is a daydream. Action without vision is a nightmare."

It should be made clear that in Taiji it is the greedy and callous actions of a small minority group that drive the evil of the local dolphin industry. The 'sin' of the majority is ignorance. And in that respect, the dynamic in Japan is actually no different to any other nation in the world, including your own. Cultural differences aside; this is a fundamental of every human race and culture. It struck me as odd that many Katsuura locals were genuinely unaware of the extent of the dolphin drive hunt and slaughter that was going on in the neighboring town of Taiji. Is it truly possible that people can live in blissful ignorance of such an event which is literally occurring on their doorstep? It appears to be inherent in Japanese culture that the government and media ensure that the population hears only a slanted spin on certain events and issues.

The greatest key to change will be in inspiring the Japanese people to stand up and speak out. In saying that, we must recognize there is an innate fear of speaking out for fear of censure by their peers. There is a traditional cultural pressure to stay quiet and to conform. Divisive thinking is frowned upon here in Japan; and therein lies the difference. *'East is East and West is West and never the twain shall meet'.* I cannot help but be reminded of Rudyard Kipling's famous words when I think of Taiji.

Despite the fact that Kipling wrote those words to describe the relationship between India and the British Empire, I can see that they have a certain applicability to the situation in Japan. And if that is so then perhaps we can take heart from the far lesser known lines from Kipling's verse: *But there is neither East nor West; border, nor breed, nor birth when two strong men stand face to face, tho' they come from the ends of the earth!*

To this end a number of activists are working in collusion with Japanese groups to foster education and change; to extend the helping hand of support. Michael Dalton's 'Eyes on Taiji' group, together with conservationist Ady Gil were in the process of establishing a powerboat operation based in Taiji harbor. Their intent is to offer the service to any Japanese groups interested in dolphin watching and marine conservation.

Many environmental groups were represented on the ground in Taiji across the drive hunt season. I do not mention them all here individually simply because I do not want to miss any of them out; their individual contributions all counted–each and every one. These wonderful people each brought with them individual ideas and methods but all were unanimous in their support of the common ideal of ending this evil industry forever, and I celebrate that union. I felt heartened to have also witnessed what may have been the first grassroots uprising by the Japanese people in defense of the whales and dolphins. That chance meeting with the young university student was a moment of epiphany for me. It may truly be the more worldly and cosmopolitan younger generation of Japanese youth that leads the way. After all, it is their country and their inheritance. It is now time for them to take the reins and lend their voices to shaping the future for Japan's dolphins.

○○○

There are some forty-one species of dolphin, and of these a full thirty-eight species are listed by the International Union for Conservation of Nature on what is known as the Red List. Of those species, nine are listed in categories ranging from 'vulnerable' and 'near threatened' through to 'critically endangered'. Just the sheer number of listings alone is a strong enough indication that dolphins in general are in serious trouble. So why exactly are dolphins endangered?

Sadly, but not at all surprisingly, their compromised status is the result of human activity. *We* are their greatest threat. Firstly, we have polluted our oceans and rivers. A major problem facing dolphin populations is the mercury concentration within their bodies. Atmospheric emissions from coal and industrial plants find their way into our oceans. The burning of fossil fuels has resulted in a progressive increase in mercury levels over the years. Dolphins are apex predators–in other words they occupy the highest level on the marine food chain.

The further up this food chain we progress the greater is the resultant concentration of mercury and other toxins within the subject life form.

Few people are aware that the body of a dead whale washed up on shore is classified as a biohazard due to its high toxicity. The carcass becomes a deadly poisonous cocktail due to the bioaccumulation of dangerous toxins over its lifetime. Tests conducted on dolphin meat taken from the waters of Taiji show dangerously high levels of mercury contamination. (On a related note–levels of mercury detected in Taiji residents have been shown to be well above the Japanese national average according to the National Institute for Minimata Disease).

Secondly, dolphins often become the innocent victims of the world's fishing industries. They fall prey as by-catch in some tuna fishing grounds due to the tendency of some dolphin species to travel with the vast tuna schools, finding themselves caught in the nets of purse-seiners, as well as falling victim to the miles of indiscriminate long-lines lacing our oceans.

And then of course there are those individuals who choose to deliberately target dolphins for slaughter. Japan alone will slaughter approximately 23,000 each year.

Mankind thus remains the dolphins' greatest predator.

I have heard all of the arguments and justifications of the pro-whaling faction. I've lost count of the number of times I have heard the old chestnut: 'You eat cows and sheep, we eat whales and dolphins.' *Wrong.*

Let's make no mistake about this, the keeping of livestock for food is fraught with problems too; land clearing for cattle grazing is a major contributor to natural habit destruction and climate change. However, the argument that dolphins are the equivalent of cattle or sheep is fundamentally flawed simply because it does not compare apples with apples. Dolphins are wild animals, and the fact remains that only a small minority of the Japanese population actually consume whale meat; so, the killing of dolphins for food is an unnecessary luxury rather than a necessity. This is exacerbated by the fact that this 'boutique' demand is further reducing. As a result of the current level of dwindling demand the price of whale meat is also decreasing and stockpiles of unwanted whale meat are on the increase.

According to an article in 'The Australian' newspaper dated January 5th 2011, Japan's stockpile of whale meat hit a record high of more than six thousand tons. Japan's Kyodo News attributed this to declining demand. The old justification of whale meat being an important part of the Japanese staple diet is rapidly losing steam and credibility. In truth it is a rationalization put forward by a minority group to justify their greedy indulgence.

Claims of culture and tradition also fall short when you compare the days of isolated community subsistence whaling with the commercial whaling enterprise of today. Furthermore, the cultural and moral high ground is lost in the unnecessary acts of animal cruelty. The cold hard facts are these; there are distinct elements of a 'pest control' mentality in operation as fishermen face the grim reality that fish stocks are declining as a result of mankind's wasteful harvest of the ocean's bounty. Time and again whales and dolphins are blamed for the serious decline in fish stocks. I have no doubt that the dolphin hunters' view of their prey as marine pests further drives the cruel and vicious large-scale slaughters. But there is really one singular underlying motivation. Monetary gain. Whilst the profit return to the dolphin hunters for the supply of dolphin meat is not great, there are substantial sums of money to be made from the capture and sale of live dolphins and this is really the driving force behind the Taiji dolphin industry. It is not the slaughter but the live capture of dolphins for re-sale which drives Taiji's hunters.

And so, let's follow the money–there is a simple economic concept underpinning and fueling all of this. It is demand that drives supply.

In simplistic terms, if there was no one willing to pay money to view these gentle creatures in captivity, the whole capture industry would collapse. Our inherent curiosity and love for dolphins has given rise to an industry of aquariums and dolphin parks which allow the general public to view the enigmatic sea dwellers at close quarters.

And of course, wherever there is money to be made there are individuals and groups who capitalize on the opportunity. 'Swim with dolphins' programs have sprung up around the world, touting the therapeutic benefits of swimming at close quarters with a dolphin. And in the same way that fast food chain McDonald's seduced and groomed a junk food generation, so the marine park and aquarium groups present a wholesome welcoming image of their trade for the benefit of well-meaning potential patrons. This becomes increasingly more important as the general perception of keeping sentient animals in captivity progressively changes.

Remember when fast food chains brought out a range of 'healthy meals' in response to changing values about food nutrition and obesity? In the same way, the marine amusement park industry faces similar changing world values. Their equivalent of the 'healthy meal' option is their increasing involvement in marine conservation initiatives and the depiction of their marine parks as 'education centers'. The marketing and presentation is very slick–happy music, happy children, happy parents. *Happy dolphins.* I have listened to the arguments of the dolphin trainers themselves: 'You don't know what you're talking about, we love our dolphins, and they love to perform. They are well fed and cared for and treated with the utmost respect'.

Many trainers respond with the rationalization that their dolphins were rescued and rehabilitated from poor conditions in the wild– illness or injury–and given food and safe haven and a chance at life, albeit in captivity. This scenario is quite often the case, particularly since many marine parks are moving towards a 'rescue and rehabilitation' culture. However, the moral high ground of marine parks and dolphinariums is quickly lost when it is revealed that they also engage in breeding programs to spawn fresh generations of captive dolphins. And then there is the incontrovertible fact that whales and dolphins' lifespans are marked shorter in captivity compared to their natural life expectancy. In the wild, bottlenose dolphins typically live between 30 and 50 years. Bottlenose dolphins in captivity only survive to an average of just over 12 years.

There is no tank in the world, no aquarium, no Dolphinarium that can come close to replacing these wild creatures' natural environment. Despite what these facilities would lead you to believe, no matter how much they dress it up with glossy lies and misleading hype, whales and dolphins *do not* revel in a life of captivity. These are wild animals, not domestic pets. Don't be fooled by the garish upbeat music and the festive carnival atmosphere. Captive marine mammals are routinely treated for depression. Of the orcas held in captivity you will see many with a collapsed dorsal fin–the once proud and impressive appendage broken and dangling limply to one side. This is the painful result of being confined in an overly small and shallow pool and thus being forced to swim continually in tight circles. The best they can hope for is a greatly reduced lifespan; often exacerbated by the stress and depression that they endure.

Forgive me if I have strayed from my original point here–it is money and demand that ultimately drive the dolphin hunts. The place to view the magnificent orcas and the playful bottlenoses is in their own playground and domain–the open ocean. Support a decent eco-tour operator who is sensitive to the needs and the essence of these wild animals.

Let these beautiful creatures enchant you and allow them to show you who they truly are. They have something to offer you. They have a teaching to impart to us. On their own terms. In their own environment. *From a place of Freedom.*

PART IV

SPIRIT

Mountain capped in snow
Towering toward heaven
Rises above cloud

CHAPTER NINETEEN

Spirit

'The reverse side also has a reverse side'
- JAPANESE PROVERB

UP UNTIL NOW I have allowed the stars of my story, the dolphins, to rightfully take their place on center stage. For this is really their story; it is the tale of their plight and their battle. It is a story that plumbs the deeper waters of spirit, and whilst I have made mention of the human players; I do so in order to further draw focus to the plight of our main characters and their world of Water. I trust that as the dolphins' envoy and mouthpiece I have done them appropriate justice here; I truly hope that I have endeared them to you, as they in turn have endeared themselves to me.

But the story of Taiji's dolphins is far deeper than a simple tale of cruelty and loss. It is not enough to simply paint Japanese culture with a selectively cruel brush. It is my earnest hope that in the telling of this story, I impart some sense of the deeper elements at work here. I hope that I have done justice to the Japanese people in general; a culture which I have come to love.

It has taken a certain amount of bravery on my part to tell you this story; in doing so I hope that I have opened up a deeper truth to you, beyond that which appears on the surface. In the process of fighting for the rights of whales and dolphins, I find myself opening to some wellspring of deeper truth. This I believe is the dolphin's gift to us; it is the gift of reconnection with the Earth and All That Is. It is a gift of healing that we need to acknowledge and assimilate into our own daily lives, and into our dealings with others. I truly believe that if we are going to save the whales and dolphins we must in the process save and heal ourselves.

In truth the one cannot occur without the other. And if this is so then what does that say of the small Japanese village of Taiji and its drive hunt industry? This is now my second visit to Taiji and the Cove. There are multiple layers of healing that need to be enacted here–between Heaven and Earth, between human and cetacean, and also between the factions of east and west; in order to foster a spirit of further change in Taiji.

I would like to begin by addressing the latter divide. It is often said, when speaking of the harsh realities of cetaceans in captivity, that the dolphin's 'smile' becomes its own worst enemy; that deceptive smile which gives off the appearance of radiant happiness is purely a function of the dolphin's fixed jawbone structure and is not indicative of the emotion that the dolphin is experiencing. This of course makes it so much harder to convince people of the pitfalls and perils of dolphin captivity; they appear to all intents and purposes to be smiling and having the time of their lives after all.

Ironically it is the polar opposite of this–the absence of physical expression or demonstrative emotion–that leads many people, particularly westerners to the conclusion that the Japanese people are a cold and unemotional race. Unlike our western notion of individualistic expression of emotion, the Japanese people position themselves at the other extreme end of the scale. Japan, typical of many eastern cultures leans towards a collectivistic attitude when it comes to emotional expression. Put in simple terms, the Japanese are highly group-centric and thus extremely sensitive to the possibility of individual thoughts and ideas upsetting the harmony within the group–be it their country, their family, their workplace or their village collective. Thus, in their dealings they remain somewhat guarded and aloof. They live in a culture which generally discourages open expression and free speech. To our western eyes, this tightly contained reservation when it comes to expressing thoughts and emotions paints a picture of the Japanese as a cold and emotionally heartless race. I can tell you that in my experience nothing could be further from the truth. Perhaps I am fortunate in that being of a Eurasian background I still retain something of that eastern sensitivity, and so maybe I see more of the reality and true depth of emotion behind the stern public mask of the Japanese.

Whilst it is true that there is good and bad in every race and nation on planet Earth, we have a natural tendency to fear what we don't understand. This unfamiliar oriental demeanor of reserve makes it all that much easier for people to feel a sense of anger and outrage towards the Japanese people in general. English author Austin Coates lived and worked extensively in the Orient during the post-war era of the 1950s. He observed that the sum effect of one European's influence on Eastern culture amounted to *"no more than a grain of salt in their ocean of salt water."* It is a sobering assessment. As outsiders here, we face something of a daunting challenge.

To foster and encourage change in Taiji, it firstly falls upon us as Westerners to understand the Japanese cultural ethic. This of course certainly does not mean that we must agree with or condone the actions of those who involve themselves in an industry of cetacean slaughter and captivity; in the same way that we do not condone the actions of those in our culture who are reckless with the environment and with animal welfare.

That being said, I would like to put a human face to some of the wonderful personalities that I met in Japan. My first real introduction to Tetsuya from the Police Special Task Force was atop Takababe Hill. In times of high emotion or stress, one often resorts to humor as a means of retaining balance. It is a concept that I am well and truly familiar with, and I must admit that without laughter I suspect my

Spirit

own sensitivity would likely be my downfall. Humor becomes my 'go to' in times of stress. It was one such moment that we shared with Tetsuya that day on the hilltop above the Cove. Possessed of a good physique and an aura of confident charm, he presented as a dashingly handsome and charismatic police patrol leader. Up on the sunlit hilltop that day were the usual factions of activists, police and coastguard personnel. Kerry had taken to filming the scene with a video cam, providing a running commentary as she did so. Panning towards me she announced me as the resident bodyguard, to which I playfully spun sideways into a mock bodybuilding pose.

Hearing a muffled commotion from the Special Task Force trio standing behind us I turned to see Tetsuya, the head of the police contingent that day, grinning broadly at me. Motioning at me and turning theatrically to his colleagues he spoke to them in very passable English:

'Someday I hope to be mus-curar too.'

In truth, Tetsuya's assessment was overly kind. I have broad shoulders courtesy of many years of competitive swimming, but I'm not perfectly muscular! Sidling up to him, and playing up to the camera, I patted my stomach and confided to him in an exaggerated stage whisper:

'Tetsuya, this isn't actually muscle. This is what we call resting muscle!'

Not to be outdone Tetsuya motioned towards his hips, buried under his uniform and flak jacket. Again, he flashed the broad grin, saying in his stilted English:

'I know what you mean. I also have the love handles!'

Despite his near perfect English inflection, the description still came out as 'rove handles.'

The unexpected English slang, coupled with the Japanese inability to pronounce the letter 'L' had us in stitches. Peals of laughter ensued, leaving the dashing young policeman somewhat perplexed as to why his seemingly innocuous comment should draw so much attention.

'Where did you learn a term like that?' I jibed Tetsuya, who remained somewhat bemused about the sudden unexpected commotion his comment had caused.

'I rearned this from watching Engrish movies' he proudly replied; his face still stretched in a cheeky yet slightly confused grin.

To a man, the Police Task Force showed themselves to be a group of the most extraordinary caring individuals; had we met in other circumstances, they would be people that I would choose to associate and socialize with. I would be proud to count them amongst my friends. Here in Japan however, their official role requires them to maintain something of a professional reserve with both factions– western activists and local dolphin hunters. Despite this their humanity and warmth is clearly evident. I am grateful that they were drawn here to this place as much as we were. I will never forget young Shota; tall, fresh faced and strongly built, he still retained traces of the awkwardness of youth. He would have been no more than twenty-three or twenty-four years of age, and was really a gentle teddy-bear in a uniform. Like the others he demonstrated an innate warmth and openness beneath the aura of officialdom that was required of his position. He really was no different to the youth in my own country, clearly having grown quickly and ably into the responsibilities of his police career, despite his youth. Shota immediately endeared himself to me, when he shuffled up to me on Takababe Hill and sheepishly apologized for what he had perceived to be a display of disrespect. He had forgotten to remove his pristine white driving gloves when he shook my hand during our first introduction earlier in the day. Though that first meeting had taken place in the pre-dawn dark at the lookout point several hours ago, the troubled apologetic look on Shota's face told me it had been playing on his mind ever since. Profusely apologizing for his oversight, he was painfully concerned that I may have taken affront to this gesture, and was desperate to explain his mistake and make amends. I was quite taken aback by this old-fashioned charm, and genuinely moved by just how deeply respectful and caring these wonderful people truly are. I could not stress enough to Shota that I most certainly did not interpret his gloved handshake as a sign of disrespect. On the contrary, I had appreciated his genuine humility and warmth when he acknowledged me in greeting in the early hours of the morning; in all honesty I did not even recall the fact that he was still wearing gloves, let alone suffer any personal affront from the act.

As the days passed and the police got to know us a little better (I suspect they actually looked forward to the lively conversation and interaction with us each morning), they would approach us with a spring in their step, their reserved professional demeanor showing the signs of breaking into grins of acknowledgement. One morning saw two of the patrol excitedly telling us with conspiratorial grins that young Shota had been spending an inordinate amount of time frequenting the local coffee shop. The reason for this had me somewhat confused and my mind settled on the stereotypical 'cops and doughnuts' theory. I posed the question as to the reason for his interest as diplomatically as I could, and it was revealed that Shota fancied the pretty waitress who worked at the coffee shop but was too painfully shy to strike up a conversation with her. To his work-mates' amusement, it seemed he was spending a goodly amount of his weekly pay packet there in a desperate effort to get himself noticed by the young lady!

On hearing this story an army of Cove angels offered to speak up for painfully shy policeman; even an offer of poetry for him to present to the object of his affection was forthcoming! I guess love is an international language understood by all isn't it? It was moments just like these that made me realize that underneath the veneer of culture and nationality we are all just human beings trying to make our way in life as best we can, with all the same yearnings and desires; the same flaws and shortcomings. It was a nice feeling to see the chill air of the mountain pass above Taiji town-site ringing with the joy of shared laughter for once. It felt like some sort of small beginning.

TAIJI

There was snow beginning to cap the peaks of the distant mountains, and our breath hung in clouds of mist as we shuffled and stamped feet to stave off the winter chill, but I was grateful for the shared warmth of the people around me that day.

The playful but quietly restrained interplay continued daily between us activists and the police. Though one group had been ordered not to befriend the police or authorities, and to view them as the enemy. It seemed that Sea Shepherd was moving increasingly towards a radical hard-left stance. It was disappointing to see them fanning the flames of racial tension; progressively painting the situation on the ground in Taiji as a warzone in an apparent attempt to procure donations from enraged followers.

Ironically Sea Shepherd's website entry described the Japanese police taskforce as monsters the very same day I witnessed the following curious event. We were making our way back down the steep stairway from the peak of Takababe Hill. Mr. D, the Police section commander led the way; turning back occasionally to ensure the ladies didn't trip or fall on the narrow flight of ancient stone steps that wound their way through the dense forest canopy. The filtered rays of mid-morning sun picked through the leafy top cover in spidery tendrils of light; playing on the gnarled roots of old trees and the upturned leaves of low bushes. Ahead of me, Leah had paused, peering at something sitting on a broad leaf. Stopping alongside her, I realized that it was a large bumblebee which she now cupped delicately in her hand. I was fascinated. I had never seen a bee that size–not in Australia anyway. In the Land Downunder we have large spiders, large sharks, large crocodiles; large pretty-much-everything that wants to take a bite out of you. Just not large yellow and black bumblebees like the one Leah was cradling gently in her palm. The bee sat there quietly, barely moving.

'It's going into shock with the cold weather,' Leah explained, 'I need to get it down into the sun so it can get body heat back.'

By this time the remaining two policemen who had lagged behind had caught up to us, and they gazed fascinated at the large bumblebee–proceeding to ask Leah all the same questions that I had done a few moments earlier. Not about the large 'pretty much everything'; just about what was the matter with the large bumblebee. Again, Leah explained that it was going into shock; telling them that if she could set it down on a flower in the sunlight it should recover.

Imagine my surprise then when what I can only describe as 'Operation Bumblebee Rescue' suddenly swung into action. The two police officers caught up with their boss Mr. D; speaking to him in rapid-fire Japanese and pointing back towards Leah who was now carefully carrying 'the patient' down the remaining stone steps and out into the open air. Mr. D carefully chaperoned Leah off the rough steps while the two junior officers jogged ahead; making a bee-line (pardon the pun) down the footpath for the Cove car park, before searching in the shrubbery just off the road for the flowers that Leah had described.

I followed the whole unlikely throng of bee rescuers back along the narrow winding roadway which led back towards the Cove beach; wondering to myself what passing locals would make of the bizarre flurry of activity. Up ahead the two uniformed police re-appeared from the bushes across the road, waving at Leah and proudly telling her in broken English that they had found the yellow flowers that she had described to them. The elderly Mr. D hurriedly ushered her across the road, checking for traffic and jogging along breathlessly with her. I can only imagine what the bumblebee was making of this executive treatment, with its escort of three Japanese Special Police Task Force officers and an international band of activists from Canada, England, New Zealand and Australia. I wonder if it realized just how special it was at that point!

Perhaps this all sounds to be a simple anecdotal story, yet it is one of those special moments that I will never forget. In that precious moment it didn't matter whether we were Western activists or

TAIJI

Japanese officials. It didn't matter whether we came from Canada, England, New Zealand, Australia or Japan. It didn't matter that the life we were trying to save was that of one lone bumblebee.

It reminded me that no matter how complex our lives become, we should never lose sight of our place here on the planet. We could all learn to give more of a damn about our home in space, and the lifeforms that we share it with.

○₃✿₈○

Overlooking the villages of Taiji and its close neighbor Katsuura is the imposing Kii mountain range, which encircles the pretty coastal village in a lofty embrace. My first impression of the region was that it was not unlike a rich deep green oriental carpet which some imposing deity had playfully flicked briskly, causing ripples of tall mountains to roll across its length. Taiji and Katsuura were left clinging to the rocky tasseled ends of the carpet for grim death, lest they be flung into the sea by this mighty stone wall.

To the east of them lies the aquamarine vastness of the Pacific Ocean, whilst the western approach is shrouded by the deep forested green of steep mountain, towering upwards toward the blue mantle of open sky. High amidst its peaks is the mystical holy land of Kumano—the doorway to the world of spirit. Here it is said that the spirits of the dead cross over to the other side. Last year marked my introduction to this holy ground; somewhat unwittingly I ventured into the mountains and found myself rocked by the sentient power of the region. Today I still hold to the notion that that sentient energy was in some small way instrumental in my call to return here. The Shinto belief is that the forest, the mighty rocks and the towering waterfall at Nachi are imbued with the manifestation of spirit. If you stand quietly enough and still your mind you may feel the living consciousness of this sacred place. The mountains themselves are postcard pretty, the air bracing and fresh. Whilst the warmth of the nearby Kuroshio Current has a moderating effect on Taiji's weather, the high mountains of the Kii Peninsula enjoy falls of heavy rain and snow as the moisture laden sea air is forced to rise and cool over them.

Less than a year ago the two worlds of ocean and sky rained devastation on Japan. In August 2011, still reeling from the tragically devastating effects of a tsunami, Typhoon Talas left its deep claw marks upon the land of Kumano and across the surrounding Wakayama prefecture. Half of the annual precipitation of three thousand millimeters fell within the painfully short space of a few days. The effect of this deluge was devastating. Driving up through the mountains in January, some five months after the tragic event, the scars marking the typhoon's path were still clearly evident. As the floodwaters cut a path down from the mountains they literally scoured away complete buildings and tall trees.

Through the village areas one could see timber framed houses still lying where Talas had left them; torn away from their foundations and thrown aside in crumpled heaps like matchwood. Almost cartoon-like, other buildings simply appeared as though they had melted and folded over to one side. In places, large stands of trees had succumbed; thrown over flat like a line of dominoes. Areas of road had subsided and collapsed in the raging current. The rebuilding of roads and houses was still in progress as we followed the winding road up through the pine and cedar forests towards the holy ground of the Nachi waterfall. We were forced to routinely stop and wait for traffic passing in the other direction to move past us; in many places the damage was so great that the main road was reduced to one lane only–half of the road had simply vanished. The local Japanese stoically took it all in their stride, their faces betraying precious little of the anguish and the suffering that they had endured. Only the incredible trail of damage and devastation relayed the truth of the savagery.

There was also a painfully tragic human cost. Although we are relative newcomers here, even we were affected by one sad loss. On my first trip to Taiji last year I had precious little information on what to expect upon my arrival. Booking of hotels was painfully difficult, and the only way of negotiating a room for the night was simply to arrive in Katsuura and make one's way to the town's Information Centre–a small tourism office located at the old timber railway station in the center of town.

Outside of the main capital cities and population centers, precious few people speak English to any great degree. Some four hours by road out of the city of Osaka, the lack of a common language proved a barrier here in the rural fishing village. The Information Centre office was small and invitingly warm; its dark polished timber floors and windows reminiscent of an old fifties' railway office. Once inside I greeted the neatly uniformed young lady at the counter in the best conversational Japanese I could muster, indicating that I was looking for a hotel room. She smiled at my clumsy attempts to conjure the appropriate words before revealing that she spoke very passable English–rather an exception out here. Introducing herself as Saki, I guessed her to be in her mid-twenties. Placing several phone calls to local hotels, she quickly negotiated a room for me for the duration of my stay in Katsuura, and proceeded to show me how to find the hotel on a map. Although Katsuura is known as a resort village, precious few Westerners journey here. In recent months the little town has played host to activists from all points of the globe, drawn here to protest the dolphin slaughter in the neighboring village of Taiji. I'm very sure that Saki knew that. She had spoken to other activists about the situation and had taken an interest in our thoughts and feelings on the matter. On discovering that I was from Australia, she asked many enthusiastic questions about my lifestyle–the weather, the beaches and the people. She proudly drew out a rough outline of

Spirit

Australia on a notepad and accurately placed on it the major capital cities along the east coast–Sydney, Melbourne and Brisbane.

That openly friendly young lady who helped me at the Information Office when I first came to Japan last year was twenty-four-year-old Saki Teramoto, the daughter of Nachi-Katsuura's mayor. Tragically Saki lost her life to the typhoon, rescue workers later finding her body when her family's house was destroyed by the torrent of water. It was just one day before her engagement party.

Mayor Shinichi Teramoto had remained overnight at the town office and just before dawn, he had received a distress call from his wife Masako desperately calling for help. Abruptly the call was cut off. Fighting back his concern, the Mayor continued to command relief operations. Japanese news footage showed the mayor speaking from his office.

'I saw the body of my daughter. The best I could do was to be by her side for half an hour. While I'm here, I don't want to show my sorrow even though I have this on my mind,' he said.

Mayor Teramoto lost both his wife and daughter that night. At the time of the TV interview his wife's body was still missing, swept away in the flood. Yet he remained at his post to save others. Such is the nature of the Japanese people, and it is a quality which I appreciate and admire.

Kerry and I paid a visit to the town Information Centre to pay our respects to the gentle Saki, who had been so openly welcoming and courteous to us both. In broken Japanese we managed to explain to her workmates that we had known Saki and were profoundly sorry to hear of her passing. One colleague, a kindly older man, motioned to the desk she had once occupied. Although he spoke no English, he went to great lengths to point out her possessions still on the desk. So deep was their grief that they had left her workspace exactly the same as when she occupied it; not a single thing had been moved. Clearly understanding the intent of our visit this wonderful man maintained his composure as best he could, carefully and meticulously showing us each of her things in turn, handling each item–pens, a stapler and desk calendar as though they were precious gemstones. There are times here in Japan where we have found the lack of a common language has proven to be a formidable barrier to communication and understanding. And then there are times like this when no spoken language is necessary. In these moments love and compassion become a common language. Hard-bitten, the tears finally welled in the old man's eyes as he concluded his examination of her desk. We shed a tear together, and we each took a measure of strength in that shared moment.

There are florist's shops in Katsuura village selling some of the most exquisitely beautiful flower arrangements that I have ever seen. Sometimes I stand in some of these quaint little curbside shops with their elegant stained timber flooring, rustic walls and window frames and feel for all the world like I'm in provincial France. We chose a beautiful little florist shop set away from the town center along a quiet street. Every inch of the tiny room was bedecked in ornamental flowers of all colors. I can't profess to be any sort of expert, but many of the flowers I have never seen before in the southern hemisphere. Settling on a beautiful spray of pinkish purple blooms which we felt typified the spirit of Saki, we returned to the town office the day before our departure, presenting them as our final farewell to this wonderful young soul who had clearly been so cherished and loved by all who met her. The old gentleman bowed his thanks and carefully placed them on her perfectly laid out desk.

TAIJI JOURNAL – February 2012

The day of our departure dawns as a cold and bleak winter morning. I marvel at the way that the ordinarily postcard pretty landscape with its heady wash of lush colors has faded in a slow dissolve into so many shades of grey. We are standing in a wintry half-light, up on the mountain pass looking down over Taiji harbor. Like a row of angry white teeth lining the mouth of some ancient predator, the streamlined hulls of the banger boat fleet bob lazily in their berths. From my lofty vantage point the reason for their dormancy becomes plainly obvious–across to my right the Pacific has dissolved into a grey-white soup, topped with frothy lines of angry whitecaps. The wind chill is high and I can no longer feel my extremities; my nose and fingers ache with that dull numbing buzz that comes with constant exposure to the bitter cold.

A white dusting of newly fallen snow caps the distant mountain peaks. The sky is a pale grey haze that blends itself into the watery froth. The air seems thinner today and it sings with a sudden banshee wail as I pull my thick woolen beanie down low over my ears. In a way I am grateful for it however, as it is a divine wind for the dolphins that have now been spared for another day; free from the sonic harassment of metal banger poles and roaring diesels. The dolphins. If pods are passing in the nearby Kuroshio, they are safely hidden from prying eyes, camouflaged in the roiling offshore swell. Not all of them are free though. Gazing down across the protected inlet of harbor waterway, I focus on the row of floating holding pens running the length of the rocky groyne across the milky grey waters.

Here the newly captured bottlenoses and Risso's are being broken into captivity. Today they are staying low in the poor conditions and I can make out only one or two dorsal fins surfacing randomly in the small enclosures. My eyes trace the rising bulk of rocky outcrop erupting along the coast behind the pens. Just behind these neighboring hills, shrouded from our view in the grey blanket of morning lays the killing cove. And beyond that, the Taiji Whale Museum with its complement of captive dolphins, now waking to the routine of another day. Faith and Hope. The Four. The whales and dolphins in the lagoon and the outside pools. And beyond that, even more captives in the floating pens at Dolphin Base. How does one walk away from a place like this neatly, without the pangs of emotion pricking desperately at one's spirit? Even with the benefit of distance from my high vantage point I am not immune.

The roadway here is little more than a slim ribbon of bitumen wide enough for one car, and it threads its way down through a series of sharp hairpin bends around the steep cliff face which overlooks the darkened harbor. My thoughts are suddenly interrupted by the approach of headlights and flashing red lights reflected by the steel crash barriers. The cavalry has arrived, and we wave in acknowledgement as the boxy police patrol car pulls in behind our vehicle, leaving precious little roadway for other cars to pass. The retro-look police vehicles always appeal to my quirky sensibilities; I half expect to hear the strains of the old TV theme from 'Dragnet' playing in the background as they pull up.

With broad smiles the three officers exit the car briskly, greeting us with polite bows which we return with boisterous enthusiasm despite the chill wind now whipping around us. Tetsuya is heading the patrol this morning, and Shota has deliberately signed on to take the early shift, knowing that this morning is the last opportunity for final farewells as we are heading directly back to meet our flights in Osaka. Despite the extreme chill, Tetsuya has elected not to wear the bulky police issue greatcoat that his two companions are now sporting. I've noticed he never wears one, and I question him on this.

'I don't like the coat. Look at them…it makes them look like large penguins!' he confides in us with a conspiratorial grin, just out of the earshot of his colleagues who like us are now shuffling in the cold to stay warm.

Their comical swaying movements only add to the graphic image Tetsuya has neatly managed to conjure up. The lively huddle of Cove angels and police talking together excitedly has suddenly dissolved into an image of the cast of 'Happy Feet'. Any moment now I'm sure they will slide gleefully one after the other down the steep cliff banks,

Spirit

to rocket themselves into the cold harbor waters below. Suddenly breaking my daydream, one of the dark blue penguins breaks loose from the noisy cluster gathered near the parked cars by the sheer cliff wall and lurches over. It is Shota, crossing the road to shake my hand in greeting. He is not wearing his white driving gloves this time and I point this fact out to him, much to his amusement. When we re-join the group, he asks us all whether we are planning to return to Taiji.

'Of course! We're all coming back for your wedding, Shota!' I jibe playfully, reminding the youthful policeman of his 'girlfriend' at the local café.

Sheepishly he dissolves into shyness as the girls all chime in enthusiastically, offering to speak to the young waitress on his behalf. His two colleagues are discreetly breaking into broad beams of quiet satisfaction as a red-faced Shota runs the gauntlet of adoration; perhaps vaguely regretting the fact he volunteered for the early morning shift.

Speaking rather officially, Tetsuya calls us together and announces that he has something for all of us. Producing his police notepad with a flourish he proceeds to explain that it is a Japanese kanji character. He draws it slowly with broad strokes of the pen so that we will remember how to re-create it; explaining it as a cluster of characters from the English alphabet, which we are of course familiar with. The shape of the character looks much like the capital letter 'A' surmounting two letters below it: 'O' and 'P'. Intrigued by this rendering of Japanese calligraphy, we ask him what it means. He simply tells us that this is the Japanese character which represents *'Life, soul and spirit'*. It is only then that I begin to realize the deep significance of the squad leader's seemingly casual act.

Because of the conventions of his official position, Tetsuya is not allowed to display an act of bias by giving us a gift; nor for the same reason is he permitted to accept one from us. Professional neutrality aside however, he has carefully and thoughtfully given us perhaps the greatest gift that I could have hoped for from someone here in Taiji–

the gift of understanding and appreciation of what we are trying to achieve. We came here to stand up for the fundamental rights of all living creatures, and the police are well aware of exactly what has drawn us here. Perhaps in some way they too were drawn here by exactly the same force. And this then is the way that East is meeting West; albeit in small steps.

We are starting to recognize one underlying shard of common ground–we are *all* human. Sometimes–particularly with the seemingly impenetrable divide of language and cultural barriers–we just need to let that humanity shine though. As I have stated before, there are some universals which require neither words nor explanations. The police speak to us about the dolphin hunters. We know that they speak to the dolphin hunters about us. We must lead by example. Or in the words of the Mahatma, *we must be the change that we wish to see in the world*. I believe we have done our best here in Taiji. With this, we shake hands as friends and say our goodbyes.

Breath hanging in a mist, I reach for the door handle. It is cold to the touch like the surrounding air. Mist and snow-capped mountains; a grey sheet of thin stratus cloud blocks the approach of the rising sun. It is a four hour drive north to Osaka. I don't want to leave this place; these people, and these dolphins. Scrabbling for the car keys I feel a touch of a hand on my shoulder–it is Shota, looking at me with the same concerned look as the day of his gloved *faux-pas*.

'You will all be coming back, won't you?' he questions, with a concerned sincerity.

'Yes, my friend we will all be coming back', I reassure him; fighting a rising lump in my throat.

Yes, I promise we'll come back. How can we not?

CHAPTER TWENTY

Big in Japan

TRUE TO MY word to young Shota and to the dolphins, I did return to Taiji. It was September of the following year, in a Japanese spring when I once again made the now familiar journey to the sleepy coastal village.

Shota, however, was not there; having been promoted to a position in Tokyo. This time I was not on my own, and accompanying me was my partner Jackie who shared my love for the dolphins and nature. Once again, the Land of the Rising Sun welcomed me. Once again, the toll booths on the motorway confused the hell out of me. And once again I felt the butterflies in the pit of my stomach as the roadside sign loomed large; the iconic black whale pointing the way into Taiji. And so here I was once again, drawn back as perfectly and completely as a hapless sailor answering the siren's song. What lay in wait for us this time?

Jackie who is a born and bred Australian, and never ventured out of her home country, immersed herself in the Japanese culture; handled chopsticks like a boss, and amused me by playing a song called 'Big in Japan' extremely loudly as we wound our way through the maze of picturesque Japanese roads in our little metallic jelly bean of a hire car.

Not a single slaughter took place in the weeks that we were in Taiji. Of course, we each knew that it would not always be that way. A string of blue days saw the twelve-strong fleet of drive boats returning empty-handed to the long harbor, day upon day. We dutifully fell into the daily routine of waking before dawn and threading our way from our hotel in Katsuura in the darkness to take up watch at the lookout at the very end of the long finger of rocky isthmus. It all carried a strange familiarity for me now; the long walk through the leafy verdant overhang of forest. The narrow path dotted with pretty little stone shrines; quiet repositories for silent prayer and contemplation set into the peaceable canopy which allowed shafts of filtered light to dance through. And all around it, the wild blue of the Pacific Ocean formed a natural backdrop; the sound of breakers rising from the Funnel below, running the length of the rocky peninsula back into Taiji harbor.

Unlike my last visit, the weather was far more favorable, sunshine and fair winds meeting us as we stood with binoculars along the lookout and surveyed the scattering of small boat traffic in the mid-distance. As usual the banger boats threaded their way out to the horizon and all but disappeared from view, and the morning passed quietly before the distinct rise of their bows could be seen heading back towards harbor in the late-morning. *No dolphins!*

The Western activists were back in force; once again, a couple of wonderful representatives of Ric's Save Japan Dolphins. Sea Shepherd maintaining their aloof, belligerent stance and waving large skull and cross-bone flags in the village streets. Again, they chose not to speak to the police, or to us for that matter. It seems other activists had now become the enemy too.

The Police Special Task Force were once again warm and accommodating, providing us with feedback about impending departures of the drive boat fleet, as well as going out of their way to explain the relevance of a couple of local festivals which were taking place. Many was the time they would join us out at the lookout, looking out for the banger boats with binoculars which we would share with them; explaining how the boats would go about the business of rounding the passing pods of dolphins. Mr. Z, the team leader was himself an animal lover and chatted to us earnestly about the importance of speaking out for a just cause. I thought back to the first year I travelled here; before the mobilization of the Police Special Task Force, and I marveled at how the attitude and the dynamic were changing. More Japanese youth were standing up and speaking out, and a large group had joined with Ric and the Dolphin Project to make themselves known on the opening day of the dolphin hunt season. *Small steps.*

In the meantime, a series of more natural and spiritual occurrences dotted our days, and sitting with Jackie at the warm natural foot spa overlooking Katsuura harbor in the late afternoon, perfunctory can of Georgia café au lait in hand; I processed the things which Japan had chosen to lay out before us on my third pilgrimage.

TAIJI JOURNAL – September 2013.
When Jac and I approached the glassed pay booth of the Taiji Whale Museum, we had come prepared. Having run the gauntlet of activists storming the Museum grounds and recording photo and video footage, the Museum was actively barring Western activists from entry. And so, dressed as colorfully as possible; the two of us present as the complete antithesis of the serious dark-uniformed activists who had been consistently turned away. In truth, we probably are something of a different breed. We looked and behaved just like tourists.

So naturally when the young counter assistant shook her head and crossed her arms over her chest to deny us entry, we feigned confusion and surprise.

'Tourist,' I explain.

'You activist?' she questions in broken English, somewhat warily. Jac and I look at each other with feigned quizzical looks.

'*Iie* (No),' I respond, 'Kumano!'
I show her the small brass icon tied with red cord, which indicated that we had hiked the Kumano trails. Recognizing this, she nodded a cautious acknowledgement and fetched the manager, pointing to us

and speaking to him in Japanese. I politely interjected and added the words 'tourist' and 'Kumano' once again for his benefit. He warily nodded his understanding and admitted us. That was our cue to scoot into the Museum and make ourselves scarce, just in case he changed his mind. Wandering around the displays I give Jac, an accomplished photographer, plenty of time to record everything on camera. There were very few visitors to the Museum that day and we pretty much had the run of the building to ourselves. I did note the manager hovering discreetly nearby several times during proceedings; keen to keep an eye on just what we are up to. We continued to act tourist-y.

Happy with our recce of the museum exhibits, we pass through the gift shop area; a mesmerizing kaleidoscope of color–soft toys, posters and books. And the jarring contradiction of a refrigerated packed with dolphin meat and fish. The glass door at the rear opens out onto the museum grounds.

To the left is the smaller performance pool housing a pair of bottlenoses and a pair of beautiful Pacific white-sided dolphins. Out to the right is the large enclosed bay; a deep green lagoon nestled against the rising ground of Tsunami Hill on one side, and fringed by a concrete walkway and a scattering of small buildings which includes the small enclosure which housed the two spotted dolphins Faith and Hope. Right at the end of the concrete pathway leading around the lagoon is the tall white Dolphinarium building, which originally housed the four bottlenoses.

A performance is currently underway in the lagoon, and Jac and I sit in the bleachers and watch the dark shapes of the pilot whales and pseudo orcas (or 'false killer whales') going dutifully about their prescribed routine; leaping and breaching together in response to the trainers' hand signals. Once again, the sing-song Japanese commentator's voice rises and echoes around the facility. It transports me back to the first time I visited this place just over two years ago, leaving me with a lump in my throat. I am anxious to know what has become of the spotted dolphins and the four bottlenoses.

We continue to watch the performance with a sense of detachment. Jac taking photographs and remotely processing the whole scene. With the performance over, the small crowd of spectators disperses along the perimeter pathway. Now out of 'performance mode' we sit and watch the big dolphins (or small whales, if you prefer) circling the lagoon area slowly. Their natural behavior is quite a contrast to the lively display of synchronized leaps and jumps we have just witnessed. We sit right at the edge of the lagoon and the pilots and pseudo-orcas casually make eye contact; studying us as they pass.

Standing slightly back from the lagoon is the small red brick building housing the small tank, and we walk up to take a look at it. A sign across the doorway describes it as a 'Sea Otter Enclosure' and advises that it is presently closed for maintenance. Where are the two spotted dolphins? Faith and Hope were originally re-located out of here into the small performance pool, but they are no longer there. Where have they gone?

The lagoon is bisected by a planked walkway and beyond the performance area, at the far end of the bay, are a number of floating pens housing more dolphins. The slate grey sides and long snouts reveal them to be bottlenoses. Here for a small price, visitors can buy a small pail of fish and walk out along the wooden planking to feed them. We decide to let the crowd die down a little before we take a closer look at the bottlenoses, and opt to visit the Dolphinarium next. Pushing through the double glass doors into the small tiled atrium, we soon discover what has happened to little Faith and Hope. They are here!

In the semi-dark Perspex enclosure, we can make out the sleek spotted flanks pulsing easily through the waters beyond the glass walls. I count four dolphins circling and weaving in the tank, but 'The Four'–the bottlenose dolphins who inhabited this enclosure–are nowhere to be seen. They have been replaced by Faith, Hope and a pair of striped dolphins.

TAIJI

'Those bottlenoses we just saw in the lagoon pens must be The Four', I tell Jac.

I feel a rising wave of anticipation. Last year, despite the connection we shared; we were separated by a thick pane of Perspex. If I can get out along the walkway to the pens, I will be up close and personal with them this time!

Watching Faith and Hope cleaving the water effortlessly provides some measure of satisfaction and comfort. It is a far cry from the two forlorn figures I found in the solitary confines of that tiny tank in the wall last year. It isn't freedom, but at least they have found some degree of peace here. They don't seem to remember who I am, but I am okay with that. I am happy that I have at least played a small part in taking them out of harm's way. It is a bittersweet feeling.

'Small steps', insists Jac gently; reading my thoughts.

We watch the pair rising to the top of the tank in unison, before firing themselves like mottled bullets into the air at the surface above us; scattering flume and froth before diving into the depths of the tank once again. It has been a journey these past couple of years. From the time I first stood here in wonderment, having been encircled in a virtual halo of four slate-sided bottlenoses. It was the dolphins that brought me here to Japan and set me on this path. That led me to question our connection with All That Is. With our environment and other life. And it would be fair to say that it was the dolphins that connected me with Jac, who has been the most perfect partner I could wish for. I can say that as much as I have given of myself to the dolphins, I have received back in return.

With that, we return to the heat of the day outside, wincing in the glare after the dark solitude of the glass-walled Dolphinarium enclosure. The afternoon sunlight is dancing prettily off the ripples created in the lagoon as the dolphins wheel and circle; stirring the surface up before diving into the murk to surface again at a distance. Many people who visit places such as this fail to appreciate that in their natural environment, dolphins and small whales tend to spend about eighty per-cent of the time underwater, and only twenty per-cent at the surface. In the artificial conditions created in captivity, they are forced to reverse that behavior; spending up to eighty per-cent of the time at the surface. When a dolphin trainer or a marine park attendant tries to tell you that they are giving you an insight into the behavior of dolphins in the wild, just remind them of that fun fact. Most probably aren't even aware of this contradiction.

The Whale Museum is busy today, compared to my past visits. It is of course the holiday season, with the favorable warm spring weather bringing Japanese families out. Katsuura is filled with Japanese couples holidaying from the bigger cities like Osaka and Tokyo. The park is deceptively vibrant, and it becomes all too easy for a visitor to be taken up in the excitement and the spectacle of the displays. In that sense that Japanese are no different to any other culture. I remember being taken to a circus as a kid, and sitting spellbound by the displays of lions and elephants parading within mere feet of me. I never even considered the plight of those animals, even when I walked past their cramped cages when the show was over.

At the lagoon, Museum staff are still selling buckets of fish to visitors. I chat to Jac about the idea of buying a bucket of fish, as an excuse to walk out to the pens and be close to the bottlenoses. I am conflicted by this; the whole thing smacks of an exercise in dominance and submission and it goes against everything in me. But I need to be close to the dolphins. Jac agrees and follows me down the narrow-planked walkway that leads to the dolphin pens. I feel like a child with a tiny metal pail full of fish in one hand. When we reach the dolphins, the whole idea upsets me. Sitting myself cross-legged on the walkway, one dolphin remains close; puffing gentle relaxed blows as it breathes easily. The slick grey snout and head surfacing in front of us. Those eyes. A hint of boredom and sadness. It is One of Four. She gazes at the bucket sitting next to me, and I offer her a fish. I am fighting back tears. She doesn't eat the fish, but plays with it casually;

tossing it end over end in her mouth as dolphins sometimes do, content to bob lazily at the surface close to us. The other dolphins come and go, openly accepting fish from us until the little pail is empty. Whilst the others circle and dissipate, once the fish have gone, One of Four simply remains close by, watching each of us.

We stay there sitting on the rough wooden planks for the longest time. The other visitors have filtered away by this, and we are now attracting looks from the trainers and the Museum staff. Not only are we the only visitors out by the pens; we are the only Westerners in the facility

Still we sit quietly with One of Four, and Jac points something rather obvious out to me. It is simple yet telling.

'Do you not realize what is happening here? She's not hungry and we have nothing else to offer here, but she *wants* to stay around us,' says Jac. 'You realize she is choosing to stay with us simply because she wants our company?'

When it is put into words like that it really hits you. *She wanted to be with us.* Isn't it strange how we can miss the most obvious things when we are confronted with a being who can't speak our language? I look into her eye and stifle a quiet sadness that rises in me. It leaves me wondering about our human condition; how we can live our lives so perfectly oblivious to the needs and suffering of others. There isn't joy for me like our last union. Neither is there joy for One of Four. We are simply content to just be. To be Here and Now in each other's company for these long moments, and the feeling is simply bittersweet.

⊂🌸⊃

Once again, I felt the insistent call from the mountains. The sacred Kumano was calling me back. In a spiritual sense my third trip was also the completion of a personal journey of discovery to the 'Other World' – the mystical Kumano triangle. Accompanied by Jackie, I made the pilgrimage to each 'doorway' of the triangle, and we paid our respects at each of the three Grand Shrines; the Nachi-, Hongu- and Hayatama-taisha.

In order to reach the mountain shrine at Nachi-taisha, you must climb an imposing stone stairway called the *'Daimonzaka.'* At three kilometers in length up the steep mountainside; walking it is no mean feat. Near to the shrine you will find a place called *'Tainai Kuguri'* ('Tainai' meaning birth canal); a cleft in the rock which is believed to be endowed with a mystical energy which is the source of the Kumano's power to purify body and soul and bring about re-birth. The Nachi-taisha, which had impacted me so profoundly on my very first visit taught me to find inner strength and courage to overcome challenges.

The Hongu-taisha had presented a completely different challenge to me when I first visited it last year. You might recall that I had completely overlooked it; hardly casting a glance at what I perceived to be simple rural land unbefitting of hosting such a sacred monument. The message of the Hongu-taisha was abundantly clear. I must learn to look carefully and humbly; without prejudice or preconceived notion and see things for what they truly are.

And what of the final point of the triangle–the Hayatama-taisha? Its teaching was only revealed to me with the benefit of hindsight and it is only now that I realize the gift it bestowed on me. Firstly, behind the Hayatama Grand Shrine lies the verdant Mount Kamikura where a large boulder called *Gotobukiiwa* can be found. Legend has it that this is the place where the gods of Kumano first came to Earth. In 33 B.C, locals witnessed what appeared to be three moons descending to Earth. When the people asked the moons who they were, the beings introduced themselves as the gods Ketsumiko, Kumano Musumi and Kumano Hayatama. The gods then instructed the people to commemorate each of them in their own shrine, namely Hongu-

Taisha, Nachi-Taisha and Hayatama-Taisha–the three sacred shrines of the holy land now collectively known as the Kumano Sanzan.

Perhaps it was fitting that I visited this place last, after the trials and tribulations of the three years and three journeys it had taken me to reach it. In the temple grounds there is a sacred Nagi tree; a species of pine. The leaves of the Nagi tree have no veins and are therefore extremely difficult to tear. Tradition dictates that a Nagi leaf is offered as a token at a wedding–a sacred wish that the relationship will not be torn.

The final gift of the Kumano, as I now realize, was a deeply personal one. It was no coincidence that I was accompanied by Jackie on my pilgrimage there.

TAIJI JOURNAL – September 2013.
Many early mornings on the trot here; waking in the pre-dawn and making the drive into Taiji village. Jac is dog-tired, partly she says due to my snoring. OK, *completely* due to my snoring. We fall into the routine of threading our way past the Cove and Taiji harbor in the pre-dawn, and watching the bangers make their way out of the harbor mouth line astern with the harbor lights still winking and glowing a dim yellow in the distance. Once again, the old routine of scanning the waters, barely picking out the bangers who have disappeared out on the distant horizon in their endeavors to find the dolphins. But the dolphins are not there. The Cove stays blue and spring sunshine bakes the rows of quaint brown and russet roofs in the village. The police come and go, exchanging pleasantries and taking a genuine interest as always.

Somehow there is always a comical element that creeps in here; perhaps this speaks to the curious duality that is Japan. Over the past days, we've noticed one particular character popping up routinely. The first time I saw him was in the makeshift compound where the Police Task Force have now established a base. In the grassy area alongside the Cove car park, a temporary demountable building has been put in this year, serving at the offices for police.

I recall as we passed the compound the other day on our way to the lookout, a stern looking character standing alone right at the small fence along the roadway. Dressed in a three-quarter length tan coat, thinning hair and circular metal-rimmed glasses; he looked just like a Japanese Inspector Gadget. He watched us with a hawkish expression as we drove past. I would hasten a guess that he was an undercover detective from the local Wakayama police force. It was those very same distinctive looks that attracted my attention to a solitary figure sitting in a tiny metallic gold car in the car-park at the lookout just a couple of days later. Yes...it was Inspector Gadget again!

He was painfully conspicuous in the virtually deserted car park. As we arrived I saw him lean over to the passenger seat and pick up a notepad, checking his watch and scrawling notes as he discreetly glanced across at our car. It didn't take a rocket scientist to figure out what was going on. He was clearly a local plain clothes officer, following the movements of the activists. This isn't unusual here. As we exited the car with our gear, he did his level best to assume a casual appearance; as casual as you can look being the only person in an empty car-park in a frightfully strange looking car. The car proved to be a major source of amusement for me. It was a model I was unfamiliar with, only being available in Japan. And it is the sort of vehicle I would refuse to be seen dead in, even on a dark night. It was basically a squashed up cube with dinky tires. No styling at all; just a biscuit tin on trolley wheels really. Walking discreetly around the back of it, I was tickled pink when I saw the badge on its rear end actually said 'Cube'! I stifled a cheesy grin, just as the severe looking occupant shot a discreet glance at me. *Sprung!* I held his glance, feeling like a naughty schoolboy, then stopped and bowed respectfully; more to indicate that his cover was blown.

Some days afterwards, we were making the drive back along the winding coastal road to Katsuura, and a familiar looking dinky vehicle caught my glance in the rear-view mirror. We were being tailed! A glance back confirmed it; the stern poker face of Japanese Inspector Gadget glaring back at me. Trying to keep my composure, I caught Jac's attention:

'Ummm...I don't want to panic you sweetheart, but we're being followed.'

'By who?' Jac shot back; rather more confused than concerned.

'By...the Cube!'

I've watched all those old TV cop movies. Somehow there just isn't anything remotely threatening about being stalked by a tiny metal cube.

The duality and the comedy that is sometimes Japan followed us to the supermarket too. I had neatly mastered Japanese currency; strangely, Japan for all its leading-edge technology tends to be a cash-based society, especially in the outlying regional areas. Having found our way to the checkout, and waiting patiently in the small queue; I rummaged through my hip bag to produce the required Japanese bank notes and coins, before a display of familiar looking chocolate bars caught my eye (potato chips or chocolate will somehow manage to do this every time). A familiar blue wrapper with a picture of a flattish chocolate bar on it drew my closer attention. It was something of an oddity in the sense that very few products have English names on their wrappers. Back home it's called a 'Crunchy' bar. Emblazoned across the wrapper was the word 'Crunky.' At the same time, Jac pointed to another familiar looking chocolate bar proudly bearing the name 'Dars Bar.' Snickering like school children, we took photos on our mobile phones before buying ourselves one of each and taking them home. And as the large sign outside the local café proudly announced in all its misspelled glory; they were *'Dericious!'*

Big in Japan

CG ✿ ಖ

The day that Jac and I left Taiji once again proved to be an emotional one. And once again we were farewelled by the Police Special Task Force. Stopping in at the police compound adjoining the Cove beach car park, we paid our respects and said reluctant goodbyes. We were urged to return, and though we are yet to do so, in my heart of hearts I know that we must.

And in another moment that will never leave me, Mr. Z finally walked us to the car and shook our hands for a second time; a heavy tear rolling down his cheek. My last memory is seeing him standing alone by the squad cars watching as we pulled out into the roadway to make the long journey back to Osaka.

Taiji for me has been a journey of discovery and understanding. Perhaps more correctly put; Taiji was an intimate encounter that formed an important part of a deeper journey which continues to this day. As much as I have a feeling of having been drawn there; I also have the deeper sense of then being 'summoned' to travel to the Other Side–the Kumano holy land. So, it is fair to ask; what exactly have I learned from my experiences? In searching for the answer to that question, I am moved to share with you some universals which have come from the experience.

There is a time to pick up the rock. There is a time to pick up the pen; to raise your voice and to speak the truth. There comes a time when injustice must be met with resistance. And then there is wisdom in knowing which course you must take. A friend told me that I went to Japan angry, but walked away a changed man. I would agree that there is some substance to that truth. I was angry at what was being done in that little village. And I was perhaps also a little blinkered.

Love as the Beatles once said, is the answer. If you're going to change the world; change it with love not with anger. Just like a coin, there are always two sides to every story. The Japanese put it beautifully in their proverb: *"The reverse side also has a reverse side."* A truly wise man recognizes this and seeks to look at both sides of the coin, before demanding a change in currency.

And the dolphins that led me to Japan? Well, dolphins will forever remain an enigma and a source of joy to me. An enigma in the sense that I am still left wondering what deeper mysteries they hold behind those knowing eyes. And a joy in the way that they remind me not to take life too seriously. To find a balance. There is a time for work and a time for play and for laughter. I don't think we can laugh often enough. What is life about after all?

With a heavy heart, I bid farewell to Japan for the third and final time.

CHAPTER TWENTY-ONE

Hindsight Is 2020

> "Nature is sending us a message with the coronavirus pandemic and ongoing climate crisis. Our continued erosion of wild spaces has brought us close to animals that harbor diseases that can jump to humans."
> –INGER ANDERSON - UN Environment Chief

TAIJI JOURNAL – July 2020.
It has been a long time since I last opened this journal. But today something occurred to me; some vague sense of epiphany which has prompted me to write this final entry in a journal I thought was long closed.

I am sitting at my desk with the morning sun insinuating itself into the room rather insistently, despite the wooden blinds being pulled tightly shut. Outside there is yet another unfamiliar world. And once again, just as I opened this book in a cramped hotel room overlooking Japan's Katsuura harbor; I am in another tiny room close to water. This time, I am in the beachside village of Sandown, on England's Isle of Wight. Narrow streets lined with old buildings; their once proud painted facades now peeling and badly faded. The incessant calls of seagulls, oblivious to the jaded line of empty old seafront hotels which seem to scowl at their freedom jealously through rows of derelict windows. A very English beach adorned with lines of gaily colored beach umbrellas and sun beds, alongside a rather tired looking Victorian pier. Perhaps in some sense I am intimately entwined as a human part of that tiredness; that wan sense of world-weariness. I am a long, long way from home. How I got here is another story in itself, and it rightly belongs in the pages of another book.

In a much broader sense we have *all* been flung into an unfamiliar world–a world wrought with increasing concerns of escalating climate change. Extreme heatwaves throughout Europe. Unrelenting bushfires on a massive scale in Australia which began in their winter months. The hottest days on record in the polar caps. The naysayers will tell you that this is all normal; that it is simply part of the planet's natural cycle. That we've always had bushfires, floods and drought.

And then there is the global coronavirus pandemic, which is still taking a toll on millions across the planet. Being right in the midst of it, we are yet to count the cost of the effect it is having on our physical and mental health, and our social and financial wellbeing. There is anger, denial and resistance. The same naysayers are telling us that COVID-19 is nothing more than a flu. That it will eventually disappear. That our immune systems are designed to handle it; and that facemasks, quarantine and social distancing measures are all overkill and a breach of our civil rights.

And of course, there is the customary finger-pointing, blame and accusation. Even the President of the United States of America, arguably the most dangerous leader on the planet right now, is in on the blame game; repeatedly and deliberately referring to it as the 'China Virus.' Many individuals and governments are taking up that same catch-cry. *Blame China!* Those dirty foreigners and their dirty ways. Eating animals that they shouldn't. Selling them in wet markets in filthy, unhygienic conditions. *They* brought all this down on us. *Those Chinese monsters!*

It all has a familiar ring. It is the 'Taiji syndrome' all over again. Please recall what I had said in the introductory pages of this book, in response to the growing condemnations of the Japanese people at the time. *We are the monsters*. And here in 2020 we bear witness to the same underlying problem writ large, and it is now affecting us all. The worldwide effect of natural habitat loss, driven by large scale clearing of land, increasingly forces wildlife into closer interactions with humankind. Climate change (which we now know is driven by the activities of mankind) is exacerbating the problem. Wild animals are forced into closer contact with us as they increasingly range and forage for dwindling food sources.

It is a terrifying world right now. And yet, *it is a world of our own doing.* If one looks past the smokescreen of media sensationalism fueled by controversial clickbait elements such as the 'virus denialists', the 'lockdown moaners' and the 'blame China' clique; you will learn that mass virus outbreaks are stemming from one simple fundamental. It comes down to mankind's interaction with the natural environment. China, just like Taiji, is only one representative element of the bigger problem. It is not enough to simply blame China for our current woes. We have collectively driven the planet to the state it is in today. *We* are the monsters.

And what has become of Taiji and the Japan dolphins? Sadly, the annual drive hunt has continued unabated up until present day. The most recent photographs captured at the cove remain as confronting and distressing as ever. A pod of gentle pilot whales roped together by their tails. A juvenile striped dolphin the size of a human baby; tossed onto a skiff for slaughter with that same rough disregard for sentient life. I will not distress you with any more graphic details. The years have fallen away, but the cruel song remains the same. *So where is Change?*

Globally, there have been signs of gradual changes since my time in Japan. For instance; in March 2016 SeaWorld USA announced that it would end their in-house captive breeding programs for orcas, following several years of pressure from environmental groups and damning publicity exposing cruel and unacceptable practices. In a public statement announcing what will effectively mean the end of orcas held in captivity by SeaWorld, CEO Joel Manby stated that they would not be releasing their current compliment of 29 captive orcas into the wild. He explains: *'These majestic orcas will not be released into the ocean, nor confined to sea cages. They could not survive in oceans to compete for food, be exposed to unfamiliar diseases or to have to deal with environmental concerns—including pollution and other man-made threats. Instead, they will live long and healthy lives under love and care of our dedicated veterinary and other trained specialists where they can inspire this and future generations to be conservationists around the world through natural presentations that are fun, exciting and will educate guests about the plight of orcas in the wild.'*

You will note that right to the bitter end, SeaWorld are still sticking to the same propaganda-like spin about *'long healthy lives in captivity'* and the *'fun, exciting presentations that educate guests about the plight of orcas in the wild.'*

I'm still left wondering exactly how putting a creature which swims hundreds of miles a day with its family into solitary confinement in a swimming pool is *'fun and exciting'* for the orca, and how this unnatural situation could in any way educate people as to their *'plight in the wild.'* By logical extension, perhaps one day we will be able to give a race of visiting alien beings an insight into how we humans live by showing them around a prison or an immigration detention center.

This all says rather more about the orcas' plight in captivity and the mentality of the human beings who keep them there. CEO Joel Manby also conveniently omitted to tell you that the life expectancy of an orca in captivity has been proven to be about half the natural lifespan that an orca enjoys in the wild. I wish Joel the same 'long and healthy life' too.

Hindsight is 2020

My colleague Leah Lemieux spoke about a wave. A wave, she said, that was composed and driven by connected and passionate individuals around the earth. A wave urging us to recognize mankind's untenable position. A wave calling for change.

In 2020 I am looking out onto a bigger ocean and I can see the wave. A growing wave driven by a sense of injustice and frustration. From those who have impotently borne witness to greed, corruption and manipulation for too long. From those who have lived their lives as second-class citizens; by virtue of skin color, religion or birthplace. From a building frustration with governmental inaction on climate change. *The wave is there.* In the rising swell of youth voices inspired by Greta Thunberg. In the cries of the thousands of Black Lives Matter protesters. These events are all inter-connected and inter-related. It is a clarion call demanding change and it is heartening to witness. We are very slowly and painfully shedding a skin. And still there is the same old resistance from those unwilling to change.

One thing that I have learned in my years around the ocean is this– water and waves are relentless. They can smooth the hardest of rocks. Given time, they will eventually weaken and collapse the most imposing of mountains. I'm proud to have been a small part of that quiet erosion.

Whatever mountain you may face, whatever ocean you ride upon; that same power lies within you – use it well, my friend.

For the Taiji dolphins. For our home planet.

ABOUT THE AUTHOR

Len Varley is a passionate advocate for the protection of human and non-human rights. His love of the oceans saw him take up the cause of raising awareness for marine conservation issues and the protection of fragile ecosystems and endangered marine species.

Len has authored scientific reports on the decline of localized dolphin populations in Japanese waters and contributed research to Australian state bodies, challenging their controversial shark cull program. He has spoken publicly at conservation events and given radio interviews in the UK and Australia.

A former commercial pilot; his aviation background led to research into bird strike mitigation measures for the aviation sector and wind turbine farms.